THE INTERPRETER

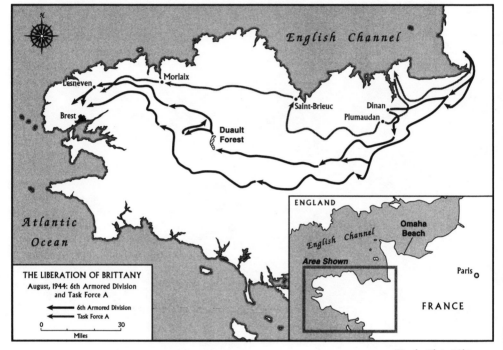

English Channel

Lesneven

Morlaix

Brest

Saint-Brieuc

Dinan
Plumaudan

Duault
Forest

Atlantic
Ocean

THE LIBERATION OF BRITTANY
August, 1944: 6th Armored Division
and Task Force A

6th Armored Division
Task Force A

0   30
Miles

ENGLAND

English Channel

Omaha
Beach

Area Shown

Paris

FRANCE

Map by Chris Robinson

— THE —
INTERPRETER

ALICE KAPLAN

THE UNIVERSITY OF CHICAGO PRESS

Chicago and London

The University of Chicago Press, Chicago, 60637
The University of Chicago Press, London, Ltd.
Copyright © 2005 by Alice Kaplan
All rights reserved.
Published by arrangement with The Free Press,
A Division of Simon and Schuster, Inc.
First published in 2005 by The Free Press
University of Chicago Press edition 2007
Printed in the United States of America

16 15 14 13 12 11 10 09 08 07   1 2 3 4 5

ISBN-10: 0-226-42425-1
ISBN-13: 978-0-226-42425-5

Library of Congress Cataloging-in-Publication Data
Kaplan, Alice Yaeger.
    The Interpreter / Alice Kaplan.
      p. cm.
    Originally published: New York : Free Press, 2005.
    Includes bibliographical references and index.
    ISBN-13: 978-0226-42425-5 (pbk. : alk. paper)
    ISBN-10: 0-226-42425-1 (pbk. : alk. paper)
      1. Hendricks, James, E. 1923–1944—Trials, litigation, etc. 2. Whittington, George
P., 1913–1996—Trials, litigation, etc. 3. World War, 1939–1945—African Americans.
4. African American soldiers—France—Social conditions. 5. African American
soldiers—History—20th century. 6. United States. Army—Officers. 7. Courts-
martial and courts of inquiry—France. 8. Trials (Murder)—France. 9. Guilloux,
Louis, 1899– I. Title.

    D810.N4K37 2007
    940.54′03092—dc22

                                                                    2006035822

⊗ The paper used in this publication meets the minimum requirements of the American National Standard for Information Sciences—Permanence of Paper for Printed
Library Materials, ANSI Z39.48-1992.

For Hattie and Mark

My role as interpreter made me feel important, of course, but equally embarrassed, worried, and distressed.

—LOUIS GUILLOUX, Memory from age fourteen

CONTENTS

—

—PART I—

LIBERATION

ONE

PLUMAUDAN

———

A T DAWN on November 24, 1944, the day after Thanksgiving, a two-and-a-half-ton American Army truck made its way from the Disciplinary Center at Le Mans to Plumaudan, Brittany. Its destination: an abandoned château down the road from the village church. The Army had chosen one of Plumaudan's only imposing structures for the ceremony. Château la Vallée was a fourteenth-century manor house, deserted for years, with rickety stone walls and gaping holes where windows had been, a round tower, a lower square building facing the road into the village, and a courtyard the size of a baseball field.

There in the courtyard, a group of Military Police unloaded their kit: large pieces of wood, slats, steps, a crossbar for the rope. The sky over Plumaudan was relentlessly gray that Friday morning and it looked like it might never stop raining. There was a wet chill in the air, the kind that goes straight to your bones—a prelude to the coming winter, so bitter cold it would freeze the rivers.

The villagers awoke to the sounds of hammering. The mayor had received his instructions two weeks earlier. The citizens of Plumaudan were to be informed, but official attendance should be limited to authorities designated by the American Army. No photographs could be taken, the Americans had said, and the local press was to omit the name of the condemned man or his unit from any of its articles.

Thirty American soldiers had also received instructions. From units stationed all over Brittany and Normandy, from

Caen to Morlaix, they were ordered to leave their posts for one day of temporary duty in a village located seven miles southwest of Dinan. They reported that Friday morning to the Commanding Officer, Seine Disciplinary Training Center. He arranged them in the courtyard, designating some as "official witnesses," others as "authorized spectators." It was only then that they learned what their duty was.

In one hour, an American soldier was going to hang. His name was James E. Hendricks. He was a black GI from a quartermaster battalion that had camped in a field in Le Percoul, a tiny farming hamlet up the hill from Plumaudan, back in August, only days after the town was liberated from the Nazis.

The soldiers who had been brought to observe knew little about the crime except that Hendricks had killed a local peasant. A court-martial had found him guilty and sentenced him to hang by the neck until dead. But they all knew the policy: GIs who committed crimes against French civilians were punished in the community where the crime occurred.

———

At 10:59 A.M., a cargo truck with its white U.S. ARMY stencil and flapping canvas top arrived in the courtyard, delivering the condemned man. General Prisoner James Hendricks was escorted by a procession of two guards and four officers to the platform on the gallows.

Hendricks was twenty-one years old, with round cheeks, gentle eyes, and dark brown skin that stood out next to his guards' ruddy white faces. He wore his uniform, but his jacket had been stripped bare of the modest insignia that identified him as a private first class in the quartermaster battalion. He had killed Victor Bignon, a decorated World War I veteran and a respected farmer who sat on the Plumaudan town council. Madame Bignon and her daughter had kept to themselves since the trial, and rumors abounded in the village about what happened to them the night of the crime.

James Hendricks had been confined to the guardhouse in

Saint-Vougay, in the western part of Brittany, since his sentencing. His closest contact there was with Lt. Robert Saunders, one of the Army's few black Baptist chaplains. The task of preparing James Hendricks to die was one of the most difficult of Saunders's Army career. Back in 1943, he had been attached to the same quartermaster battalion as Hendricks at Camp Van Dorn, Mississippi, a training camp for black GIs. The poor conditions at Camp Van Dorn had so appalled the forty-year-old chaplain that he tried to resign his commission. He understood, better than anyone, what Hendricks's life had been like since he was drafted into the segregated Army. At Saint-Vougay the two men had prayed together on Thanksgiving. Now, on the gallows at Plumaudan, they were still side by side.

Saunders was not the only black man at Plumaudan on November 24. Three African American enlisted men from service units other than Hendricks's had been ordered to attend the ceremony. It was lip service to the so-called "separate but equal" policy of Army segregation, which stipulated in the memorandum on hangings that there were to be black witnesses present along with the whites.

Hendricks's own Army buddies were spared the gruesome privilege of seeing their comrade hang. The 3326th Quartermaster Truck Company, which had played a key role in Brittany by transporting the supplies crucial for winning the Brest campaign, had moved on to Belgium and Holland. With them was Hendricks's commanding officer, Lt. Donald Tucker, who had testified in court to the young man's fine behavior before the shooting. Hendricks's defense counsel, and two officers from the court-martial who had requested that his death sentence be commuted to life in prison, were also in Belgium, en route to Germany.

———

After Hendricks's feet were bound, the ceremony proper began. The commandant asked him the requisite question:

"Do you have a last statement to make before the order directing your execution is carried out?"

"No, sir."

Chaplain Saunders began to recite the Twenty-third Psalm: "The Lord is my Shepherd, I shall not want. He maketh me to lie down in green pastures; he leadeth me beside the still waters. He restoreth my soul . . ."

The commandant interrupted the verse; it was time for Saunders to ask Hendricks his own official question, as dictated by the strict protocol of the hanging memorandum.

"Do you have a statement to make to me as Chaplain?"

"Thank you for what you've did for me," James Hendricks answered. "Tell all the boys not to do what I did."

———

Amidst the carnage of World War II, the spectacle at Plumaudan was a minor incident. Only a dozen men had been at James Hendricks's trial. The crowd that came to watch him hang was small. Once they were gone, who would remember what he did, what happened to him, or what it meant? Ordinary crimes such as his are not part of the story of D-Day or the legacy of the Greatest Generation. They seem destined to fade in memory, then disappear forever. Except that one man could not forget. He was a Frenchman and writer named Louis Guilloux.

Guilloux was not at the ceremony on that rainy November day, but he knew more about Hendricks's crime and punishment than anyone at Plumaudan. He had attended James Hendricks's court-martial as an interpreter, translating the testimony of the French civilian witnesses into English for the Americans. He had witnessed many acts of war and occupation—cowardly acts and heroic ones—but these American military trials haunted him for decades. He remembered Hendricks's story in all its details.

There were a few things people always liked to say about Louis Guilloux. He had a perfect ear for language, and a perfect sense of justice. His ear for language came through in the dialogue he wrote, and in his ability to translate. He spoke English beautifully, though he had only been in England once, as a boy.

His sense of justice was just as sharp. It didn't have to do with ideology, but with a kind of lucidity about the world, about what mattered, what was fair and unfair. When Guilloux sensed an injustice, he wouldn't let it rest. His friends still remember him, cradling a pipe in his left hand, tilting his head, his eyes sparkling with discernment. He didn't care if you agreed with him or not. He liked to ask uncomfortable questions, and he wasn't satisfied until he understood the answers, in all their complexity.

After a month working for military justice in the U.S. Army, Louis Guilloux began to sense that something was very wrong: "The guilty were always black," he mused, "so much so that even the stupidest of men would have ended up asking himself how it was possible that there be so much crime on one side, and so much virtue on the other."

Postwar Army statistics confirm Guilloux's intuition. In an After Action Report, the Judge Advocate General's Department revealed that seventy men were executed for capital crimes in the European Theater of Operations between 1943 and 1946. Fifty-five of them were African Americans. That's 79 percent in an Army that was only 8.5 percent black.

Guilloux thought about it for twenty years, then he began to write. He had served as interpreter in four cases. He had seen six black GIs condemned to life in prison for rape and two more black GIs sentenced to hang for rape and murder. In his final trial, a white officer, on trial for murder, was acquitted. It took him twelve years of work and as many drafts to turn the memories of his time with the Americans into a novel. He concentrated on the trial of the black private James Hendricks, who was condemned to hang at Plumaudan, and the white officer George Whittington, whom the Army found innocent.

Although he wrote in French, Guilloux was always an interpreter at heart. He wanted the language and spirit of the GIs to be central to his story, so he gave his book a title in American English. He called it *OK, Joe.*

TWO

OCCUPATION AND RESISTANCE

—

L OUIS GUILLOUX was forty-five years old when the
Americans liberated his hometown of Saint-Brieuc on
the northern coast of Brittany. He had lived under
German occupation for four years, and by the time it was
over, he was emaciated and weakened, both physically and
mentally.

Louis Guilloux had always been thin, with a high forehead
and a long, aristocratic nose. In the 1930s he was natty and
bohemian in his tweeds. You might have mistaken him for
Fred Astaire except that he was disheveled—he couldn't be
bothered with proper grooming. *"Une belle tête,"* people said
about him; "a beautiful head." By 1944, he was unrecogniz-
able: scrawny, stooped, and hesitant, wearing a ragged sweater
and a peasant's beret. He hadn't had a haircut in months, and
his thick black hair was matted onto his neck. The discomforts
of daily life under the occupation, the lack of food, the risks he
had taken, the deportation and execution of comrades and
friends, and the constant threat of his own arrest were all to
blame. The Occupation was an affront to everything he valued.

Guilloux had inherited his political passions from his father, a cobbler also named Louis Guilloux, whose life's work
had been to found a union hall, the *Maison du peuple,* in Saint-
Brieuc. Guilloux was supposed to follow in his father's trade.
But when he was an infant of two, he contracted a tuberculo-
sis of the bones, which deformed the fingers on his left hand.
His parents realized that he would never be able to do a cobbler's handiwork.

The elder Guilloux had already started his apprenticeship as a shoemaker by the age of thirteen. Young Louis, who had no prospects in the trade, was allowed to stay in school at thirteen and beyond. He won a scholarship. "You won't be a cobbler, but you won't have to be a soldier, either," his mother liked to say. By abandoning his father's trade and becoming an intellectual, Guilloux left his own kind. There was a sadness for him in the distance he now felt from the working people with whom he had grown up, and his apartness was one of the qualities that made him a sensitive translator. He never felt quite comfortable in the world of letters either. He had lived in several worlds without settling in any.

Guilloux had a special empathy for people without a home and a keen eye for politics. In the 1930s, in his native Saint-Brieuc, he had organized shelter for thousands of refugees from war-torn Spain and Nazi Germany. In 1935, he published a novel, *Le Sang noir*, a Dostoievskian epic that explored the devastating effect of World War I on the people of Brittany. The book had nearly as strong an impact in France as Remarque's *All Quiet on the Western Front* had had in Germany. In 1936, André Gide invited Guilloux and several other trusted intellectuals to accompany him on an investigative mission to the Soviet Union. Guilloux, who had had high hopes for the Communist experiment, returned from the trip a skeptic.

———

His country had fallen to the Germans in June 1940 after a six-week battle, a colossal military defeat that sent over 2 million Frenchmen to German POW camps. To consolidate their victory, the Nazis immediately occupied over half of France, including Paris, the North, and the coastal regions. They left the interior for later. Brittany, a peninsula jutting out from the Northwest, was vital to Europe's defense, so the Nazis located their naval base there, in the port of Brest, at the western tip of the peninsula. All along the Brittany coasts, from Saint-Malo in the north to Lorient and Saint-Nazaire in the South, the Germans built seawalls, gun nests, cement barracks, to protect their possession from an Allied invasion from across the Channel.

Guilloux's native Brittany saw one of the earliest and heaviest influxes of German soldiers of any occupied region. In households in every village and town of the province, the Nazis requisitioned room and board for their officers. German soldiers stayed in rooms left vacant by the French, first by the sons who had been drafted in 1940 and taken prisoner, later by the thousands of men and women the Nazis forced to Germany for "obligatory work service" in factories and fields throughout the warrior nation.

In a policed world of restrictions and zones, international travel became impossible for the writer, and even travel within France was now extremely difficult. Guilloux's usual rhythm throughout the 1930s had been a constant back and forth movement between Saint-Brieuc, where he lived with his wife and daughter in a comfortable modern house on the rue Lavoisier, and a solo bohemian intellectual life in Paris. For the four years of the Nazi occupation, Guilloux was limited mostly to Saint-Brieuc. In his attic study, lined with books, he looked out toward Brittany's rocky granite coasts in one direction and toward the roofs of Saint-Brieuc in the other. He often wrote standing, at a wooden lectern he set up near the window with the sea view.

The Occupation was a time of political action but also a time of reflection for Guilloux. Although he complained that he wasn't getting any writing done, he nearly completed the manuscript of an 800-page novel, in the form of a series of tales set in Saint-Brieuc during the Occupation, full of picturesque characters and adventures, constructed as a labyrinth, with one story leading to another. In his diaries Guilloux recorded details from his daily life, but it was too dangerous to write about his own resistance activity. Any name he mentioned, any plan, could lead to the arrest of a comrade or the destruction of an underground network.

Instead, in anguished detail, he recounted his dreams:

February 14, 1944:
. . . I saw some long, fat fish swimming just below the surface of a river. Then I noticed that these fish turned into cats, got out of the water, walked along the river bank in single file—I counted eight or nine of them. They soon returned to the water.

February 20, 1944:
I'm at Baratoux School (occupied by the Germans since their arrival). On the threshold of a door that doesn't actually exist, and which, in my dream, opens to the left of the front gate, I find a kind, cheerful German soldier—no longer a young man—with whom I start up a conversation, telling him that I used to live in that school, that my father was a concierge there for two or three years, and that I'd really like to see where we used to live. To which he answers that nothing could be easier or more natural, and he escorts me to our former quarters, which I walk through, muffling my sobs in a handkerchief rolled up into a ball, which I bite and stuff into my mouth. . . .

Fish leap out of the water and march along the river like cats; Guilloux's childhood home has lost its door; and the cheerful enemy inside has been living there long enough to have grown old. It's hard to imagine more perfect allegories for life under Vichy.

The establishment of the Vichy government meant not only that France was occupied but that the country had chosen to collaborate with the enemy. For unlike Belgium, Holland, or Poland, which had also fallen to the Nazis, France maintained a semblance of self-rule. In 1940, when the Germans captured Paris, the French ministries moved to the spa town of Vichy, where a French government continued, ruled by the most reactionary political elements in the country. Vichy signed a pact of collaboration with Hitler, and Vichy law and policies often echoed the Nazis in form and spirit. Vichy suspended the French constitution, stripped French Jews of their professional affiliations and civil rights, and eventually cooperated with the Nazis in massive deportation schemes. Seventy-six thousand Jews and a nearly equal number of resistance fighters were deported from France. Five thousand Bretons were deported or executed as hostages. And in a country where millions of men were absent in POW camps or obligatory work service, Vichy promoted motherhood and family values and made administering abortions a crime punishable by death.

Although Saint-Brieuc was controlled in large part by the German military, the administrative structures of Vichy were visible at the police and the Prefecture, the regional representative of the French state. Vichy-controlled police were constantly on the lookout for the enemies of the regime, Jews, Freemasons, and Communists, whom the regime's nonstop propaganda blamed for France's fall. Given his political visibility in the 1930s as a leading intellectual of the left, Guilloux was a marked man.

By 1941, in the country at large, organized resistance to the Nazis and the repressive Vichy government began to take shape. Charles de Gaulle, virtually unknown in 1940, organized a free France out of London with dissident elements from the French military, who had refused the armistice and collaboration with Germany. Within France, the interior resistance strengthened as conditions in the country deteriorated. In Brittany, the dense population of Nazi soldiers had inspired a healthy resistance movement from the beginning. Saint-Brieuc was an important center of resistance activity for the northeast section of the region, the Côtes-du-Nord.

Guilloux's role was central, even though he was not what one would call a resistance fighter. Forty-one years old when the Occupation began, Guilloux was valued within the movement as an elder statesman, someone who knew how to set an agenda when the stakes were high and the conflicts deep. Guilloux's house on the rue Lavoisier became a meeting place for

diverse factions of the Resistance and a refuge for young mili-
tants involved in dangerous street actions—underground
printing and pamphleteering, rescue of comrades, sabotage of
German property. For these men, Guilloux provided shelter
and direction.

In January 1941, in the very earliest phase of resistance to
Nazi occupation, Guilloux met with l'abbé Chéruel and l'abbé
Vallès, two future leaders of the Catholic Resistance in Saint-
Brieuc. He noted the meeting in his diary but said nothing
about what was discussed: "If only I could say half of what I
thought!" He was forging a coalition among Catholics, Social-
ists, and Communists in the Saint-Brieuc Resistance. His own
affiliation was with the Front National, a federation of resistance movements linked to the Communists. The Front distributed tracts, organized demonstrations, and carried out acts of
sabotage against the Germans.

Though his actions took place behind the scenes, rather
than on the street, Guilloux was a wanted man. In March
1943, the Vichy police searched his house on the grounds that
the writer was a Communist sympathizer, likely to be involved
in subversive activities. He was taken to police headquarters
for an interrogation, but no charges were brought against him.
Later that year, when he and his daughter were visiting a
nearby town, a car came to the rue Lavoisier to arrest him. By
the time he returned to Saint-Brieuc, the car was gone.

In February 1944, with the threats against him mounting,
Guilloux went into hiding in his wife's childhood home near
Toulouse, in the Southwest. He stayed nearly a month.

Throughout 1944, the Germans abandoned any pretense of
moderation in their administration of the French territory. The
collaborationist Vichy government, too, had grown desperate
in its attempts to ward off the growing Resistance movement.
It had formed a law and order squad called the *milice*, "the
militia," to wage armed combat against the Resistance fighters, whom it labeled "terrorists."

As Vichy and the German occupiers became more violent,
the interior Resistance gained more strength, its various politi-

cal branches cooperating for the common cause. In Saint-Brieuc, the Communist, Socialist, Christian Democrat, and Gaullist factions of the Resistance that Guilloux had helped to unite had federated into one Departmental Committee of Liberation. They were hopeful.

This newfound strength and unity of the Resistance was connected to the larger war effort. The strategic question for the Allies had always been to figure out in what order they needed to invade Europe and the Mediterranean so as to defeat Germany as quickly as possible. The first step in the process of liberation was the Allied invasion of French territory in North Africa on November 8, 1942. The Germans responded to the Allies' North Africa invasion by crossing the demarcation line separating the occupied from the non-occupied zones of France: by the end of November 1942, they occupied all of France.

Next came Italy. In July 1943, Benito Mussolini, leader of the second Axis power after Germany, was overthrown and held captive by the Italian monarch. Freed by a German commando, he formed a puppet Nazi government in the north of Italy. The Allies landed in southern Italy in September, and while the regular Italian government soon surrendered to the United States, the Germans responded by occupying the rest of the country. Though the Italian campaign was extremely difficult, the slow advance of the Allies toward the north reinforced the optimism of Guilloux and his colleagues. It was only a matter of time, they agreed, before the Germans would be defeated. The collaborationist Vichy government would fall with them.

Guilloux and his colleagues in Saint-Brieuc knew that as soon as the Allies landed on the northern coast of France—whether it was in their own Brittany or in Normandy, to the east—their time would come. It would be a matter of weeks, maybe days until the Americans reached them, and the Germans would be forced to retreat.

In that heady spring of 1944, in one of the meetings at Guilloux's home on the rue Lavoisier, the Saint-Brieuc Committee of Liberation began making plans with the town's future mayor, Charles Royer. Royer would take up his rightful place in city hall as soon as the forces of liberation arrived in Saint-Brieuc and the Vichy-appointed mayor was expelled. Royer promised to bring in Guilloux as his official English-language interpreter.

Guilloux's passion for English was well known in Saint-Brieuc. As a schoolboy, he had loved to go down to his town's port, Le Légué, and speak to the British sailors. Later he befriended a visiting journalist who invited him home to England for the summer of his thirteenth year. And since the 1920s, he had made ends meet as a literary translator.

The Resistance leaders understood that they would need to communicate with the Allies from England and the United States, who were sure to play a part in their town's postwar recovery. With his fluent English and his political experience, Guilloux was perfect for the job.

THREE

THE LIBERATION

———

UNTIL IT HAPPENS, liberation feels impossibly distant, even to those who hope for it most. The final days of the Occupation in Saint-Brieuc were a time of terror and of waiting. Everyone knew that the Allies might land any day, but no one knew exactly when or where. In the meantime, the desperate Vichy government sent out its militia squads to terrorize the Resistance. As they felt themselves losing the war, the Germans stepped up their requisitions of Frenchmen to forced labor camps; executed hostages; and arrested and deported Resistance fighters and Jews at a great pace—among them Guilloux's dear friend, the poet Max Jacob. Paradoxically, as liberation approached, conditions became worse for the French, and the accumulated weight of four years of occupation felt heavier than ever.

Nor did the prospect of liberation come without its own anxiety. Guilloux worried that the Allied landing might take place on the Brittany coast at Saint-Laurent, where his aged mother was living. There would surely be huge civilian casualties after the liberators landed. A bomb aimed at the Nazi seawall or at an ammunition depot might just as easily hit a home. Meanwhile, Hitler had given orders to his commanders that the ports of Brittany were to be considered fortresses, to be defended to the death. In the spring of 1944, the Germans ordered anyone living on the coasts who was older than sixty to evacuate. Louis Guilloux's mother left Saint-Laurent and moved in with Guilloux's sister in Ablis. A month later, tired of waiting, she returned home.

Throughout northern France, reports filed by the local prefects to the central administration described an anxiety about the landing that was nothing short of a "psychosis." A much-hoped-for landing on March 15, 1944, never materialized; a local intelligence report quipped: "We are constantly waiting for the landing and it isn't coming." By now, Allied planes were flying from England to northern France on regular bombing missions, hoping to inflict damage on German munitions, transport vehicles, and troops. French civilian casualties were an inevitable by-product of these bombings. French intelligence reports describe flashes of anger on the part of French civilians after the Allied bombings, anger that subsided only when the French realized that the Allied bombers had casualties of their own.

Finally, on June 6, 1944, the Allies launched their ships across the Channel. "Operation Overlord" was under way. On that "longest day," in Cornelius Ryan's mythical phrase, there were nearly 10,000 casualties on Omaha, Utah, Juno, and Gold Beaches, where 130,000 men braved land mines and a storm of bullets from the Germans stationed high on the bluffs above them.

We often think about those soldiers, but we forget the French, whose strange privilege on June 6 was to welcome a brutal assault on their own country. One of the most poignant scenes in the movie *The Longest Day* is the speech given by Adm. Robert Jaujard aboard the Free French cruiser *Montcalm*, which crossed the Channel with the USS *Arkansas* to cover the men on Omaha Beach. Jaujard is supposed to have addressed his men on a loudspeaker as the assault began: "It is a terrible and monstrous thing to have to fire on our homeland, but I am asking you to do it today."

For Americans, D-Day marks the liberation of France. But for anyone who took part in the operation, and for any French civilian who remembers life in northern France during the summer of 1944, June 6 was only the beginning of a war to expel the Nazis that raged on for several months, and the unleashing of a process that would be bloody and painful.

———

Between June 6, 1944, when the Allies landed in Normandy, and August 18, when the Nazi siege at Brest finally ended, the people of Brittany were pawns in a ferocious battle. In the Breton countryside there was an atmosphere of civil war, as the Vichy *milice* attacked the underground Resistance *maquis* who were fighting the Nazis in the countryside and the forests. Among the German troops at large in the countryside were Russian collaborators who had joined the German army in the eleventh hour, hoping for better treatment from the losing Nazis than from their own army. They were known for their violent behavior among civilians. Pillage, rape, and terror were commonplace.

Back in Normandy, immediately following the landing, the Americans were having trouble breaking through the Nazi lines. The news reports were bad, describing the Army's tanks blocked by the massive and muddy hedgerows that enclose fields in that part of the country. They were under constant attack by the Germans, and there was much bloodshed among soldiers and civilians. By July 7, the towns of Caen, Lisieux, Vire, Coutances, Saint-Lô, Flers, and Condé-sur-Noireau were, in the words of the historian Hilary Footitt, "virtually reduced to dust" by Allied bombs. Throughout the countryside, the stench of dead cattle was intolerable.

———

The people of Brittany waited for the Americans to arrive on their western peninsula. Although the U.S. Army's ultimate goal was to move east, to cross the Rhine into Germany, its leaders were also determined to move west to Brittany. This westward turn was motivated by two factors: the Allies needed to secure the ports of Brittany so that they could bring in supplies for the march toward Germany. And they needed to expel the Nazis as far west as Brest; otherwise, they were vulnerable to an attack from behind.

Bombing raids punctuated the month of June; soon there was no more electricity and no more gas; curfew was set at 9 P.M. Guilloux never knew if the sounds of grenades and gunfire he was hearing were those of the Resistance or the *milice*.

On June 14, Guilloux noted that forty-one Resistance fighters from his region had been condemned to death by a German military tribunal and executed. On June 26, he received an official paper ordering him to work on the roads for the German occupiers. A medical visit furnished him with an immediate exemption: he was weak and seriously underweight. He was not alone; the calorie count for the average city dweller in France, after four years of insufficient food, was half what it had been before the start of the war.

By July, Guilloux was describing his physical and mental state in desperate terms: "the least effort is costly; I often have trouble dragging myself from one place to the next; I go to bed tired; I wake up tired. Work is going badly, this work that is endless and will never end." "Work" meant his work as a writer, but he might also have been referring to the difficult work of liberation.

Finally, in August, the German retreat began. As they fled Saint-Brieuc on August 3 and 4, the departing occupiers destroyed everything they could—their own papers and files, the town's supplies of food and weapons. They burned Guilloux's own lycée, which they had been using as an ammunition depot.

Where did the Germans go? One U.S. veteran of the northern France campaign described an odd situation. A retreating German battalion crossed paths with his advancing American battalion, and two traffic patrols, German and American, found themselves face to face. It was a lighthearted memory of a conflict that took 200,000 German lives in Normandy alone. Other German soldiers were arrested by the liberating armies and herded to Allied POW camps in convoys of flat-bottom trucks.

The U.S. Army was a vast moving operation, fanning across the entire length of the Brittany peninsula in less than a month, bringing armored divisions, infantry divisions, and administrative units to every town and village, occupying the same châteaux and administrative buildings that the Nazis had left only days before. The Army's rear guard was composed of administrative support organizations, including Civil Affairs, in charge of relations with French civilians, and a Judge Advocate Unit, in charge of legal matters. The Army needed the help of men like Guilloux, for the encounter of American troops and French locals was a fragile event, on the individual as well as the political level. Boys who had never before left the United States, fatigued and disoriented, longing for relief from war, were coming into daily contact with natives whose language and customs were strange to them. The goodwill of French civilians was central to American strategy, and if the Americans were perceived as occupiers, rather than liberators, the battle was lost.

As early as 1943, Civil Affairs prepared Zone Handbooks for each region the Allied Army would enter, to guide British and American officers in their dealings with the local populations. They made clear the cultural gap Guilloux was expected to fill.

The typical Breton presents the following marked characteristics:

—the Breton is introspective. He is not a Latin, and lacks Latin gaiety. He is quiet, even taciturn—something of an introvert. In his country, *"la joie elle-même y est un peu triste."* But sometimes, at feasts or on holidays, he breaks out violently into an extreme merriment. He is apt to be querulous when in his cups.

—He dislikes foreigners. Although hospitable by force of long tradition, he is fundamentally hostile to foreigners. He does not like Englishmen, but he hates the occupying

Germans to such an extent that he will welcome the English in their capacity of allies.

In a formula that would come back to haunt the Army, the handbook propagated the perennial cliché of the easy native woman:

> One should not pay much attention to the lapses of Breton women with the Germans—the race is naturally erotic.

As they arrived in the Côtes-du-Nord, a special Information Bulletin alerted U.S. officers not to make insulting comments about housing and hygiene in the French countryside. In Brittany, they were warned, they were likely to find man and beast dwelling side by side on many farms.

Four

The Interpreter

—

ON AUGUST 7, 1944, the day after Saint-Brieuc was liberated, the Americans set up their Office of Civil Affairs in the Collège Ernest Renan, the local girls' school. The new mayor, Charles Royer, had assumed his duties, and, as he promised, had appointed Louis Guilloux to serve as his interpreter.

That evening, Guilloux, his wife, Renée, and their twelve-year-old daughter, Yvonne, walked down to the school gates to meet the liberators. The streets in the center of town were covered with shattered glass, and an entire block near the train station had been leveled by bombs. There wasn't a window remaining in the municipal library or the fire station. Half the lycée was in ruins. But the Nazis were gone.

For Guilloux, the Liberation meant, among other things, that he could resume doing what he had always loved to do best when he wasn't writing: wandering the streets of Saint-Brieuc and starting up conversations with strangers. "*Je suis un buveur de rues,*" he once said of himself; "I'm a drinker of streets." His wanderings were the source of countless scenes and impressions that he transposed into his writing. The more respectable citizens of his town, who knew nothing of the literary esteem with which he was held in Paris, were suspicious of his aimlessness. Guilloux, to them, was a man with too much time on his hands, an eccentric, if not a bum.

But on August 7, the rest of the town was out on the streets with him. Everyone in Saint-Brieuc wanted to speak to the friendly GIs replacing the Nazis who had stood at the same gates only days before with grenades in their belts and guard dogs at their sides. Louis, Renée, and Yvonne crossed the crowded square in front of the Collège. Yvonne held out her sketchbook to the soldiers she met milling about. They signed their names: Robert H. Anderson, Birmingham, Alabama; W. B. French, Springfield, Minnesota; Michael Ostrow, Little Rock, Arkansas; Hyman Katz, New York City; William Cormier, Chicago, all crowding around her, smiling, handing her presents of gum and Nescafé.

Guilloux struck up a conversation with Bill Cormier, the young Chicagoan. It was a meeting that affected both men. Years later, Guilloux made Bill Cormier a character in *OK, Joe*, the idealistic young American who believed he was coming to France to change the world. Cormier wasn't a writer, but like Guilloux, he was keeping a diary of his war experience. That night, he wrote about his first encounter with the Frenchman:

> The slight little fellow with long disheveled hair covered with a typical French beret was speaking with a British accent. . . . He spoke excellently. An interruption enabled me to speak to his wife and I learned the news that he was Louis Guilloux, quite an accomplished author. . . .

Cormier, a sergeant in the Army's VIII Corps, soon introduced Guilloux to his superiors, who were looking for a man who could help them communicate with the local population. And this is how Guilloux came to leave the services of Mayor Charles Royer and join the Judge Advocate Office of the VIII Corps as their official interpreter. Cormier and Guilloux, fast friends, were bemused by one another: Cormier found Guilloux dissatisfied and pessimistic to the point of nihilism, while Guilloux found his American friend optimistic to the point of naïveté. As they argued their different views of the world, their friendship grew, nourished by many evenings of conversation.

Because so many of the American soldiers who served in World War II were of German descent, it wasn't difficult for the Army to find interpreters to help them in Germany. But in France and Belgium the Army had to rely on civilians, and there was a dearth of French civilians who knew enough English to communicate successfully with the Americans. To make matters worse, the Army's rate of pay was so low that the position of interpreter was not attractive to anyone with advanced training. After the war, Army Military Justice officials reported that the situation had "affected both investigations and trials deplorably."

The Army was lucky to have found, in Louis Guilloux, a person of enormous curiosity and passion for causes, as well as an experienced literary translator. The war, with its paper shortages and crisis in communication, had put his work on hold, but by 1940 he already had three book-length translations to his credit. The most interesting of these was Claude McKay's Harlem Renaissance classic, *Home to Harlem* (1927), the story of a black veteran of World War I who makes a new start in the jazz dives of 1920s Harlem.

McKay's novel uses Harlem slang. Guilloux translated it into Caribbean French. The work inspired him, for at the same time as he was translating, he was also planning his World War I saga, *Le Sang noir*, a novel using the Gallo dialect spoken in the east of Brittany. Guilloux's notebooks from the 1930s contain conversations in slang and lists of local expressions. Maïa, the main character, speaks in a patois as thick as one of McKay's Harlem characters.

There is yet another connection between Guilloux's *Le Sang noir* and McKay's *Home to Harlem*: their focus on Brittany during World War I. It's easy to forget that McKay's story begins in the port town of Brest, where the main character, Jake, has enlisted in a troop of black soldiers, a service unit. Brest, in World War I, was a vital port for supplies and for manpower. Thousands of African American soldiers served as stevedores, unloading shipments and building the barracks that circled the Breton peninsula.

Jake's description of the plight of black soldiers alerted Guilloux, well before World War II, that there were race problems in the American Army:

> He sailed for Brest with a happy chocolate company. Jake had his own daydreams of going over the top. But his company was held at Brest. Jake toted lumber—boards, planks, posts, rafters—for the hundreds of huts that were built around the walls of Brest and along the coast between Brest and Saint-Pierre, to house the United States soldiers. Jake was disappointed. He had enlisted to fight. For what else had he been sticking a bayonet into the guts of a stuffed man and aiming bullets straight into a bull's-eye? Toting planks and getting into rows with his white comrades at the Bal Musette were not adventure.

Frustrated and humiliated by an army that wouldn't let him fight, Jake breaks the rules, risking a court-martial or worse.

Little could Guilloux have imagined in 1933 that a decade later, another world war would bring black enlisted American soldiers to Brittany again.

———

The VIII Corps Judge Advocate Journal for the month of August 1944 records the event: "Mr. Louis Guilloux (French) was employed by JA Section, Hq VIII Corps, Rear Echelon, as an interpreter." Guilloux's diary says simply: "I left with the lieutenants."

With prosecutor Joe Greene, his new boss, and an Army driver named Sam, Guilloux made his way along inland roads from Saint-Brieuc west to Morlaix—eighty-six kilometers.

Once he joined the Americans, the entries in Louis Guilloux's diaries became sketchy. "Only time for 'headliner,'" he wrote, meaning, "Only time for the headlines." He used an English word instead of the French *titres,* as if to underline the fact that he had entered a new linguistic universe.

Guilloux was delighted to be in Morlaix, charmed by all that was new, by his situation, by his conversations with the American officers. It is difficult from our perspective today, given the vast influence of American culture on all aspects of European life—food, dress, language—to realize how exotic the Americans looked and acted to this Frenchman and his fellow Bretons in the summer of 1944. Their large size, their gum (that mysterious substance that wasn't a food but something you chewed to pass the time), and their white straight teeth were strange. Even the way the GIs spoke and gestured— quick, direct sentences, constant smiles, and instant ease— bore little resemblance to their more familiar British cousins.

Later, when he began his novel about the summer of 1944, Louis Guilloux made lists of the words, both military jargon and everyday expressions, he had learned from the Americans: "mother's pets or mashed potatoes" for MPs (Military Police), "GI" for government issue; "Jerries" for Germans; "dear me!" and "good egg." And he added: "but who wasn't a good egg in this democratic army?" He was fascinated by the ritual "hellos" and "how are you doing?" and "oks" and "all rights" that he had heard in Morlaix. In an early draft of his novel, he carefully reproduced this exchange:

See you later, alligator.
In a while, crocodile.

Some evenings Guilloux spent with Joe Greene, the Army lawyer who hired him; others with Bill Cormier. Bill had dined at his home in Saint-Brieuc and had become a friend of the family. Greene, Guilloux's boss, was a brilliant, fast-talking New Yorker, stocky and handsome, with black hair and shining eyes, a lawyer who also prided himself on his talent as an amateur violinist. He was full of ideas for Guilloux's next novel. When Guilloux turned him into a character in OK, Joe, he described the American's hairy knuckles and his graceful violinist's hands. A fellow soldier remembered Greene as a man who was awkward at the ordinary tasks of soldiering and a smooth genius in the courtroom.

"I am really enjoying my new situation, great rapport with the lawyer, Lt. Joseph D. Greene—last night, long chat with him and the colonel, in the colonel's office," Guilloux wrote in his diary, the first day at Morlaix. And he added: "I admire the Americans' democratic spirit: even in uniform, they never stop behaving like civilians." It was a surprising vote of confidence for a man whose hopes and beliefs were so shaken by the war.

Guilloux slept in Morlaix on August 31, in the boys' school that had become the VIII Corps headquarters. On September 1 at 9 A.M., he left with Lt. Joseph Greene and Lt. Ralph Fogarty, his colleagues on the court-martial, on the long ride to Plumaudan, in eastern Brittany, to investigate the murder of the farmer named Victor Bignon by an African American GI named James Hendricks.

FIVE

JAMES HENDRICKS

—

I N HIS famous article on "Moral Luck," the contemporary American philosopher Thomas Nagel mentions three kinds of luck: luck in our upbringing or personal attributes, luck in our life circumstances, luck in the outcomes of our actions. This luck, or lack of it, creates the conditions by which we are judged, but we can't be judged solely on the basis of our luck. There has to remain a way to determine our responsibility for actions—responsibility that goes beyond upbringing, circumstances, or even outcomes. What part of the bad things that happen to us is within our control?

James Hendricks wasn't born lucky. His mother died giving birth to him on April 29, 1923, in Drewry, North Carolina, south of the Virginia border. His father, Eddie Hendricks, sent James and his sister Lou to live with their Henderson cousins on a farm in nearby Macon; Lou died soon after. Two other siblings stayed with their grandparents. Several years later, James's father died in a freak accident. A splinter stabbed him in the eye while he was chopping wood. The stick penetrated his brain and killed him instantly. By the time James Hendricks was a teenager, he was an orphan, separated from two surviving siblings he barely knew.

Nonetheless, in many ways, his life was a privileged one for an African American child growing up in the 1920s and 1930s. In Macon, James's adoptive parents, Ed and Annie Henderson, had escaped the fate of so many African American farm laborers in the years after emancipation: they weren't trapped in the sharecropper economy. They owned their own farm, in a part of Macon where several prominent black families were landowners and where the whites were poorer than the blacks. The community was called Embro, after "embryo," for new beginning.

The Hendersons farmed a large plot of land. They grew cotton and tobacco for cash, wheat and corn to feed their hogs. They made their own flour and corn meal, grew their own sugar cane for sugar and molasses, and the fruit they ate came from their own orchard.

James went to the Embro school, a three-room yellow schoolhouse within walking distance of the farm. It was a Rosenwald School, one of the hundreds of schools for rural African Americans funded in the 1910s and 1920s by the Chicago philanthropist Julius Rosenwald. Three teachers, ten children to a class, lessons indoors and out. Reading, writing, arithmetic, geography, history, and prayer.

James's only surviving schoolmate and neighbor, Robert Daniels, remembers his friend Jack Hendricks as an impulsive boy, prone to violent temper tantrums: "He'd fly all off." James's niece Geraldine, who grew up with him on the Henderson farm, remembers Hendricks as a "jolly type of person who liked to joke and carry on all the time." His five stepsiblings were jealous of all the love he got from their mother, his stepmother: "Don't hit him," Annie Henderson would say to her husband, "he's not my child." Ed Henderson would retort, "That's what's wrong with him—you let him have his way." Geraldine remembers that her mother, Hattie, and her aunt Geneva—James's stepsisters—would "pet him up." He was beloved, even spoiled by the Hendersons, but he would always be their guest, never a full-fledged member of the family.

Like many of the young black men in Macon, James Hendricks went north to look for work after ninth grade. He moved to Washington, D.C., where he lived with his stepsister Geneva (Ed Henderson's daughter) and her husband, Crosby Irby. They were religious people who discouraged drinking, and the atmosphere in their home was warm and friendly. In the evening, they played cards together.

Hendricks found a job with the Government Printing Office, but he hated having to wear a coat and tie to work. Crosby couldn't even get him to wear a shirt and tie to church.

After avoiding a first round of the draft by faking an illness, Hendricks was finally drafted in February 1943. He was inducted at Fort Meyer, Virginia, then sent to Camp Van Dorn, Mississippi.

The name "Camp Van Dorn" conjures what Ulysses Lee, in the U.S. Army's official history of the employment of Negro troops in World War II, called a "harvest of disorder." Low morale, inadequate leadership, inferior facilities, and the humiliation of segregation led to an escalating series of race riots at training camps like Camp Van Dorn. Many of these camps were located in the South and Deep South, since the climate was considered conducive to field training.

Camp Van Dorn, Mississippi, had a reputation as one of the very worst training camps in the nation. The physical environment was grueling for black and white troops alike, who had to contend with humid tropical weather, digging ditches in standing water that was a breeding place for snakes, mosquitoes, and chiggers. For African American GIs, the situation was exacerbated by the rule of Jim Crow, on the base and off. In the nearby town of Centreville, with a population of 2,100, facilities for African Americans were nonexistent and the atmosphere was thick with racism.

Some 6,500 black soldiers trained at Camp Van Dorn when James Hendricks was there: a black infantry unit, the 364th; two quartermaster truck regiments; a service battalion; a medical ambulance battalion; and a quartermaster laundry company.

Hendricks's Army papers say he was assigned to the medical battalion, the 791st Sanitary Company. By the time he sent a photo home from Mississippi, he had been transferred. He wrote on the back: "Private James E. Hendricks, Company C, 272nd Quartermaster Battalion." In the Sanitary Company, he learned first aid and gas mask techniques, but he also dug garbage pits and worked on mosquito and roach control. In the unit history, his commander noted that the men were expected to learn to read field medical records, although some of them could neither read nor write.

There is no record of Hendricks's transfer to the 272nd Quartermaster Battalion, but it was doubtless heavier work, physical labor to prepare him for the truck-driving duties he'd be given overseas.

Hendricks had been at Camp Van Dorn for over a month when trouble broke out. The 364th Infantry Regiment, the camp's single black infantry company, had transferred to Camp Van Dorn from Arizona. The men, many of them from the North, rebelled at the conditions in Mississippi. They caused a disturbance at the Negro Service Club, broke into the post exchange, and misbehaved in the nearby town of Centreville. On May 30, 1943, a black soldier from the 364th clashed with Military Police outside the gates of the camp. A local sheriff arrived on the scene and shot and killed the soldier. Men from the company, learning of the shooting, broke into a camp supply room and armed themselves with rifles. A riot squad of black MPs fired into the crowd of armed men and wounded one of the soldiers. The riot was barely contained.

For many years, there was a rumor that the army had killed over a thousand black soldiers from the 364th Infantry Regiment and buried them at Camp Van Dorn. Perhaps the terrible conditions that existed at the camp and the very real suffering of the men who trained there were breeding ground enough for such rumors, which were never substantiated. The fires of the legend were later flamed by a novel about Camp Van Dorn called *The Slaughter*, published by a white Mississippi writer named Carrol Case. Case claimed that his book was grounded in historical fact. After the publication of *The Slaughter* in 1998, the NAACP asked for an investigation. In 1999, the Army issued its report, based on archival sources and interviews with black veterans. The Army's research determined that only four soldiers of the 364th Infantry Regiment had died between May and December 1943 while stationed at Camp Van Dorn. Everyone else was accounted for. But the willingness of the public to believe the worst about the Mississippi training camp, in the absence of any proof, is a mark of tensions and hatred that still run high. The enduring Camp Van Dorn legend is an emblem of all that hasn't been resolved about the African American experience in the armed forces.

What the record shows is that the number of violent episodes in the African American training camps grew, beginning in 1941, when the first African American draftees entered the Army, and came to a head in 1943, the year James Hendricks was inducted. In April 1941, a black soldier was found hanging from a tree at Fort Benning, Georgia. Authorities at the camp thought it was a suicide, but his fellow soldiers believed he had been lynched. In August 1941, a white bus driver asked for MP protection when a crowd of rowdy black GIs boarded his bus heading for Fort Bragg, North Carolina. The white MPs used their nightsticks on the black soldiers. One of the black GIs grabbed an MP's gun and started shooting into the crowd. In the ensuing riot, one white MP and one black GI were killed; two white MPs and three black GIs were wounded.

Sometimes it was the black troops who started the altercations. In Camp Stewart, Georgia, black soldiers from the North, appalled by their treatment at the hands of white military and civilian police, rioted after hearing a rumor that a Negro woman had been raped and murdered by white soldiers who had killed her husband. What followed was an inevitable cycle of violence—armed mobs of black GIs, gunfire by white MPs, black and white men wounded and killed.

In 1942, the African American newspaper *The Amsterdam Star-News* analyzed the problem from the point of view of black enlisted men:

> They [Negro soldiers] cherish a deep resentment against the vicious race persecution which they and their forebears have long endured. They feel that they are soon to go overseas to fight for freedom over there. When their comparative new-found freedom is challenged by Southern military police and prejudiced superiors, they fight for freedom over here.

About Hendricks's specific situation at Camp Van Dorn, we know this: In December 1943, he got sick enough to be transferred from the Camp Van Dorn hospital to Foster General Hospital in Jackson, Mississippi. He spent a month in the hospital.

In February 1944, he shipped to England as private first class in a quartermaster truck company, then crossed the Channel to France. There, he did what he was trained to do: he drove trucks and slept in fields. He even managed to learn a few words of French. James Hendricks was a fully trained servant of liberation in a white man's army. Life could have been better; it could have been worse. Until the August night when everything changed.

—Part II—

UNITED STATES
VERSUS PRIVATE
JAMES E. HENDRICKS

S IX

THE INCIDENT

—

O N AUGUST 20, Gen. George S. Patton, Commanding General of the Third Army and the man who oversaw the Brittany campaign, sent a fierce memo to all Army units under his command: "I am gravely concerned with the increasing number of crimes of violence against French civilians which are being committed within the Army, particularly by service troops."

Patton's remarks were pointed: by "service troops," he meant black GIs. Eighty percent of all African American soldiers were assigned to non-combat service units, performing menial tasks. Black soldiers in the quartermaster, trucking, and ordnance companies moved weapons, food, and supplies from sea to port to battlefield. The liberation of Europe was a war of supplies, and their contribution was vital. At the same time, members of these service units were being arrested in greater numbers than any other sector of the Army for murder, rape, and theft. Patton deplored their crimes and underlined for his men the Army's commitment to civilian relations:

> American forces, with our allies, are now engaged in the liberation of France and the destruction of our common German enemy. Our purpose and deeds have won for us the enthusiastic welcome and cooperation of the French people. It is not to be tolerated that a comparative few shall, by their criminal conduct, bring discredit upon us. The continued prevalence of these offenses cannot fail

measurably to affect the manner in which our forces are now regarded.

Patton ordered each commander at all levels of Army organization to ensure that his troops were duly assembled. Company commanders were to inform their men that offenders were being tried by court-martial and that severe sentences, including the death penalty, were being imposed for the crime of rape. Severe sentences would continue to be imposed. The commanders themselves were under explicit orders to control the contact of their troops with the civilian population and thus prevent further criminal action.

The commander of James Hendricks's 3326th Quartermaster Truck Company assembled the 120 men under his command and read them Patton's warning. It was now his responsibility to control the behavior of his company, and his responsibility to prevent further criminal actions.

Twenty-four hours later, James Hendricks and four of his buddies were relaxing in a trailer at their campsite, sampling the hard liquor given to them by the local farmers. It was caramel brown, like cognac, but much stronger. *La goutte* is what the farmers called their own brand of calvados. The GIs could get as much of the hard stuff as they wanted. They traded gasoline to get it, as the farmers of Brittany were desperate for gas to run their threshing machines that August. Hendricks, a small man at five feet, seven and a half inches, weighing 140 pounds, had drunk his share.

He had been sent to the unit a week and a half earlier as a replacement. He served as an assistant truck driver, riding up front, hauling supplies. The 3326th Quartermaster Truck Company, a black company with a black commanding officer, Lieutenant Tucker, had been assigned to the task force headed toward Brest. Although they were classified as a service unit, they'd been operating in the combat zone since July. They'd seen plenty of action, including strafing by the enemy. In July, two of their men had gotten Purple Hearts. You didn't need to be in a combat unit to get wounded or killed.

Hendricks had only been in the company eleven days, not enough time to get to know the others. When he was training at Camp Van Dorn, in Mississippi, he was known as the "pet." He'd always gotten on with his COs. The men in the 3326th liked Hendricks, but they thought he was a little strange. Some days he would talk, other days he wouldn't say anything.

At 10:30 P.M. on the night of August 21, after getting drunk, Hendricks got up to leave the trailer. He said to his buddies, "I'm going out to get some." He was dressed in his regulation Army uniform—a beige shirt, a tie, a raincoat. He wore a helmet on his head, carried a rifle at his shoulder. All the drivers headed to Brest had been issued M-1 rifles and instructed to carry them. The orders were specific: seven rounds of ammunition only, and no round in the chamber. They were supposed to keep the safety on. James Hendricks crossed the field where the 3326th had been camped for a week, past tents and trailers and vehicles. He'd worked as a farm laborer most of his life, and the Breton wheat fields were a familiar setting, although the land was hillier and the soil blacker than the flat red clay of his native North Carolina. It had been raining on and off all day, but the rain had stopped now. The air smelled of cut wheat and manure. In Brittany in August the sun didn't set until almost eleven. During the last hour of light, the sky turned the deepest blue, the color of indigo dye.

Hendricks walked through the muddy fields. He was about a mile from Plumaudan when he came to a hill overlooking the village with a neat row of stone houses on either side of a narrow dirt road. There was a barn alongside one of the houses. Hendricks ventured inside and stayed there for a while. When he came out, he crossed the yard and knocked on the door of the adjacent stone farmhouse.

Inside was the Bouton family—three brothers about his age and their two parents. The brothers opened the door for him.

Hendricks asked them for the "Mademoiselle." The Boutons said there were no Mademoiselles in the house. Hendricks circled around the table toward Madame Bouton, gesturing that he wanted to kiss her. René Bouton took Hendricks by the shoulder to prevent him from getting any closer to his mother. Raymond Bouton offered the GI two eggs and his brother, Charles, offered a glass of cider. Hendricks declined the cider, but took the eggs, put them in his raincoat pocket, and left.

By the time he came out of the house, it was pitch dark. He crossed to the other side of the road, where he saw a smaller stone house with a wooden door. Because the window was blacked out, it was impossible to tell if there was a light on inside.

He pounded on the door, but no one opened for him. *"Boches,"* he cried out—he knew the French slang for "Krauts." "Boches!" he yelled over and over. If he did hear the people inside yell back at him, he couldn't understand what they were saying. He started asking for a Mademoiselle again. "Ouvrir, Mademoiselle!" "Ouvrir, ouvrir, Mademoiselle," he cried, pounding on the door. He pounded for two or three minutes, first with his fist, then with the butt of his M-1 rifle. Then he fired into the closed wooden door of the house.

Still no one opened. Hendricks pounded at the door for another three minutes before firing a second shot. This time there was a shriek from inside. Hendricks kicked the door ajar and discovered Victor Bignon collapsed behind it, his blood and his brains in a pool on the floor around him. Shards of wood from the gunfire had injured Bignon's wife, Noémie. Her face was bleeding. There were two other people in the room: Roger Robert, the farmboy, and Jeannine Bignon, the Bignons' eighteen-year-old daughter.

When Hendricks grabbed at Jeannine, she pulled away, ripping her blue and white pinafore. She and her mother and the farmboy ran across the road to the Boutons' house—the house where Hendricks had just been. Hendricks ran after them, and as he approached the house, he saw Charles Bouton standing in the yard. Hendricks motioned to him with his rifle to get away. Charles ran as fast as he could into the fields behind his house.

By the time Hendricks got inside the Bouton house, the young girl had disappeared. Her mother Noémie Bignon, René Bouton, and the farmboy Roger Robert stood in the main room, a living room that also served as a bedroom for the modest farm family. Hendricks pointed his gun at the two men and motioned for them to get into bed. He shouted at them in English and they answered in French, with no understanding of each other's words.

Hendricks pushed Noémie Bignon alongside a third, empty bed, laid her down, pulled up her dress, and exposed himself. Noémie cried out to Hendricks to leave her alone. She managed to keep him at a distance by struggling and fighting with her bare hands.

Hendricks jumped off the bed, aimed his gun at the three French peasants, but didn't fire. Finally, he fled from the house, running until he reached the shelter of a wheat field.

Back at the campsite, Lieutenant Tucker had heard the shots and screams. He gathered eight of his men to go out on patrol. As they came up toward the little farm hamlet, they thought they saw a figure in the dark and started shooting. A man fell into a ditch. When they approached, the man came out of the ditch and stumbled onto the road, then fell again. Two of Tucker's men picked him up. It was James Hendricks, the new man in the company. One of the soldiers shouted, "What the hell are you doing up in this area?" Tucker was irritated. "I'm the one doing the questioning," he said.

"What are you doing out of camp?" Tucker asked Hendricks.

Hendricks told him that he had been on water duty. The truck had left him behind while he was taking a leak, and he was just trying to find his way back to camp.

Tucker knew exactly who had been on water duty and knew his enlisted man was lying. He told him so.

Hendricks immediately changed his story: He hadn't been on water duty, but he'd been walking down the road with two other men from the company, trying to get back to camp. He remembered being in the field, but he didn't remember how he got there.

While Tucker was questioning Hendricks, one of the soldiers in the search party went up to the farmhouse with the open door to investigate where the scream might have come from. He looked past the threshold and saw the body of Victor Bignon. He called for Tucker. Tucker went to the open door and found Bignon's body, saw the hole in his head and his blood and brains on the floor.

Tucker sent for the MPs. He went back to Hendricks in the yard and confiscated his rifle. Tucker sniffed at the chamber and determined that it had been fired recently. There were five shells—two missing. Tucker asked Hendricks if he knew about the shooting, but Hendricks just stared at him as though he didn't know who Tucker was. Tucker told him to go over to the house and look at the body.

When Hendricks returned, he was shivering, as though he had the chills. He sat down on his helmet in the yard of the Bignon house, facing his commanding officer. Lieutenant Tucker stood over him. Tucker told him that if he made a statement, it would be used against him in a court-martial. He asked Hendricks to let him know if he was involved in the shooting in any way but added that it was up to Hendricks whether or not he made a statement. Hendricks decided to talk. "I'll tell you what I know about it," he said.

This time Hendricks told a different story. He had knocked at the door of the Bignon house to get directions back to camp. When no one answered, he'd fired a shot through the door. When he knocked again and nobody answered, he fired another shot. He couldn't remember anything else until he heard the men coming up the road.

As Hendricks was telling his story to Tucker, two jeeps arrived from Military Police headquarters in the nearby town of Dinan. It was 12:30 A.M. One MP guarded the crime scene while another joined Tucker in guarding Hendricks; a third MP went across the road to interview the French witnesses at the Boutons'. Word of the shooting had already reached the mayor of Plumaudan, who alerted the French gendarmes that a crime had taken place at the Bignon farm at Le Percoul. The gendarmerie informed the regional prefect and the town doctor, and two gendarmes arrived at Le Percoul to investigate, alongside the Americans. Both French and American authorities took statements from Noémie and Jeannine Bignon, and from the Bouton brothers.

It was 2:30 A.M. by the time the MPs finished their work with the civilians and were ready to drive Hendricks and Tucker to Military Police headquarters in Dinan for the official arraignment. The Military Police searched Hendricks and emptied his raincoat pockets. They found a billfold and some matches. Inside the billfold were snapshots and a condom. They also found one of the two eggs Raymond Bouton had given Hendricks. Strangely, it was unbroken.

Tucker turned in Hendricks's rifle as evidence. An MP named Lieutenant Naiser advised Hendricks of his rights. Tucker stayed with him, but the MP did all the questioning. Hendricks was allowed to have a smoke. By now it was 4 A.M.

"Did you fire the rifle?" Lieutenant Naiser asked him.

This time Hendricks told a very different story. His rifle had gone off because he had tripped as he was approaching the door of the Bignon farmhouse to ask for directions. He had reached down nervously to put the safety back on and his rifle had gone off again. The door had come open and he'd seen a man lying on the floor covered in blood. He'd crossed the road and found a farmhouse with its front door already open, so he just walked in. An old lady in the house offered him cider and he drank it. That was all he remembered until Lieutenant Tucker came after him with the other men.

In the conclusion to his statement, Hendricks took responsibility for killing Victor Bignon but called the shooting an accident:

> I'm sure it was my rifle that shot the man. I further state
> that I was drinking before this accident occurred. I certify

that I make this statement of my own free will and that
this may be held against me.

James Hendricks's one-page statement was the only official
declaration he ever made about his crime. It was typed up by
the Military Policeman at the headquarters in Dinan at 5 A.M.
It said nothing about chasing the Bignon women across the
road or about assaulting Noémie Bignon in the Bouton farmhouse.

As became clear at the trial, accounts of Hendricks's behavior in the Bouton house were based on the testimony of
only one witness. Many details were never corroborated. This
story, reconstructed using pieces of testimony from a handful
of people who saw James Hendricks that night, is the closest
we can come to knowing what actually happened on August
21, 1944.

SEVEN

THE COURT-MARTIAL

———

J AMES HENDRICKS'S general court-martial was scheduled for September 6. On September 1, Lt. Joe Greene, who'd been assigned to prosecute Hendricks, set out to investigate at the scene of the crime, accompanied by Lt. Ralph Fogarty, Hendricks's defense counsel, and their new French interpreter, Louis Guilloux.

Plumaudan was ninety miles east of Morlaix; a three-hour journey. Once they reached Saint-Brieuc, their driver, whom Guilloux calls "Sam" in his diaries and "Joe" in his novel, had to take the back roads, sunken lanes lined on either side by the ancient hedges that sheltered the crops from the wind—the infamous hedgerows that had almost trapped the American Army in Normandy a month earlier and that still offered perfect hiding places for German snipers. Although the region had been liberated for nearly three weeks, trouble could still be lurking around the corner, and everyone knew it. Guilloux marveled both at Sam's sangfroid and his sense of direction; he acted as though he was driving these lanes for the hundredth time instead of following the U.S. Army's detailed maps.

In *OK, Joe,* Guilloux recounts the sad scene of welcome at the Bignon farm:

Lieutenant Stone walked up to the door, briefcase in hand. He knocked. A tall country woman of about fifty, rather stout, dressed in black, opened it. We all cringed at the sight of the woman: her face looked almost as if it had been skinned; her forehead, her left cheek, and her chin were covered with scarlet spots.

"I know who you are," she said softly, stepping aside. "Come in."

The house consisted of a single room with a dirt floor. At the back of the room a young woman was busy tending a stove. She didn't join us.

The pre-trial investigation papers in James Hendricks's general court-martial file recount much the same process that Guilloux describes in his fiction. Greene and Fogarty arrived with their interpreter at the Bignon house on September 1. They asked Noémie and Jeannine Bignon a series of questions about the night of August 21; Guilloux translated. They took note of each bullet hole in the door and on the ceiling of the farmhouse. They found a bullet. They visited the local physician, Dr. Drouet, who supplied them with an affidavit about the cause of Victor Bignon's death. Guilloux translated the document into English.

The next day, September 2, Guilloux made a second round trip in the U.S. Army jeep from Morlaix to Plumaudan with Lieutenants Greene and Fogarty. Their objective this time was to transport the witnesses back to Morlaix. Noémie Bignon, Jeannine Bignon, their neighbors René and Charles Bouton, and the farmboy Roger Robert traveled in the Army jeep to the boys' lycée, where the Judge Advocate had arranged for a lineup.

Yet when they faced a group of black men and were asked to pick out the man who had entered the two stone houses and caused so much trouble on August 21, no one was able to identify James Hendricks. The failure struck Louis Guilloux as highly significant, and moved him to paint the scene in his diary:

This morning, in the courtyard, the lineup [*la confrontation*]—six black men lined up against a wall, while three men from the military police aimed their rifles at them and a fourth man aimed his machine gun. The witnesses walked past the men, one after the other, and examined them, one after the other. No identification.

It was an exceptionally long entry for this busy month of September, when, on a given day, he usually wrote only a line or two.

Guilloux was positive that the court-martial wouldn't be able to condemn a man for murder if the witnesses could not identify him. He pitied the victims, especially the poor French peasant girl who had lost her father. And so he concluded:

The guilty man will doubtless save his skin. The trial is scheduled for Wednesday.

James Hendricks was tried for having violated two separate Articles of War: Article 92, murder, and two counts of Article 93, housebreaking and assault with intent to rape. The charge that would send him to the scaffold would be based on a combination of three separate crimes. A general court-martial met to hear his case on September 6 from 9 A.M. to 5:30 P.M. and on September 7 from 9 A.M. to 3:45 P.M., with breaks for lunch.

Justice is supposed to be immutable, but a military tribunal in a time of war is anything but. Even the courtroom itself was makeshift. The Judge Advocates had chosen the common room at the boys' lycée for their court-martial—the *salle des fêtes*, a place where students danced together and teachers awarded end-of-year prizes. There hadn't been a proper party there since the Germans had first requisitioned the school several years earlier. Now this big hall had to be transformed into a space suitable for a trial.

Outside, it still sounded like war, not liberation. The campaign to take Brest was in full force, the battle raging to the west of Morlaix. You could hear Army trucks in the courtyard, planes buzzing overhead, and the occasional bomb going off.

For the makeshift tribunal, someone found a table long enough to accommodate all the members of the court-martial and covered it with a cloth to make it look official. Years later, as he was writing his novel, Louis Guilloux drew on his memory of that space: the large windows on both sides of the room that let the late summer light pour in; the table covered with a green cloth; the chair for witnesses in front of the table; a smaller table for the court reporter and his new-fangled transcription machine, almost noiseless.

———

Much has been written about the shortcomings of military justice—it is to justice, according to the famous saying, what military music is to music. But the difference between the systems is not merely a matter of quality. In its essence, military justice has different goals than civilian justice. The historian Elizabeth Hillman has put it succinctly:

> Courts-martial are part of a disciplinary scheme relied upon to maintain good order among troops, to preserve the obedience and conformity deemed necessary to successful military action, and to eliminate from the military those individuals who pose a risk to other service members or to national security itself.

In the specific situation of the U.S. Army in France, a crime against a civilian represented a grave breach of Army discipline that threatened the liberating army's relationship with the local population, crucial to the war effort.

Soldiers were judged in this system not by a jury of their peers, but by a commission of officers appointed for court-martial duty by their commander. The court-martial acted as judge and jury in one.

James Hendricks's court-martial had ten members. In the middle of the table sat the president and presiding officer, a colonel from Georgia named Claud T. Gunn. He was fifty-two years old, ten or fifteen years older than the other men on the court. Next to him on the left sat the Law Member, Lt. Juan A. A. Sedillo. The eight other officers who sat on either side of them, by order of rank, were lieutenant colonels, captains, and first lieutenants, officers representing various units of the VIII Corps rear echelon stationed at Morlaix: the Cavalry, the Military Police, the Adjutant General Department, the Finance Department, and the Quartermaster Corps, James Hendricks's branch. At the end of the trial, all ten men would cast a vote as to Hendricks's guilt or innocence. Their votes counted equally. The ballot was secret and a unanimous vote was required for a death penalty conviction.

The Hendricks court-martial, like the U.S. Army, was a melting pot. The men on the court were from Illinois, from Wisconsin, from Georgia, from New Mexico; they were Catholic, Protestant, Jewish; they were of Spanish, German, English, and Russian descent. But it was a white melting pot. Guilloux, remembering the scene, described the accused, terrified, "the only black man in this assembly of whites."

By far the most intriguing man and certainly the most influential on the Hendricks court-martial was the designated Law Member, Juan A. A. Sedillo, the member of the panel empowered to rule on judicial matters, such as the admissibility of evidence, during the trial. Discovered by a Fox Studio executive when he was in law school at Georgetown, he had played a Cuban detective in the 1929 film *Girl from Havana,* his only Hollywood role. In 1930 he published a short story in the *New Mexico Quarterly* about an old man in the hills of New Mexico who didn't want to sell his land. "Gentleman of Río in medio," anthologized countless times, became part of a canon of Chicano Studies as that field was constituted in the 1970s.

Sedillo himself, a suave ambitious man whom Guilloux portrayed with thick hair, a large head, and a languid gaze, was an elitist who had always insisted on his white, European origins. In 1930, he wrote to the *New York Times* to insist that the first white child was born in Colorado in the eighteenth century, not in the nineteenth, as a book reviewer had claimed.

He was descended from a New Mexican family of lawyers that proudly traced its origins back on both sides to the Spanish royal family. His sport was polo. He had married and divorced a Danish countess whose first language was French. His name had appeared regularly in the *Washington Post* society pages in the first years of the war: he squired admirals' daughters. His work on the Hendricks case was the stepping stone to great legal responsibilities in the postwar era, on war crimes tribunals and international courts.

Lt. Ralph Fogarty, James Hendricks's defense counsel, was as modest as Sedillo was flamboyant. The son of a clerk at an electrical motor works in Wausau, Wisconsin, he grew up in a neighborhood of German immigrants. In 1944, thirty-two-year-old Fogarty was two years into a long career with the U.S. Army Infantry during which he would rise to the rank of lieutenant colonel. We can imagine him, much as Guilloux described the character of the defense lawyer in *OK, Joe,* as well groomed and smiling affably: "As soon as you saw him, you understood that he must have excellent manners, always and in every situation."

Fogarty had completed officers' basic training at Fort Benning, Georgia. His training included no instruction in military justice. It was Army custom, before 1951, to assign junior officers in combat units, rather than Army-trained Judge Advocates, to serve as defense counsel in general courts-martial. If the men had legal experience in civilian life, so much the better, but it wasn't a requirement, even in death penalty cases. The situation in the VIII Corps court-martial was better than the norm: Col. William Scully, the Judge Advocate, had managed to get men with law school experience assigned as both trial and defense counsel in the Hendricks trial. Fogarty had graduated at the top of his class at the John Marshall Law School in Chicago in 1940. By 1944 he wasn't yet a member of the bar, and his work experience seems to have been limited to the insurance business. He gleaned his knowledge of the military justice system from his experience in the court and from his reading of the 1928 *Manual for Courts-Martial.*

He pleaded not guilty for his client on all counts: murder, housebreaking, and assault with intent to rape. Hendricks had chosen a man named Norman W. Porr from an engineer combat battalion to act as an assistant defense counsel, as was his right, but Porr did not speak during the trial and seems to have played no significant role. Fogarty performed unevenly in his defense of Hendricks. He appeared overpowered by the prosecution at the start of the trial, but he excelled in his cross-examination of Hendricks's commanding officer. In choosing Fogarty to defend James Hendricks, Judge Advocate Scully may well have named the second most experienced officer available, though he named a defense counsel who was clearly less experienced than the man who would prosecute the case.

Lt. Joseph Greene, the Brooklyn lawyer who chose Guilloux to serve as his interpreter, prosecuted Hendricks. In military legal parlance, he was known as the Trial Judge Advocate. By all accounts, Greene was a live wire who loved performing in a courtroom. The tougher the legal challenge, the happier he was.

Greene was born Joseph Greenberg in 1906; his immigrant father worked as a dress retailer in Brooklyn, but he had wanted better things for his son. Greene studied the violin as a boy. He attended law school at Fordham and practiced in Brooklyn after he was admitted to the bar in 1931. Joe Greene remained a bachelor and lived with his parents on Ocean Parkway until the war. Like many Jewish men of his generation, he believed in the American dream of assimilation. In 1937 he had petitioned to change his name from Joseph Greenberg to Joseph Glencort. The petition was approved, but he didn't go through with it. The name change was too radical, he decided—the name Glencort might alienate his Jewish clients. In 1941 he decided on a more modest change, from Greenberg to Greene, and he petitioned his local court a second time. There were too many Greenbergs in New York, he argued, including seven Greenberg attorneys in Brooklyn alone, and the confusions wreaked havoc on his legal business and his personal life. He was drafted as Joseph D. Greene and entered the Adjutant General Department as a lieutenant in 1943. By then the Army had begun to train lawyers for its Judge Advocate Department in a special school in Ann Arbor. But in the absence of enough trained judge advocates to go around, and given his legal experience in civilian life, Greene found himself assigned for immediate duty with the VIII Corps office of the Staff Judge Advocate, taking on the mantle of prosecutor in some cases, defense lawyer in others. He was thirty-eight years old in the courtroom at Morlaix, six years older than Fogarty.

Everyone who watched him perform in the courtroom was impressed by Greene's brilliant and aggressive legal strategies. But what Guilloux always remembered about Greene was how much he loved the violin. He didn't have his instrument with him in the Army, and he was suffering without it. Of all the images of Greene that Guilloux captured in his novel, one stands out: the elegant gesture this musical prosecutor made with his hands as he presented to the court the physical evidence that would send James Hendricks to the gallows:

> At the end of his speech, Lieutenant Stone took a tiny object, shining like a jewel, out of his pocket and raised it in front of everyone in a quasi-liturgical gesture. Holding the jewel between his thumb and his index finger, raising high his elegant violinist's hands, he walked the whole length of the table, taking small steps so that all the officers could see it clearly.
>
> "Here is the bullet!"

EIGHT

THE CASE AGAINST JAMES HENDRICKS

———

A S THEY pieced together the testimony of American soldiers and French civilians, the officers on the court-martial tried to understand how James Hendricks had gotten in trouble.

Corp. Robert Manns from the 3326th described drinking with Hendricks in the trailer and hearing him say he was going out "to get some." The Bouton brothers said that Hendricks had come to their house and tried to kiss their mother, accepted the eggs, left the house peacefully. The Bignon women described the pounding at the door of their farmhouse, the voice crying: "Boches!" then "Ouvrir, Mademoiselle!" Victor Bignon had shouted back in his own language from behind the thick stone walls: "We're good French people!" and "There are no Mademoiselles for you here!" When the pounding continued, both Victor and his wife and daughter had gotten out of bed. Victor lit a lamp. It would have seemed logical for him to have hidden in the back of the house after the first shot was fired through the door, but that was not what Victor Bignon did. He was leaning against the door to keep the intruder from getting in when the second bullet struck him in the head. Both Noémie and her daughter, Jeannine, described fleeing to the Bouton house, with Hendricks following close behind. Jeannine was able to hide in the cellar while Hendricks threatened the others with his gun. Lieutenant Tucker, Hendricks's commanding officer, gave the details of his enlisted man's arrest and interrogation.

Throughout the trial, as each witness took the stand,

Greene, Sedillo, Fogarty, and the other members of the court pointed to Hendricks and asked if this man, the defendant, was the same man the witness had seen the night of August 21. Each witness responded that it had been too dark to tell.

No one could identify the perpetrator, yet everyone was sure of his race. Jeannine Bignon, Victor Bignon's daughter, told prosecutor Joseph Greene that the man who had first knocked on the door of her home was black. She couldn't have known that before the shooting, since the door was locked and the single window of the Bignon house was blacked out. Although Fogarty, the defense lawyer, was objecting regularly to Greene's direct examinations, he didn't object here. Colonel Gunn, the president of the court, wanted to know if Noémie Bignon recognized Hendricks's voice. How could she? In the courtroom, she hadn't heard him speak.

Sixty years is a long time to remember accurately the details of testimony, especially testimony given after a trauma. But even sixty years later, Jeannine Bignon still remembered the insistent questioning by the Americans, and she remembered her answer: "How was I supposed to recognize a black man in the dark [*un noir dans le noir*]!" She recalled her father's dread of the black soldiers camped across the way; he told his family he had fought with black soldiers in World War I and didn't like them. Each night after their arrival at the field in Le Percoul, he had bolted the door of the house and urged his family to go to sleep early. On August 22, he had assumed that the man yelling outside his door was from the nearby black American unit.

After the trial was over, the Judge Advocate Board of Review considered the problem of identification in the trial, and explained it through cultural difference: "the [French] witnesses are not familiar with Negro characteristics and faces."

There was another possible explanation for the inability to identify the assailant, which had nothing to do with race. The farmhouses of Plumaudan had no electricity, only candles and gas-lit lamps. When the witnesses said it was "too dark" to recognize the black man, Greene did not ask them whether they could have identified a white person in the dim light. In his questions, he kept insisting on the assailant's race—"the black soldier you were fighting with"; "the black American"; "the colored man who attacked you." Sedillo, the Law Member, also referred to the accused as "the black man." Only Fogarty, the defense lawyer, left the racial epithet out of his questions, referring to Hendricks as "the soldier."

In the end, none of the French witnesses ever linked the crime to Hendricks—only to a generic black man.

———

In the absence of a positive identification, the burden was on the prosecution to argue that circumstantial evidence proved Hendricks's guilt beyond a reasonable doubt. Here, Joseph Greene's job was easy. Jeannine Bignon had found a twisted .30-caliber bullet on the floor of her house, the day after the murder—the same type of bullet issued to Hendricks for his M-1 rifle. In conjunction with Hendricks's own admission that he had fired through the door, the bullet was proof enough to convict Hendricks.

But of what? Was James Hendricks guilty of manslaughter, or of murder? The difference between the two charges, for the young soldier, meant the difference between a long prison sentence and an execution.

Manslaughter, according to the Army's *Manual for Courts-Martial*, involved killing that hadn't been premeditated or planned. The manual outlined two types of manslaughter: voluntary and involuntary. Hendricks might have pulled the trigger of his gun believing that the safety was on. He might have shot through the door thinking that the house was empty; or, more likely, hoping only to frighten the inhabitants into opening their door for him. These scenarios were arguments in favor of a charge of involuntary manslaughter. Voluntary manslaughter, alternatively, meant an act of homicide committed in the heat of sudden passion, after provocation. If Hendricks had been adequately provoked by Victor Bignon in some way, his attorney might have argued for a charge of voluntary manslaughter. All of these charges would have spared Hendricks's life. Indeed, it was difficult to argue that Hendricks had planned to kill Victor Bignon when he shot through the door of the farmhouse the night of August 21.

Yet Hendricks was charged with homicide murder. Homicide murder implies that there was a deliberate intention to kill—in the language of the law, "malice aforethought." The arraignment sheet attached to his record of trial specified that James Hendricks had shot Victor Bignon, "with malice aforethought, willfully, deliberately, feloniously, unlawfully, and with premeditation." The murder charge in itself was aggravated by the second set of charges: housebreaking and attempted rape.

Here was the heart of the case against Hendricks: He had committed not one, but two felonious acts. Shooting through the door alone might well have gotten him convicted for manslaughter. But criminal law had a special doctrine involving an interaction of felonies. If you killed someone *while* you were committing a felony such as rape or housebreaking, the killing could no longer be considered manslaughter. It was "felony murder"—a homicide with intent to commit a felony. The French considered this situation an "aggravating circumstance," which would increase the penalty but not necessarily lead to a death sentence. In an American court in the 1940s, however, whether civilian or military, conviction for a felony murder meant an almost certain death sentence.

The intertwining charges of murder, housebreaking, and attempted rape formed the basis of Joseph Greene's prosecution. To make these felonies add up to felony murder, Greene needed to focus the court's attention not on the shooting itself, but on what happened afterwards—the events at the Bouton farmhouse that James Hendricks said he didn't remember.

NINE

NOÉMIE BIGNON'S TESTIMONY

—

IN ITS postwar report on sex offenses in the European Theater of Operations, the Judge Advocate Department acknowledged the extent to which translation problems had created obstacles in cases of sexual assault:

> As was to be expected, much trouble was often experienced by interpreters in court-martial trials in the use of particular technical words like "penetration" when non-English speaking witnesses were on the stand, because of the difficulty or impossibility of making a precise translation of the English word into the foreign languages.

A woman couldn't say to a court-martial, "He raped me," or, "He tried to rape me." To convict someone of rape, the burden was on the victim to prove that an actual penetration had taken place against her will. The victim of a sex crime was required to produce two kinds of testimony. She had to describe the incident of sexual violence using anatomically detailed language, and she needed to show that she had not complied with the sex act. Courts-martial of the 1940s were as bad as American civil courts in obtaining this information; both tended to put victims of sexual assault on trial along with the accused. The Judge Advocate understood the issue as a problem of translation. From the point of view of the foreign victim, the issue was respect. Noémie Bignon and her daughter had no way of knowing that a Zone Handbook for Allied officers had described Breton women as "naturally erotic," but they knew that they felt ashamed and misunderstood throughout the trial.

Madame Bignon, Victor Bignon's widow, was the first witness called to take the stand against James Hendricks. She testified for two and a half hours—longer than any other single witness except Lieutenant Tucker. The court spent several minutes questioning her about the shots that were fired through the door of her house. But the bulk of her testimony concerned James Hendricks's attempted rape.

Prosecutor Joseph Greene's disdainful attitude toward Noémie Bignon constitutes one of the mysteries of *U.S. v. Hendricks*. When Noémie Bignon would not discuss sexual details in response to his questions, he was dismissive and abrupt. Throughout his questioning, Greene remained impatient and aggressive with her. He never expressed sympathy for the fact that she had just lost her husband through an act of violence or that she had been disfigured by the gun fire that had killed him, or that she had been assaulted. There could have been no more traumatized or confused witness than Noémie Bignon that September morning. She had seen her husband killed in her own home less than three weeks earlier. She had run from the assailant, who attacked her on a bed while the other men in the room hid under their covers and her daughter hid in the cellar. She arrived in court wounded and in mourning.

When Fogarty first objected that Greene was leading his own witness, Greene asked the court's permission to use leading questions because Noémie Bignon was "a simple-minded peasant." "It is difficult," he added, "to get a clear, connected story from a simple-minded woman."

Increasing her burden was the fact that the Americans had taken her away from home at harvest time. With no husband, finding a neighbor to take over her farmwork wasn't easy. She sat in the makeshift court, overwhelmed by the huge lycée, a bigger building than any that existed in Plumaudan, the village where she had spent her entire life.

In her own way, she was as far from home as James Hendricks. And unlike Hendricks, she was surrounded by men speaking a foreign language. Noémie Bignon spoke a mix of French and Gallo, the dialect used by the Breton peasants in her region. Her interpreter Guilloux, with his citified French, stood behind her chair, the only link to the world she knew.

When it came time to explore Hendricks's attack on Noémie Bignon, Greene asked the court once again to allow him to lead his witness. "I may have to use some leading questions because apparently I can't get into her mind the thoughts that are in my mind," he said. "I'll make another attempt to see what I can do about it." It was a throwaway line for Greene that is certainly more revealing than he intended it to be. He wanted to control the foreign woman, who was vital to him in establishing the attempted rape charge.

Joseph Greene might have gotten a clearer testimony from Noémie Bignon if he had shown more sympathy. But she remained a vehicle for his prosecution; a means to an end, rather than a suffering woman.

Noémie Bignon understood well the pressure she was under and resisted: "I told you about ten times already what he tried to do," she said to Greene, through Guilloux. "He tried to force me. That's all I can say."

Faced with her resistance, Greene asked for a five-minute recess. When the court was reconvened, he announced that he had asked the interpreter, Guilloux, to instruct the witness about what he wanted and needed for his prosecution of Hendricks.

———

It must have been a painful conversation for Guilloux. Greene, blustery and demanding, impressing on Guilloux, the intellectual, that he needed Noémie Bignon to talk explicitly about sex.

And it must have baffled Guilloux that Greene was concentrating on Hendricks's intent to rape. Because while a killing had occurred, a rape hadn't.

The issue of wartime sexuality was fraught in World War II France, and weighed on the conscience of many Frenchmen that summer of 1944. Public figures from the Communist poet Paul Eluard to the songwriter Georges Brassens would later speak out against Resistance gangs who took out their vengeful rage on women who had had relations with Germans. Uppermost in Guilloux's own mind were the scenes he had just witnessed in his own town of Saint-Brieuc. Outside the local inn, Guilloux had watched a young girl forced to sit on a chair while her hair was sheared, the mark of shame that gangs imposed on women who had German boyfriends. One of her legs shook the whole time—"shaking as violently as if she were pedaling a bicycle," he wrote later. The men threatened to take her out back and rape her, but they didn't. Afterwards, Guilloux felt guilty that he hadn't interceded.

Now, in this American courtroom, as he translated questions with their escalating attention to sexuality, he was feeling a similar sense of ignominy. He wrote, much later, "I never should have let myself be dragged into this mess."

Joseph Greene wanted Louis Guilloux to become the interpreter of Noémie Bignon's shame. He asked his interpreter to coerce the witness to say in detail what she didn't want to say, to repeat her trauma. Guilloux was caught between his duty to translate individual words and sentences and his desire to protect a woman who depended upon him for the very words she uttered.

The Hendricks trial loomed large in Guilloux's mind when he began to explore his feelings of unease about his work as interpreter for the Americans in the first drafts of *OK, Joe*:

> . . . I was plunged into a sort of bizarre inertia, I was at the mercy of what was happening from one minute to the next, I did nothing but I wanted to do something, telling myself it was not my concern. Or was no longer my concern. It seemed to me that I had lied my whole life, lied to myself. I was no longer sure of anything, but I was not yet, I would never be, detached or strong enough to be anything other than a spectator. A spectator! What would become of these two unhappy women. . . . And the mur-

derer of the father who would finish his young life of twenty years at the end of a rope? I felt as though the world were becoming too difficult for me.

Guilloux recalled another arrest scene he had watched from the streets of Saint-Brieuc—a girl suspected of collaboration who had dared to talk back to the man from the Resistance pounding at her door to arrest her—"just as the black soldier had pounded on the door of the little farmhouse," he wrote. The logic of his thoughts, the analogies that came to him, had little to do with right and wrong. As he wrote, he assembled images and feelings that corresponded to his sense of intrusion and invasion.

After the trial resumed, Joseph Greene directed Louis Guilloux to ask Noémie Bignon: "Did he, at any time, insert his private part in your private part?" The thirty-eight-year-old attorney from Brooklyn spoke even more quickly than usual. He was embarrassed. Guilloux described him in *OK, Joe*: "He let his arms go lax as though he were thinking 'There, that's it, I actually said it . . . '"

Guilloux did as he was told: he translated. It is difficult to imagine how he rendered the euphemism in French. "Private part" does not translate. He may have used the formal French word for male or female sexual organs—"*sexe.*" More likely, he used the everyday expression "*sa chose*" (his thing).

In any case, her answer was no. Noémie Bignon testified that James Hendricks had forced her alongside the bed. He had exposed himself and she had held his penis in her hand. "I took his private part in my hand to keep him away from me," Guilloux translated her response. Greene asked Noémie Bignon if the soldier had a discharge. She said yes, although her hand wasn't wet and she didn't know if the floor was wet. It was dark. She was certain that Hendricks hadn't touched her genitals and hadn't entered her.

In retrospect, it's puzzling that she described a discharge but no seminal fluid. Did she even understand the word "discharge"? And did Guilloux understand the words he was translating? He made plenty of other small translation mistakes: "she flew" instead of "she ran away"; "we were mad" instead of "we were frightened." It's possible he didn't correctly translate the term "discharge," and that Madame Bignon was answering a different question than the one Greene had asked.

For all his pressure on Noémie Bignon to talk explicitly about sex, Joe Greene did not pursue this curious disparity. He seemed much more interested in proving sexual assault than in understanding what had actually happened.

When Fogarty's turn came to cross-examine Noémie Bignon, he did not seize the opportunity Greene's questions provided. How could there have been an ejaculation with no semen? While Greene was disdainful, Fogarty treated Madame Bignon with kid gloves. He asked her if Hendricks's raincoat was buttoned when he came into the second house. She didn't remember. She only saw his genitals when he came after her.

Did Fogarty want to argue that Hendricks couldn't have exposed himself while wearing his Army raincoat? He doesn't say. It's one of many times in the Hendricks trial where Fogarty appears to be on the verge of contesting an assumption made by the prosecution, then drops his protest as soon as he fails to get a perfect response to his first question.

Later in the trial, Greene asked that a condom found in Hendricks's pocket be entered as further evidence of intent to rape: "I am going to offer the rubber, or condom, in evidence," he announced. "I know it is an offensive item, but I think it is necessary in a question of intent."

Fogarty objected. Sedillo, the Law Member, pointed out that every soldier carried condoms. Yet Greene wouldn't take no for an answer, and Sedillo had to repeat himself several times. Sedillo was an extremely elegant man, relaxed in his gestures, and it was unusual for him to express this much impatience: "Gentlemen, let's cut this argument short. . . . Asking the court to take this condom into evidence, and offering it as evidence of rape is going too far. . . . Now let's forget about it."

For Greene, the condom represented one more item in the sexual arsenal he had assembled for his argument. If Guilloux hadn't understood before, he could now see the shape of Greene's prosecution. In the story Greene was telling the court, all of Hendricks's words and actions before the crime—his line to Corporal Manns about going out "to get some"; his behavior at the Bouton house; his crying, "Ouvrir, ouvrir, Mademoiselle," at the door of the Bignon house; even his carrying of a condom—proved that the GI had set out from his base camp with the express purpose not just of having intercourse but of raping a Frenchwoman. For Greene, the Hendricks case was not about killing, it was about sex. And when Noémie Bignon finished her testimony, however halting it was, the vision the court had of James Hendricks was of a sexual predator.

TEN

THE DEFENSE

—

GREENE'S STRONG prosecution had muddied several basic facts about the case: First of all, James Hendricks was drunk. Second, he had probably never intended to kill. He shot into a closed door and had no way of knowing Victor Bignon stood in the path of the bullet. Third, he did not rape Noémie Bignon but he did sexually assault her.

Only the doctrine of felony murder could have moved such fundamental facts to the background. According to the structure of felony murder, Hendricks's intention didn't matter as long as he killed Victor Bignon in the course of an attempted rape. He had engaged in a criminal act and was liable for its terrible consequence. He might as well have been a cold-blooded murderer—the legal consequences were the same. Furthermore, felony murder bound his homicide to his attempted rape in a single charge: Hendricks could not have pleaded innocent to the charge of first-degree murder and guilty to the charge of attempted rape.

In 1944, the appropriateness of the felony murder rule was taken for granted; felony murder was a cornerstone of American criminal justice, inherited from English common law. Today, the English have abolished the felony murder rule, as have a number of states. Organized opponents throughout the United States argue that the rule is unfair, because it frees a prosecutor from having to consider intent or moral culpability in a murder case.

Handicapped by his lack of experience in civilian criminal cases, Fogarty had an uphill battle. His only hope of saving

James Hendricks was to establish the exact sequence of events on August 21, dislodging the logic of a felony murder that had bound all of Hendricks's actions together.

Strangely, Fogarty did not challenge the felony murder charge. Greene claimed that Hendricks's intent to rape was "cumulative." Fogarty didn't contest this idea; in fact, he never addressed the issue of Hendricks's intent. A more zealous attorney would have jumped at the opportunity, for there were obvious weaknesses in the felony murder charge as Greene had presented it. Hendricks had assaulted Noémie Bignon *after* firing the shots that killed her husband. A proper charge of felony murder would have depended upon the idea that Hendricks had intended to rape *before* he committed the murder. In a standard felony murder charge, the murder occurs in the course of the felony. If the sexual assault came after the shooting, and the shooting was accidental, could the shooting really be considered part of the felony?

Fogarty might have asked the court to consider when Hendricks's intent to rape started. Was it when Hendricks said to his buddies that he was "going out to get some"? Was it when he arrived at the Bouton farmhouse and appeared to want to kiss Madame Bouton? Does bragging about "getting some" show intent to rape? Does wanting to kiss a Frenchwoman show intent to rape? If so, most of the U.S. Army would have been guilty.

Even the argument that the felony had started when Hendricks cried "Ouvrir, Mademoiselle" outside the door of the Bignon house was problematic. Certainly crying out, "Mademoiselle, open up!" is no more proof of intent to rape than carrying a condom is. Hendricks probably did have sex on his mind, and maybe in the form of rape. But it was an extraordinary thing to prove, and an extraordinary means by which his shot through the door implied murder.

Fogarty missed a number of strategic opportunities. He did not emphasize the linguistic situation. Hendricks knew only a few words of French, and he could not possibly have understood what was being said to him, either by the Bouton brothers or by Madame Bignon. And while Joseph Greene gloated over his circumstantial evidence, there was a flaw in his arsenal: Donald Tucker testified that one of the eggs given to Hendricks by the Bouton brothers was still intact when Lieutenant Naiser searched Hendricks's raincoat pockets in Dinan. Tucker felt it important enough to emphasize in his testimony that the egg had only cracked after it was entered into evidence. It's a significant detail. How could an egg in Hendricks's pocket have remained whole if he had attacked Noémie Bignon violently on the bed in the Bouton farmhouse? Fogarty never even commented upon the fact. Perhaps Hendricks's attack wasn't so violent; perhaps he stopped short of rape because he wasn't murderously bent on sex after all. Perhaps he was just drunk.

There was more. The possibility of an insanity defense, never raised by Fogarty, haunts *U.S. v. Hendricks*. On the second day of the trial, Corporal Manns told Greene that Hendricks often acted a little funny. Manns recalled that when he had arrived in the 3326th, a replacement just like Hendricks, the other men told him right away that Hendricks was "half-cracked." Tucker, Hendricks's commanding officer, testified that after Hendricks saw Victor Bignon's body, he started shaking and no longer recognized his CO. Although drunkenness did not qualify as an extenuating circumstance in the *Manual for Courts-Martial*, Fogarty still might have argued that Hendricks had lost his rational judgment when he shot through the door of the Bignon farmhouse. But to do that, he would have needed to request a psychiatric evaluation of his client.

Psychiatric evaluations in many general courts-martial during World War II were racially determined, in effect if not intent. The Third Army, more and more attuned to the psychological stress of war, had begun to require psychiatric evaluations of all soldiers in combat units who were brought before a general court-martial. Because Hendricks was black, he had been assigned to a service unit. If he had been in a combat unit, he would have had an automatic psychiatric evaluation before appearing in court. It might have saved him. But because he was in a service unit, such an evaluation was optional; he could be tested only at the court's discretion. The quartermaster major in charge of the pre-trial investigation had used the standard language on the form he submitted in his report: "I have no reasonable ground for belief that the accused is, or was at the time of any offense charged, mentally defective, deranged, or abnormal." There is no sign in the court record that either Fogarty or any other member of the court-martial disagreed with this view. If they had, the court would have adjourned the trial until an evaluation was furnished.

Hendricks's shivering, his looking at Tucker as if he didn't recognize him, the devastating effects of 140-proof alcohol on a 140-pound man, the rumor among the soldiers in the 3326th that Hendricks was "half-cracked," all were passed over in his trial.

Almost as puzzling as the avenues Fogarty did not pursue were his misguided attempts to damage Greene's case. He objected every time an assumption was made by a witness that Hendricks was Hendricks, harping on the lack of a positive identification in the pre-trial lineup. He argued that nothing proved that the soldier who pounded on the Bouton and Bignon doors crying "Mademoiselle" was the same man as the person who fired his gun through the door. His claim smacked of sophism, given that Hendricks had confessed to firing the shots.

Greene's stubborn confidence came to the fore in his response to Fogarty's nitpicking: "As I stated in my opening," Greene reminded the court, "this case will be based on circumstantial evidence; we will connect the accused with the occurrence in that manner."

To which Fogarty protested:

"If the court please, the court is interested in knowing if this witness could identify the person on the date this incident occurred."

Greene remained unperturbed: ". . . we make no claim via eye-witness identification that he is the man merely because he looks like the man. We claim nothing other than a circumstantial case."

Eleven

Hendricks's Commanding Officer

—

B Y THE afternoon of the first day of the trial, Ralph Fogarty was steadily losing ground in his defense of James Hendricks. Joe Greene had won every procedural skirmish—even the lack of a positive ID of Hendricks didn't matter to the court. But Fogarty had a strategy in reserve, gleaned from the *Manual for Courts-Martial*. If he could prove that Hendricks's confession had been coerced, he might be able to save his client. The key man for his strategy was the person who had obtained that confession, Hendricks's commanding officer, Lt. Donald Tucker.

There were two problems with Tucker. If Tucker had been white, Fogarty could have argued that racism had prejudiced the CO against his enlisted man. He could have drawn on a sociological argument: It was common knowledge in the Jim Crow Army that southern white officers, regularly assigned to the command of black units, gave their men a hard time. But Donald Tucker was a black officer, which made it trickier for Fogarty to argue coercion or mistreatment. Worse, Fogarty needed to call Tucker as a character witness to defend Hendricks's good record, once the commanding officer finished testifying for the prosecution about his arrest of Hendricks. Fogarty couldn't attack Tucker too fiercely in a cross-examination and then expect him to cooperate in the interests of the defense.

Ralph Fogarty must have believed that challenging Tucker's arrest of Hendricks represented his only option in a very tough case. When Joe Greene called Lt. Donald Tucker to the stand as his star witness, Fogarty leapt forcefully into his cross-examination. Anyone who had witnessed his performance earlier in the day would have been surprised by the change in his persona.

———

When Lt. Donald Tucker first took the stand for Joe Greene on the afternoon of September 6, the color of his skin set him off from every other officer in the room. In the segregated Army of 1944, he was one of only 700 black officers in a Quartermaster Corps that counted 31,000 officers in all. This statistic was actually a marked improvement; a mere five years earlier, the entire Army had counted only five African Americans among its total population of commissioned officers in all branches, and three of these officers were chaplains.

The Quartermaster Corps, the service and supply corps in charge of feeding, supplying, transporting, and clothing the troops, had a higher percentage of black enlisted men than any other branch of the Army. Black soldiers made up nearly half the Corps. As violent episodes increased in segregated Army training camps and as the morale of black soldiers plummeted, the Army hoped it could bandage its problems with more black officers.

Very little is known about the men in Donald Tucker's situation, but it is certain they were made acutely aware that they represented the exception. They served as exemplars of black achievement in an Army that doubted the capacities of black men to be soldiers. At the same time, these exceptional black officers were never allowed to forget their second-class status. In some training camps, the Army built entire barracks for one or two African American officers so as not to have to integrate white quarters. When this wasn't possible, black officers shared quarters with their black enlisted men. The arrival of a black officer in a white officers' mess created a hush, if not a scandal. No black officer in any unit could outrank a white officer in his company; a white officer of a higher rank was always placed in close proximity to a black officer. In the rigid hierarchy of the military, race outranked rank.

In a rare account of life for a black officer in World War II, Thomas Russell Jones—later a Supreme Court judge in the State of New York—described his joy at being billeted with a French farm family in Normandy. They treated him with more respect than did his fellow officers.

Hendricks's commanding officer, Donald Tucker, the son of a laundress and a construction worker, came from Kansas City, Missouri. In 1941, commissioned as a member of the Army Reserve, Tucker attended Quartermaster's Officers Candidate School as well as Ordnance School, where he specialized in the operation and maintenance of motor vehicles. His quartermaster regiment crossed the ocean from New York to Glasgow in March 1944. In July, after four months of hauling supplies and troops to ports in England and Wales, he and his men made the short voyage to Utah Beach, Normandy, beginning ten months of intense service in the post–D-Day supply war.

We can imagine that Lieutenant Tucker's exceptional status bred pride, protectiveness, and a hypervigilance where the discipline of his men was concerned. He was well aware that the Army saw units like his as the source of crimes against French civilians. Patton's August 20 memo had said as much, and Hendricks had committed his crime only hours after Tucker's strong speech to his men about the consequences of criminal actions. Nothing could have been more of a slap in the face to Tucker's command authority than what James Hendricks had done at Plumaudan on August 21. For this black officer, his enlisted man's crime was not only tragic in itself; it also signified his own failure.

Now, in the courtroom at Morlaix, as the star witness for the prosecution, Tucker was in the hot seat, called upon to account for Hendricks's misdeed. Like the French peasant woman Noémie Bignon, he was given a hard time. Unlike Noémie Bignon, he was defending himself to fellow officers, but officers who were white. His standing as a leader of men was at stake.

Fogarty's hope for Hendricks lay in the following clause in the *Manual for Courts-Martial* concerning coerced confession: "A confession made to a military superior . . . will ordinarily be regarded as requiring further inquiry into the circumstances." The manual insists: a confession induced by fear is involuntary, and involuntary confession is not acceptable as evidence. If Fogarty could show that Tucker had badgered Hendricks into confessing, the court would have to rule out everything Tucker had told them about Hendricks's lies and contradictory statements the night of his arrest.

Fogarty had shown a lack of confidence in his earlier exchanges with Greene, but now he was energized, almost fierce, as he cross-examined Lieutenant Tucker. The pace of the trial quickened.

"When you had that conversation with the accused, what was his condition?"

"Well, he had been drinking."

"Was he nervous?"

"Very nervous."

"Was he shaking?"

"Sort of like he had chills."

"And at that time you stated that you warned him of his rights, and told him that he would not have to make a statement?"

"Right."

"Just what was the nature of your warning at that time?"

"Well, I told him that if he had anything to do with this, if he wanted to make a statement, he could, or if he didn't want to, he didn't have to. I told him that with him in the area, it looked bad for him."

"You are his commanding officer. Is that right?"

"I am."

"It is necessary, on many occasions, for you to order him to do things. Is that right?"

"That is right."

"How many times did you have to ask the accused if he had anything to do with the matter in question before you got an answer?"

Even before Tucker could answer the question, Greene leaped in with an objection: Fogarty was drawing conclusions. The men argued. Later, after another barrage, Greene interceded again. "Give him an opportunity," Greene said to Fogarty. "He was just starting to talk." When Fogarty continued to pound, Greene tried to slow him down: "I am objecting to counsel. He doesn't give the witness a chance to talk. I am not making any objection to the question."

Law Member Juan Sedillo took Fogarty's side and explained why: "The court is very anxious to find out the exact details of the circumstances surrounding [Hendricks's] admissions." Following a poor start, Ralph Fogarty was coming into his own.

———

After he finished cross-examining Tucker, Fogarty asked the court that Tucker's entire testimony for the prosecution be stricken from the record of trial "on the grounds that no proper warnings of [Hendricks's] rights were given to him; and the conditions surrounding the conversation would seem to place the accused in fear."

Sedillo dismissed Fogarty's motion immediately. But he acknowledged Fogarty's concern by testing the hypothesis that Hendricks had been badgered into confessing.

"Did you threaten the accused?" Sedillo asked Tucker.

"I did not threaten the accused."

"Did you bawl him out?"

"I didn't bawl him out."

"Did anybody lay hands on him?"

"No, sir."

"Did anybody 'cuss' him?"

"Not at all, sir."

The court called no character witness, either to vouch for Donald Tucker or to assail him. The black lieutenant may well have displayed cruelty toward his men or created a climate of fear in his company, or he might have been generous to a fault. We don't know. Although eight of his men had watched Tucker arrest James Hendricks, the court took Tucker's own word about what had happened.

Fogarty's idea was a good one—Tucker might have pressured Hendricks into confessing. What is more difficult to understand is the transformation of the hesitant, affable Fogarty into a confident and aggressive challenger, once Tucker is on the stand. Between the two officers was a subtle issue that may well have played a part in their exchange. Donald Tucker was a first lieutenant in the Quartermaster Corps; Ralph Fogarty was a second lieutenant in the Infantry. In theory, Tucker outranked Fogarty. By putting Tucker through his paces, Fogarty might have been proving himself to the court-martial, or even asserting his superiority with a more experienced officer. The psychological issues at play were complex, but so was the legal reality. Fogarty was risking his entire defense on an officer who had everything to lose by confirming Fogarty's theory.

After grilling Donald Tucker throughout most of the afternoon of September 6 and the subsequent morning, the court was satisfied that James Hendricks had been adequately informed of his rights. Tucker was dismissed as a witness for the prosecution. Then, after a five-minute recess, Fogarty recalled Tucker to testify as a friendly witness for the defense. For the next half hour, Fogarty abandoned his role as a hostile cross-examiner and transformed himself into an encouraging and friendly guide.

Fogarty asked Tucker to speak about Hendricks's character. Tucker praised the soldier, who had only recently joined his unit as a replacement:

> I was very pleased to have him in the company. . . . The man was clean cut, and his appearance was always as I desired it. He was as clean as possible. We had no trouble

with him as far as non-com trouble; and he was always willing, as I stated before. When he did come to the company, I had a chance to transfer several men. Well, I kept him in preference to several of my old men because he seemed more of a soldier than these old men did.

But Hendricks had only been under Tucker's command for eleven days. Eleven days was not much of a basis for him to offer a convincing version of what is known as the "good soldier" defense—the kind of defense that can benefit a soldier with a long distinguished service record.

In his response to the court, Lieutenant Tucker expressed himself fully. His testimony for both the prosecution and the defense lasted for four hours, a third of the trial. He was highly professional in fulfilling his role as officer. He made the about-face from prosecution witness to defense witness with grace. We know what he thought and how he acted the night Victor Bignon was killed. Although he had every reason to be angry and ashamed of the behavior of his enlisted man, and every reason to be defensive after his grilling by Fogarty, there was nothing untoward in his testimony. He spoke of Hendricks on the night of the crime with horror, and he referred to the Hendricks he had welcomed into his company with respect. It was an impressive balancing act.

———

A single question suggests the problem with the proceedings: White or black, why should Lt. Donald Tucker have been the expert on James Hendricks's state of mind? It leads to Fogarty's other major decision in his defense of Hendricks—the decision not to have Hendricks testify.

The decision about whether to put an accused man on the witness stand is always a difficult one for a defense counsel. Hendricks had already made two contradictory statements the night of his arrest, and he had been caught in a lie when he said he was on water duty. He was unreliable, he had a ninth-grade education, he was twenty-one years old, and he was afraid. Fogarty must have believed that Hendricks could not hold up to the tough cross-examination he would surely face. So he had cross-examined Tucker instead.

Hendricks had three options in court. First, he could make an unsworn statement—oral or written—in his own defense. He could not be cross-examined on that basis, but he chose not to make such a statement.

Second, Ralph Fogarty could make an unsworn statement—oral or written—on Hendricks's behalf. Fogarty did not elect to speak or write on behalf of Hendricks. James Craighill, the young Judge Advocate lieutenant who later reviewed Hendricks's case, recalls that he himself won many a difficult case for the defense in World War II and Korean War trials by making an unsworn statement on behalf of a client who was frightened or intimidated by a court-martial. What counted in such a statement was less the legal argument than the sympathy it conveyed for the defendants. Fogarty's decision to neglect this option may well have been a significant strategic error.

Hendricks's remaining option was to remain silent, in which case, as the saying goes, "his silence could not be used against him."

The third option is the one Hendricks chose.

He had pleaded not guilty to all charges, but his plea went entirely unexplained. Given his silence, the court had no chance to know him—to learn something about him. What would he have said about his moods that others described: his tendency to speak and then say nothing; his looking as though he didn't recognize Tucker after seeing Victor Bignon's corpse? How did he react to strong alcohol? What remorse did he feel about the shooting? The court had no chance to hear him tell how he was apprehended, nor what it was like to be taken to MP headquarters in the middle of the night and to sign a statement at 5 A.M. Everyone except Hendricks had told, in detail, what they had experienced the night of the shooting of Victor Bignon. All the other witnesses had accounted for Hendricks's actions. We can only imagine what Hendricks might have felt or thought.

Guilloux, with his writer's intuition, describes Hendricks at the start of his trial with an image that conveys the poignancy of a man who has elected to remain silent. Hendricks was a worried, silent cat—the "cat who didn't even dream of taking a leap."

—

Fogarty's own shortcomings in defending James Hendricks add up, not to any obvious problem in his attitude, but to his relative lack of experience in court by comparison with Greene, the seasoned litigator and showman. Fogarty made no attempt to lower the charge from homicide to manslaughter or accidental death or to challenge the felony murder charge. He offered no evidence or testimony designed to justify the not-guilty plea. He didn't make an unsworn statement on Hendricks's behalf.

Fogarty's role in *U.S. v. Hendricks,* however, was part of a much bigger problem. As early as March 1944, a memo circulated in the VIII Corps, requesting that Negro officers be appointed to serve on courts-martial where Negro soldiers were being tried for violent crimes, all the while acknowledging that Negro officers were very difficult to find. At the same time, the memo directed commanders not to reproduce or distribute the order—it was to be carried out by word of mouth. A major general's perception that black officers ought to vote on the guilt or innocence of black soldiers offered one indication that the Jim Crow system was starting to crack from inside.

The system in which James Hendricks was tried was about to be reformed. In 1946, the Vanderbilt Commission, appointed to review the practice of military justice in World War II, decried the use of legally inexperienced officers to defend soldiers brought up before general courts-martial. New Articles of War ratified in 1948 in response to the Vanderbilt Commission's recommendations gave every accused soldier the right to have a judge advocate or at least a qualified lawyer as his defense counsel if the prosecutor was also a judge advocate or qualified lawyer. In 1969, the protection was strengthened further: both defense counsel and Trial Judge Advocate (Fogarty and Greene's positions) in every court-martial were required to be schooled by the Army and designated as Judge Advocates.

Those reforms came too late for James Hendricks. In 1944, his life depended upon a man of goodwill, four years out of law school, who was learning about military justice and race through hard-won experience.

———

Ralph Fogarty's closing statement was not included in the trial record—no closing statement is. All we have left is Guilloux's fictional version, and there is no way of knowing how faithful the French writer was to what Fogarty actually said. Guilloux makes Hendricks twenty years old rather than twenty-one, and he changes Fogarty's name to Bradford. He imagines a guilty plea. In Guilloux's fictional speech, Fogarty/Bradford pleads only for Hendricks's life, resting on the American pillars of democracy and religion:

> As awful as it was, the terrible thing of which he was ac-
> cused was simply an accident. He was not an assassin, he
> had premeditated none of it. Furthermore we were deal-
> ing with a young life of twenty years. Men of conscience,
> free men, citizens of a great democracy must think twice
> before sending this hugely irresponsible young man to the
> gallows. Certainly he deserved punishment, but let this
> punishment be imprisonment for as long as they liked.
> Spare him the noose! By sparing his life, give him a
> chance to redeem himself. Lieutenant Bradford had inter-
> viewed the defendant at great length in his prison cell and
> he could assure the court that the work of repentance had
> already begun. We must not interfere with God's work on
> a human soul!

TWELVE

THE HANGING

—

T HE VERDICT was swift and unanimous: The court found James Hendricks guilty of all charges. At 3:45 P.M. on September 7, he was sentenced to hang by the neck until dead.

At the moment of sentencing, Fogarty requested clemency based on Hendricks's clean record. The crime at Le Percoul was his first offense. A week later Law Member Juan Sedillo and Capt. Frederick Orr, two of the ten officers on the court-martial panel, asked that Hendricks's death sentence be commuted to life imprisonment. Perhaps they were touched by Fogarty's closing statement. They gave no explanation for their request.

Three different post-trial reviews completed by officers from the Judge Advocate Department approved the guilty verdict and the death sentence. "No errors injuriously affecting the substantial rights of the accused were committed during the trial." The sentence was approved by Troy Middleton, commander of the VIII Corps, and by Dwight D. Eisenhower himself, commander-in-chief of the U.S. Army in the European Theater. Only Eisenhower had the authority to grant the clemency requested by Orr and Sedillo. Eisenhower's order for execution was dated October 27, 1944, and the hanging ceremony at Plumaudan was carried out almost a month later.

In the first Judge Advocate review of the Hendricks trial, James Craighill emphasized the strong role played by Lt. Donald Tucker in bringing a criminal to justice and made his own recommendation:

> Insomuch as First Lieutenant Donald F. Tucker, the commander of the accused's unit, by his timely and efficient action on the night of the offenses, contributed so valuably and so materially to the solution of the crimes and the positive connection of the accused therewith [,] it is recommended that an official letter of commendation be dispatched to him.

Tucker was not only exonerated of any suspicion cast upon him by Fogarty; he was commended. On October 16, five weeks after the trial, he received a promotion from first lieutenant to captain.

The requisite unit history Captain Tucker filed for the 3326th in January 1945, after his men reached Maastricht, Holland, notes the missing soldiers who happily returned to camp or the occasional injury. It mentions no deaths, either by enemy fire or by hanging.

Louis Guilloux spent two days in the courtroom in Morlaix. After translating the testimony of Noémie and Jeannine Bignon, Charles and René Bouton, he had plenty of time to contemplate the proceedings. The guilty verdict left him shaken.

In his role as interpreter, he was condemned, as he said in drafts of *OK, Joe,* to be either an accomplice or a spectator. He had watched James Hendricks throughout the trial, and as he listened to the others speak, he had a terrible sense of what was missing. It was Hendricks himself: "He remained as immobile and mute as he had since the beginning of the session, his gaze always as empty, you might have said that things were happening without him and that he himself was consenting. As if he was no longer anything but an object."

Louis Guilloux did not see James Hendricks hang. By the time the quartermaster private went to the gallows, Guilloux was back in Saint-Brieuc. In his novel years later, he managed to capture the desolation of an event he never witnessed:

Incidentally, where were they hanged? And who was the hangman? It probably took place at dawn, as everywhere in the world where people are hanged, where people are executed, where heads are cut off. People were still sleeping at that hour—myself along with the others, wrapped warmly in my three blankets, surrounded by my roommates, Stef, Pat, Robert, and Gus, also sleeping soundly. No one ever knew. The thing was long done by the time we opened our eyes.

It was the Army's recording officer, Albert Summerfield, who described the actual scene on the gallows on November 24, 1944, for the historical record. It wasn't dawn after all, but 11:02 A.M. in the courtyard of the Château la Vallée in Plumaudan when James Hendricks died:

> The trap mechanism functioned correctly and the prisoner dropped through and hung suspended in the lower screened portion of the scaffold. There was no muscular movement of the body and only a slight swaying on the rope. During the next twelve minutes there was complete silence around the gallows. There was some audible conversation among a few civilians who had stopped on the road in front of the Château, but this did not affect the solemnity of the proceedings. No emotional reaction from any one present could be observed.

Emmett Bailey, Jr., a white sergeant in the Graves Registration Company, was sitting in his truck on the road beyond the stone wall bordering the château that morning, waiting for the guards to cut the noose from Hendricks's neck. When he received the signal, Bailey approached the scaffold, pushing aside the curtain. He wrapped James Hendricks's corpse in a mattress cover. The guards carried the body to the truck on a stretcher.

Bailey then headed east to Marigny, to the temporary American cemetery set up near the Normandy beachhead following the June invasion. There was a special row of graves at

Marigny for general prisoners, separate from the graves of men killed honorably in action.

Bailey was a technician; he designed the gravesites and supervised the interment of the war dead. He didn't dig James Hendricks's grave. That job was left to the enlisted men in Graves Registration. But on November 24, 1944, after James Hendricks's grave was prepared, after the young man's body was lowered into the Normandy earth in its striped mattress cover, Sgt. Emmett Bailey, Jr., said a prayer over General Prisoner James E. Hendricks, just as he did for all the GIs he put to rest.

THIRTEEN

VERDICTS

———

ON SEPTEMBER 8, 1944, Louis Guilloux woke up in the officers' billet at the Lycée Kernégues in Morlaix and wrote in his diary: "Friday. Yesterday and the day before yesterday at the court-martial. The young black criminal was condemned to hang." It was his first job with the court and it changed his mood for the worse. "I should have lots of things to jot down in this notebook," he added, "but I'm incapable of it, because of a sort of melancholy that grabbed me yesterday and still has a hold of me today. . . . "

He was worried about his wife and daughter back in Saint-Brieuc and took a day's leave from Morlaix to visit them. He found his daughter sick in bed with asthma. In the evening, he returned to Morlaix and dined in the officers' mess with Bill Cormier, his American friend. "Am tired," he wrote in his notebook—"vague anxiety."

Guilloux wasn't called back to court duty for two more weeks, but he stayed busy with pre-trial investigations. Then, on September 20, seven black GIs went on trial for a gang rape. They were condemned to terms of life at hard labor. S. T. Fellows, one of the young soldiers who had only observed the rape, received the same sentence. Col. William Scully, the Staff Judge Advocate for the VIII Corps and the man who hired Guilloux, reviewed the case. Scully was enraged not by the harshness of Fellows's sentence, but by the court's leniency toward the six men who had committed rape. What had happened to his officers' toughness? The VIII Corps court-martial had already sentenced two men to death on a rape charge on

August 29, and they had given James Hendricks a death sentence on September 7. He expected them to condemn the rapists with the same sentence.

"The perpetrators are not worthy of the names of men," Scully wrote in his review of *U.S. v. Davis, Nathan, Roland, et al.* His outrage extended to the sentencing of S. T. Fellows. He felt the other men, by comparison, should have received the death sentence:

> The court utterly failed in its duty when it failed to impose the extreme penalty on each of the seven convicted accused. It did not even differentiate (which might have been a supportable ground of distinction) between those that had forcible intercourse and those that did not.

Scully recommended to the high command that a letter be sent to the members of the court-martial castigating them for failing to impose the death penalty. Col. Claud Gunn, president of the court-martial, would be required to read the letter to the men who had served on the panel.

"*Colère du Colonel S,*" Guilloux scribbled in his diary—the Colonel was furious. John Silbernagel, a member of the court, still remembers the day that Colonel Gunn reconvened the members and read them the reprimand from Troy Middleton, Commanding General of the VIII Corps, the man in charge of the entire Brittany campaign. Middleton had taken Scully's suggestion to heart, and he must also have had the words of Patton's August 20 memo in mind when he wrote to the court:

> I am completely at a loss to understand the reasons for the sentences in the case in reference. The same court but recently imposed three sentences of death in similarly serious cases. Yet when seven accused set upon a lone and defenseless woman they are virtually rewarded for the combination. As officers of the United States Army I would have expected a far clearer recognition of duty and

the dictates of justice from the members of the court. The membership as a court failed even to follow what would possibly have been a supportable line of distinction between those who had intercourse with the victim and those who did not. A more repulsive, inhuman, debased, and revolting scene than that portrayed by the evidence cannot be imagined and completely beggars description.

Guilloux had no contact with Major General Middleton, though the fifty-five-year-old career military man, brought back from retirement to lead the Battle of Brest, would have made a fine character for his novel. The highest-ranking officer in Guilloux's entourage was Colonel Scully. In *OK, Joe*, Guilloux used Scully's outrage to dramatize the American Army's zeal for the death sentence:

> . . . the very polite Colonel [Scully] who had received me as a social equal and had given me the papers guaranteeing my status as an official interpreter had thrown a fit of anger when he learned the verdict. He had even railed quite crudely against the members of the court who didn't have the balls to pronounce a death sentence.

It must have been shocking for Guilloux to hear the death penalty referred to as a viable sentence in a rape case. The French state had administered capital punishment by guillotine since the Revolution, and wouldn't abolish the practice until 1981. France had just discontinued public executions when World War II began, and the French use of the death penalty was certainly not measured. In 1943, in an infamous case, the Vichy government had sent a woman to the guillotine for administering abortions. But the French criminal code did not prescribe the death sentence for the crime of rape.

For men like Scully and Middleton, the death sentence for rape was part of American legal, and extralegal, culture. Rape remained punishable by death in the United States until 1977, when the Supreme Court ruled that the punishment was cruel and unusual, according to the Eighth Amendment. The racial factor in executions for rape was blatant, and, in southern states especially, there was often a fine line between these executions and lynching. The statistics speak for themselves. In North Carolina, James Hendricks's state, sixteen men were executed for rape between 1940 and 1945; thirteen of them were African Americans, and three were Native Americans. As the death penalty scholar Stuart Banner argues, "the death penalty was a form of racial control."

Three days after the seven black GIs received their life at hard labor sentences, Guilloux was back in the courtroom. Two more black GIs were on trial for rape and murder. It was a clearer case of felony murder then the Hendricks case. The two GIs had entered the home of a farmer in Locmenven, in the western part of Brittany where the Breton language is spoken. One man held the farmwoman down on the bed while the other waited his turn. The woman's husband, alerted by a neighbor, came running home from the fields to stop the rape. As the Breton couple fled their house, one of the GIs fired his rifle and hit the young woman in the abdomen. She died several hours later. William Davis, the GI who fired his gun, was sentenced to hang; his accomplice got life at hard labor.

———

When William Davis was sentenced to death, Guilloux had been with the court for almost a month. He was immersed in American culture, learning more and more new American phrases and an emphatic, cheerful way of using them. "You're doing a good job!" Joe Greene liked to tell him.

The Army appreciated Guilloux. In addition to translating testimony in court, he served as a guide to the French civilian witnesses during their stay in Morlaix. These men and women, peasant farmers, most of whom had never ventured far beyond their village and who rarely heard a language other than Gallo or Breton, depended on the interpreter to help them through a judicial process that was totally foreign to them. They were in mourning, or traumatized by an assault. And in the best of circumstances, they would have been frightened to appear before a board of strange men in uniform—men who spoke a language they couldn't understand.

After the trial, it was Guilloux who took them to the Army bursar to receive their witness pay: $1.50 for each travel day; $3.00 for each day spent in court. It was Guilloux who picked them up at the Hôtel de l'Europe in the center of Morlaix, Guilloux who accompanied them to the Army jeep that would return them to their farm, where harvest work awaited them that August.

After Pvt. William Davis's trial, Guilloux went a step further. He advised Jacques Pouliquen, whose wife had been killed by Davis, to apply to the Army for a pension for himself and his two-year-old daughter. The inter-Allied agreement included provisions for money to be paid out in the case of acts of violence against civilians that were not related to combat. Within its Judge Advocate Department, the Army had established claims commissions, where civilians could apply for reparations concerning damaged property or loss of life. Jacques Pouliquen was awarded a pension from the U.S. government, and his two-year-old daughter, Jacqueline, received a stipend until she turned eighteen. The Army paid for Germaine Pouliquen's marble gravestone in the church cemetery at Guiclan, the village next to Locmenven. "The peasants needed me," Guilloux wrote, "if only to go to the bursar's office."

His loyalty was to them, to his countrymen. But things were never that simple for Guilloux. It was his curse and his gift to be able to empathize with both sides of a drama—to understand criminal and victim as figures in a larger human tragedy.

A French patriot, Guilloux was also a committed internationalist, sensitive to struggles beyond his own national boundaries. The man who had translated Claude McKay's *Home to Harlem* felt sympathy for the black Americans on trial. And while their crimes troubled him, so did their punishments: "Sentenced to hang by the neck until dead." He had heard it twice in the U.S. court.

———

Guilloux was struck by the similarities in the cases he had seen so far. The same ingredients were repeated: contact with civilian women, rape or attempted rape, violence, the firing of shots, a civilian found dead. Or rape alone. Invariably, the GI was drunk. He had bartered liquor in exchange for gasoline, like Hendricks's squad. Or he had accosted a woman on her bicycle and thrown her into the bushes. Or he had returned to a farmhouse after doing errands for the farmers earlier in the day. Only this time the husband was out in the fields, and the farmwoman was alone. Guilloux had seen black GIs in court, but black soldiers were not the only soldiers committing these crimes.

On August 16, 1944, as the fierce battle in the Mortain Forest was winding down, two white GIs killed a farmer in the Breton town of La Bazouges-du-Désert, due east of Plumaudan. The French police report on the crime resembled the Hendricks case in many details. The soldiers were drunk, and they were after a woman.

> On August 16, 1944, around 10 P.M., two American soldiers in a state of inebriation entered the house of Mademoiselle VELE, a farmer in the village of Epine, a commune of La Bazouges-du-Désert. When these soldiers tried to kiss her, Mlle Velé fled. Her brother, who tried to intervene, was mortally wounded by the bullets fired by the soldiers. The American authorities arrested the murderers.

Unlike Hendricks, these white men had been invited into the farmer's home earlier in the day to celebrate the American military victory. The family offered them their homemade calvados. Trouble came later. While sixty-six-year-old Auguste

Velé and his son were working in the fields, the American soldiers, now drunk, returned to the farmhouse and frightened
Pauline Velé, Auguste's sister, with their advances. A neighbor
woman, fearing the worst, took the Velés' daughter to safety.
The Velé men returned from the fields, and a fight ensued. Unlike Hendricks, the Americans fired directly at their French
hosts. One of their bullets struck Auguste Velé, who collapsed
and later died.

After the GIs were taken into custody by American Military
Police, Pauline Velé and her son, who had witnessed the shooting, were taken to Rennes to identify the culprits. They were unable to pick the white soldiers who shot Auguste Velé out of the
lineup. The Army paid for Auguste Velé's burial. That was the
last that the Velé family heard from the Americans.

No GI was ever executed for the murder of Auguste Velé.
We know this from the record of death sentences in the Euro-
pean Theater. Nor is there a description of any crime in La
Bazouges-du-Désert among the many cases reviewed by the
Judge Advocate General Board of Review, which reviewed
murder and rape cases that resulted in a harsh sentence.

It was up to the men's commanding officer to determine
how far the investigation of their misconduct went, and to de-
cide if they were to be tried by a court-martial or simply sent
back to battle. The lack of positive identification in the Velé
case may have been enough to keep the white GIs out of court.
Possibly, the men were acquitted of a lesser charge of involuntary manslaughter and their case was never examined by a
Board of Review. In either scenario, though, the two white GIs
were spared a capital trial for murder with intent to rape. Military justice, it appeared, was selective.

—PART III—

UNITED STATES VERSUS CAPTAIN GEORGE P. WHITTINGTON

FOURTEEN

LESNEVEN

———

A UGUST 22, 1944, began as an ordinary day, if any day in a war zone can be called ordinary. Patton's memo, ordering his commanding officers to do everything in their power to prevent their soldiers from committing crimes against civilians, was only forty-eight hours old. Young James Hendricks had signed his confession statement at Military Police headquarters in Dinan in the early hours of the morning and was already in confinement, awaiting a murder trial.

In the westernmost part of Brittany, around the town of Lesneven, 120 miles from Dinan, massive numbers of troops had been gathering for weeks for the siege of Brest. The men of Task Force A, the 4th and 6th Armored Divisions, and the 2nd, 8th, and 29th Infantry Divisions were scattered in encampments to all sides of the port city.

Lesneven was officially classified as the rear of the Brest combat zone—it was behind the lines. The town was a commercial center, organized around a square where an open market was held every week. At one end of the square was Lesneven's best hotel, the Hôtel de France, an ornate seventeenth-century structure which had served as a nobleman's home, then as an Ursuline nunnery. The hotel had been requisitioned by a group of U.S. Military Intelligence officers who were on the alert for German spies rumored to have infiltrated the countryside around Brest in search of information on Allied war strategies. Lesneven was declared off limits to any American soldier who wasn't either Military Intelligence or Military Police.

On August 22, a captain in the 5th Ranger Battalion named George Whittington was camped in a field at Tregarantec, two and a half miles southeast of Lesneven. Whittington was a D-Day hero, the recipient of the Army's second highest honor, the Distinguished Service Cross. The 5th Rangers, for whom the casualties at D-Day were still a recent memory, were getting into position to make the final attack on Brest.

Captain Whittington had explicit orders to stay put, but he convinced his friend William Runge to take the two-and-a-half-mile walk into town. Runge, who was known as a goody-goody, the "Boy Scout" of the battalion, might have thought he could keep an irascible buddy out of trouble. By the time they got to town, both men were AWOL.

At about 6:30 P.M., they sat down in a bar on the ground floor of the Hôtel de France called Le Western Saloon, a play on the fact that Lesneven was in the Far West of France. The allure of the once glamorous bar had been diminished by war. There were the usual mirrored walls, but the shelves where the bottles should have been were completely bare. The liquor was in the cellar. The intense bombings in the area, reverberating like a hundred earthquakes a day, would have sent every bottle crashing to the floor.

A man had been in and out of the bar all afternoon. He was tan, with thin lips, slick black hair, a long, hooked nose, and a dark, intense gaze, which he focused on the pretty young barmaid, a country girl named Yvonne Pichon. He was a confusing sight, dressed in a combination of British and American uniform—a U.S. Army flannel shirt, a 6th Armored Division patch on his sleeve, British combat trousers, British combat shoes and leggings. And he spoke with a strange accent. Francis Morand had first gone to the Hôtel de France around three or four in the afternoon with a few comrades from the local resistance, the Forces Françaises de l'Intérieur. He stayed until five-thirty, then went to a nearby café with FFI leader Paul Jacopin.

Morand and Jacopin sat in the café on that warm summer afternoon, exchanging war stories. Jacopin had buried four of his comrades during the battles for the liberation of Lesneven that had taken place two weeks earlier. Soon he would leave Lesneven with the forty-five men in his unit to join a Ranger battalion fighting on the Crozon peninsula. Morand explained that he was originally from the French Alps, a Special Air Service paratrooper trained in England who had hooked up with the 6th Infantry after his unit was raided by Nazis. He planned to rejoin a unit from SAS, who were regrouping in Vannes. The two men had dinner together, and there was more talk of the battles to come. Jacopin described the situation around Brest: the roads were packed with convoys of German prisoners and the local hospitals were filled to capacity with casualties from the Allied bombings. The final move on Brest was only days away, and Gen. Bernhard Ramcke had just ordered all French civilians to evacuate the port city. Refugees were crowding the streets of Lesneven, looking for shelter. In the skies overhead, the men could hear the buzz of hundreds of Allied bombers.

Morand returned to the Hôtel de France at 10 P.M. and found a smattering of American officers enjoying their drinks. Rangers Whittington and Runge were sitting at a table drinking cognac. At the bar were two officers from Military Intelligence, Lt. Charles Zuccardy, an interpreter, and his sergeant, Michel d'Etamper, who was born in France and spoke French like a native. The two Americans were drinking Covant liqueur, a thick, sweet after-dinner drink.

Morand sat down at the table with Whittington and Runge and started drinking cognac with them. They ordered a bottle of champagne, then another. Whittington was proud he knew the French word for "bottle," and carried on a halting conversation in French with Morand. His buddy, Runge, couldn't understand a word they said. Switching to English, Whittington entertained the men with talk about Ranger techniques. The soldiers invited Yvonne, the barmaid, to join them, and the young woman shared a few glasses of good champagne.

The atmosphere was friendly when Morand left the table, walked up to the bar, and laid down his carbine, pointing the barrel of his gun in the direction of d'Etamper and Zuccardy. Lieutenant Zuccardy asked him in French to turn the carbine in the other direction. Morand said, "What's the matter, don't you trust me?" Zuccardy answered that it wasn't a question of trust. He approached Morand and repeated his request three or four more times, each time in French. Morand shoved him aside.

Now Runge and Whittington joined in. Still sitting at their table, they too asked Morand to turn the carbine away. It was to them that Morand finally responded. He turned his carbine from Zuccardy and d'Etamper and started fiddling with it, fingering the stock. Around him, everyone was nervous.

Yvonne Pichon left the table where she'd been drinking and took up her place behind the bar. Lieutenant Zuccardy, his suspicions raised, asked Morand to show him his papers. At first Morand refused, telling Zuccardy he was an officer, too, and that Zuccardy hadn't come over to France to teach him the rules. Sergeant d'Etamper piped in: "You know what it is to refuse to show one's papers for the American Army?" Morand said, "Yes, quite well."

Morand was becoming more and more offended, while the American officers were becoming more and more suspicious. D'Etamper asked Morand why he spoke with such a heavy German accent, and then whispered to Lieutenant Zuccardy that he thought the man was probably German. He sounded like he came from the Württemberg region, and when he spoke English, he said "*mit*" instead of "with." Zuccardy pursued the matter. He addressed Morand in German. When Morand responded fluently, Zuccardy asked him how it was that he spoke the language so well. "I studied it," Morand said, and d'Etamper quipped that his German was much too good to have been learned in any school. The strangely dressed soldier took a white paper out of his pocket attesting that he was a member of the 4th French Parabattalion of the Special Air Service, temporarily assigned to the 50th Armored Battalion of the 6th Infantry. Everyone knew that the Special Air Service had parachuted hundreds of men into the interior of Brittany and Normandy after D-Day to support the French *maquis* and prevent Nazi troops from reaching the coasts. It was as impressive a credential as a Free Frenchman could have that summer. Morand flashed his paper for a few minutes, then put it back in his pocket. "I regret, but you won't see the rest," he said.

Perhaps the papers reassured Zuccardy and d'Etamper. Perhaps they decided they could interrogate Morand later. In any case, Lieutenant Zuccardy spoke to Morand in a spirit of reconciliation. "We will have a glass more. We will drink and then you will forget the doubts we had about you." Morand turned to the barmaid Yvonne in confidence. How strange, he told her, that this American lieutenant had doubts about him. She had doubts about him, too. That afternoon, she'd heard Morand tell the boys from the FFI that he was a lieutenant, but he had bragged to her that he was a captain and said he'd been in England for three years. Now, in the presence of the Americans, he was lowering his rank back to lieutenant again.

Everyone had another drink. Then, at 11:10 P.M., Morand left the café, with a gallant *"Bonsoir"* to the French speakers and a friendly "Good night" to the English speakers. He had been there for an hour of intense drinking with the Americans.

With no explanation, Whittington followed him out the door, closing it behind him, and stepped into the courtyard of the hotel.

Capt. Jacques La Rus, also from Military Intelligence, was sitting on the hotel's only toilet in a lavatory on the second floor. The door to the WC was open to the hallway, and an open window was near enough so that he could make out voices in the courtyard.

He heard footsteps, then a conversation. Two men were speaking: each seemed to be making an effort to speak the other's language.

The first man said, in his best accented English: "I am very sorry that you do not believe that I am really Free French, but I assure you that I really am."

The other man answered in French, with a strong American accent: "Well, it doesn't matter. Glad to have met you. Good night."

The first man answered: "Goodbye and good night. Good luck to you. Maybe someday we'll meet again."

There were five or ten seconds of silence, then six pistol shots rang out. La Rus heard a groan, a sigh. Then there was silence again.

He ran from the WC down the stairs to the courtyard to find George Whittington standing over Francis Morand's body. "A man has been shot in cold blood," La Rus yelled, and he called out to one of his men in the bar to get an MP.

"When any son of a bitch points a gun in my face," Whittington muttered, "I'm going to kill him."

Whittington walked back into the bar, and, while he waited for the MP to arrive, he told his side of the story. Morand had pulled a gun on him. As Whittington demonstrated to everyone there, he had dropped to the ground, just as he was taught to do by the Rangers, pulled out his pistol, and fired.

FIFTEEN

GEORGE WHITTINGTON

—

GEORGE WHITTINGTON, the man who shot Francis Morand, had a childhood befitting a great soldier. He was born in Hot Springs, Arkansas, on October 5, 1913, the second son of the local prosecuting attorney. When he was seven, his mother became worried about his older brother's health, so she moved George and David to a friend's ranch near Carlsbad, New Mexico. It was a boy's dream: there were horses to ride, animals to hunt, roundups and chuck wagons. Formal schooling came a few years later. Both brothers attended the New Mexico Military Institute, where George discovered his talent for boxing. In 1934, his senior year in high school, he won the Southwest Golden Gloves regional championship in the light-heavyweight division. He could have gone professional, but he found the sport too corrupt.

With what would turn out to be a characteristic indifference to convention, George Whittington cut his high school education short a week before graduation. He went on what one friend referred to as "a spree." Whatever the spree may have involved, it was against the rules. Young Whittington was expelled from the New Mexico Military Institute without a diploma. He hopped a train for California and joined the Marines, who sent him to China.

As a China Marine, Whittington was part of an operation sent to protect U.S. interests in the international enclave at Shanghai, and to guard U.S. trade ships along the Yangtze River during a period when Chinese city and countryside alike were threatened by Japanese attack. In China he acquired a tattoo: a tiny question mark, placed a few inches below the crease on his left arm.

After five years with the Marines, Whittington enlisted in the Army and served in the Coast Artillery Corps. He activated his reserve Army commission when the United States declared war on Japan, and rose in the ranks from second lieutenant to first lieutenant, and then to captain in the 10th Armored Division. In 1943 he volunteered for the 5th Ranger Battalion, the all-volunteer unit being trained to serve as shock troops in the risky landing the Allies were planning on the coast of France.

In his quest to become a Ranger, Whittington received the most rigorous training the Army knew how to give. The 5th Rangers began their preparations for war in September 1943 at Camp Forrest, Tennessee, and continued on the beaches of Florida. They wrestled and boxed, swam, marched, drilled, and practiced raids and house-to-house fighting. They became expert marksmen. They were fast and they were smart—elite ground troops with the mental and physical agility of paratroopers.

In January 1944, the Rangers crossed the ocean for a destination on the British Isles secret even to them. They set up base in a camp in the hills of Scotland, where they endured even tougher marches and exercises, and where, as 5th Battalion Ranger Henry Glassman wrote in his history of the 5th, "Rangers were made or lost." On the Scottish coast, they practiced assault landings on beaches strewn with barbed wire. They tried to anticipate every kind of obstacle the Germans might think of placing on the French beachhead.

There, in the midst of intense training, Whittington and two other men in the 5th challenged the authority of their battalion commander. They thought he was incompetent. There's not much detail available about the incident, except for the fact that the commander immediately reassigned the three men to a distant unit. But Whittington's exile proved temporary. He soon learned that the higher brass had replaced the commander he'd disliked with Lt. Col. Max Schneider. Schneider invited Whittington and the two other men to rejoin the Rangers.

———

Whittington was valued as a soldier, though he continued to create controversy among his superiors. John Raaen, one of his fellow officers, remembers his hot temper, and his boxer's readiness to fight:

> Whitt, that's what we called him, had been an old China Marine for five years (1934–39). During that time he was the fleet heavy weight boxing champion, or so we all believed. He acted like it, thumbing his nose and sniffing loudly as he shadow boxed around the room. Trouble with that was, it was normal conduct for him to act like a punch drunk fighter warming up for a fight. And don't startle him or you'd end up on the floor with a sore jaw. As a matter of fact, don't cross him or you'd end up the same way.

When D-Day finally arrived, Whittington was captain of Company B, one of four companies in the 5th Ranger Battalion. His men crossed the Channel on the *Prince Leopold*. At 4:30 A.M. on June 6, 1944, they boarded an LCA (Landing Craft, Assault), a small plywood boat manned by British coxswains, who deposited them on Dog White Beach, due west of Omaha. The 5th Rangers' mission was to capture the enemy's guns, secure a sector of the beachhead, and forge an exit from the beach. Every exercise, every task George Whittington had accomplished over the past twelve months had been carefully designed to prepare him for that moment—6:30 A.M. on "D-Day, H-Hour"—the first wave assault on the Normandy beaches, and the beginning of northern France's liberation.

On Omaha Beach, stretches of sand soon give way to steep limestone bluffs. Atop these bluffs the Nazis had carefully constructed their network of bunkers and "pillboxes" to defend against invasion by sea. An air strike by the Allies on the morning of the 6th was supposed to destroy this defensive wall before the boats landed, but the bombers missed their target and struck further inland instead. A new, unexpected German infantry division was stationed on the beaches, ready to fight back. The Americans who landed on Omaha Beach on June 6 presented easy targets. D-Day, in the words of a corporal who fought under Whittington, was "a duck shoot."

Whittington and his men stepped off their landing craft onto a beach carpeted with land mines, where hundreds of bullets kicked up the sand. Tangled masses of barbed wire blocked their movements toward the seawall, so they used long metal pipes filled with TNT—bangalore torpedoes—to blast an opening in the wire. With the Germans firing down, Whittington led his men through the opening. "George Whittington was a hell of a man . . . one of the first ones over that goddam seawall," remembered his corporal, Carl Weast, who felt he owed his life to Whittington. Company B scaled the 100-foot cliff without a single casualty.

It was a scene that became an American myth. Steven Spielberg would re-create the moment in his film *Saving Private Ryan* from the point of view of a Ranger captain named Miller, who also braved the beach, scaled the cliff, and vanquished the enemy at the top, while all around him, men were dying.

Later, when Whittington's battalion commander criticized him for unnecessarily exposing himself in battle, Whittington reminded him: "You saw it happen back on that goddam beach. Now you tell me how the hell men [lead] from behind them, you let me know. It just does not work."

———

Once they reached the top of the cliff, Whittington's men could only advance by crawling under the machine-gun fire. They blasted the artillery batteries and killed the soldiers who tried to stop them. In the chaos, three Germans suddenly emerged from their gun nest, crying, *"Bitte, bitte"*—"Please, please." Whittington gunned them down, then he turned to his men with a straight face, and said, "What does *'bitte'* mean?" At least that was the legend that made its way into the movie version of Cornelius Ryan's *The Longest Day*, with Whittington played by the actor Tommy Sands.

Fifth Ranger Battalion Capt. John Raaen, who was on Omaha Beach with Whittington, heard a different version of the incident. "Some Rangers were bringing a German colonel off the bluffs near Les Moulins and figured that he'd be wonderful for interrogation," Raaen recalled, "and as they went by, Whittington murdered him." American soldiers had risked their lives to capture a German officer, who was now dead, useless for interrogation. The Rangers were in the thick of an intense battle, and there were very few witnesses to what Whittington had done. No one thought a charge would stick, since, after all, he had killed an enemy in battle and could easily have argued that the prisoner had pulled a hidden weapon. "His peers thought that he violated the rules of land warfare, but there could have been only one or two actual witnesses to the incident. But the story sure made the rounds." Whittington's actions took place during a week when German soldiers killed twenty Canadian prisoners of war.

George Whittington received the Distinguished Service Cross for his gallantry and heroism on D-Day. The Army commemorated the ceremony with an official photograph of Whittington with Lt. Col. Max Schneider, his battalion commander, and the six other Rangers who received the coveted decoration. Wearing his helmet, short and muscular, he looks every bit the boxer. He already had a Presidential Unit Citation Badge, a Combat Infantryman Badge, and a Marine Corps Good Conduct Medal. Now, as he crossed the Brittany peninsula toward Brest, he wore the Army's second highest decoration for valor.

Two months later, George Whittington went AWOL in Lesneven. He walked into the hotel bar, met Francis Morand, then shot him six times.

SIXTEEN

THE INVESTIGATION

——

J AMES HENDRICKS fired a shot through a door, after many drinks, and killed a man. George Whittington shot a man in an open courtyard, after an argument and many drinks. Hendricks confessed to his commanding officer and signed a statement for the Military Police. From MP headquarters, he was taken straight to the guardhouse. He remained silent throughout his trial. George Whittington spoke up for himself at the scene of his crime and never stopped speaking.

After the events of August 22, Captain Whittington was held by the Military Police for two days, then transferred to a U.S. Army hospital in Rennes for psychiatric observation. An Inspector General of the VIII Corps took charge of investigating the case. Capt. John Raaen filed a second report with information provided by fellow Rangers. Together, the reports would determine whether Whittington would be brought up before a general court-martial for killing Francis Morand.

Thomas Petrich, the medical officer for the 5th Rangers who had been with Whittington since training camp in Tennessee, did not mince words in his statement for Raaen's report. Whittington could not exercise his full powers of discretion because of an old boxing injury, obvious from the almost continuous twitching of the left side of his face. The man had already proven himself mentally unsound before the shooting:

> When the officer in question, for instance, has indulged in
> alcoholic beverages and has become, to normal standard,

slightly inebriated, he has been a potential menace to everyone in the nearby vicinity. In several instances he has pointed a loaded pistol at a person's head threatening to shoot, in another instance carelessly discharged a loaded pistol in amongst a group while drinking with them.

Whittington's commander, Maj. Richard Sullivan, concurred: "I believe the man is insane for numerous reasons. I think you will notice that yourself."

Petrich and Sullivan's words are harsh, but their motives might not have been. In the Third Army, it was standard procedure to check the sanity of any soldier in a combat unit who was standing for trial. A guilty sentence in a murder trial would mean a dishonorable discharge, a long prison sentence, or even the death penalty, but an insanity defense could save Whittington from standing trial in the first place, although the Ranger captain would surely have hated the tactic.

If an insanity defense was Petrich and Sullivan's strategy, it didn't work. The 127th General Hospital declared George Whittington sane and fit to stand trial. The hospital commander, Colonel Murchison, annotated the standard hospital form after speaking with the chief of neuropsychiatric services, an accomplished young clinician from Oak Park, Illinois, named Melvin Blaurock: "spoke with Blaurock on September 6; testify to sanity—a sadist." It was tantamount to saying that Whittington liked to kill.

The Inspector General's report summed up the evidence against Whittington. First, the Ranger officer was absent without leave in the town of Lesneven. His claim that he had killed a Nazi spy was unconvincing. No one doubted the authenticity of the British army service paybook found on Francis Morand's body, and U.S. Army officials had been able to verify the Frenchman's temporary duty with the 50th Armored Infantry Battalion.

Nor did the Inspector General believe that Whittington had acted in self-defense. For a killing in a situation such as

Whittington's to be considered an act of self-defense, the *Manual for Courts-Martial* required that the person under threat must believe the threat to be imminent and "retreat as far as he safely can." Whittington had not retreated from danger; he had deliberately followed Morand into the hotel courtyard. His behavior suggested malice aforethought, a condition for the charge of murder.

Finally, Whittington had contradicted himself. After showing the people in the bar how he had dropped to the ground under attack, he made an emphatic statement to John Raaen that he had fired all the shots while standing. The report by the Inspector General recommended that charges for murder be brought against Capt. George Whittington.

———

Whittington was released from the hospital on September 1 and returned to duty under guard while he awaited trial. On the 29th, his 5th Rangers had left their base at Tregarantec for Brest, where they began their heroic contribution to the final siege, assuring the defense of a main road into the city, driving off German assaults, attacking forts. The battle they had been preparing for since D-Day finally came to a head on September 16, when the Americans entered Brest en masse. The Americans scaled the city's ancient fortress walls, then forced the Germans out of their hiding places with smoke grenades. Most of the town's citizens had been evacuated three weeks earlier, scattering across Brittany in search of refuge. No one was left but the soldiers. After two days of intense street fighting, the Germans surrendered.

Louis Guilloux was traveling down a country road that day in a U.S. Army jeep with his driver and the two lieutenants from the court-martial when he noticed the quiet. "The deepest silence," he wrote in *OK, Joe,* remembering how, after weeks of endless racket, he could suddenly hear nothing but the whinnying of a horse. A few hours later, the silence was broken by the rumble of flatbed trucks packed with German prisoners. Since the siege of Brest had begun, the Americans had taken 37,000 prisoners of war.

The day after the surrender, Guilloux jotted down the only dream he recorded during his time with the Americans:

> I was with some officers, all of them young. One of them entered into a room, I saw him at the door, from the back, and suddenly I knew it was Tolstoy. I started shouting, "Long live Tolstoy!" And the others around me began to do the same. Then I woke up.

It's hard to say, for any writer, when the idea of a new book is born, but the appearance of Tolstoy in his dreams might indicate that Guilloux had started, at least unconsciously, to work on his novel about the Liberation. He probably loved Russian literature more than any writer of his generation, and Tolstoy, for him, was not only the author of *War and Peace,* he was also the soldier who had taken part in the siege of Sebastopol, the port city on the Black Sea, during the terrible Crimean War. Sebastopol, 1854; Brest, 1944: Tolstoy's *Sebastopol Sketches* show a city collapsing, a soldier and his comrades growing progressively disillusioned with war.

Maj. Gen. Troy Middleton, who commanded the VIII Corps, presided over a ceremony on September 20 to hand back Brest to the city's mayor. As Jonathan Gawne, historian of the Brest campaign, put it, "there was not much of a city to hand back." Air and artillery bombing had gutted the old city and the Germans blew up the port facilities before they surrendered. Military historians still debate whether or not the surrender of Brest could even be considered a military victory for the Americans. All was quiet in the Breton countryside, but, as General Ramcke had promised, the port city ceded by the Nazis was entirely pulverized.

On September 21, Louis Guilloux was back in the Army jeep, accompanying Lieutenants Greene and Fogarty from Morlaix to Lesneven to get ready for another trial. He knew little except that a Ranger officer had killed a French Resistance fighter at a bar. After nearly a month working for the Judge Advocate office, Guilloux was seeing his first and only case involving a white soldier, and an officer. Military Intelligence officers in Lesneven had taken the pre-trial statements from the French civilians, and the bulk of the pre-trial report had been delegated to the Inspector General. The JAG lieutenants seemed nervous about the case. For the first time since he had joined the American team, Guilloux felt excluded from the proceedings. He didn't understand why the preparation of this trial was so different from the others.

———

Members of a court-martial cannot hold a rank inferior to the man on trial. The officers assigned to sit in judgment on George Whittington were colonels, lieutenant colonels, and majors. One member of the court immediately recused himself because of pre-formed judgments on the case; another, who had presided over James Hendricks's trial, was challenged off the court by the defense. James Montgomery acted as president and Juan Sedillo as Law Member. Joseph Greene, the violin-playing lieutenant and aggressive prosecutor of James Hendricks, served as George Whittington's defense lawyer; Ralph Fogarty, who had defended Hendricks, assisted Greene.

Whittington had the right to choose an additional attorney to act as his individual defense counsel. He was lucky: help was nearby. On September 11, George wrote to his older brother:

Dear David,

At present I am at VIII Corps Headquarters awaiting trial under the 92nd Article of War, Specification, killing.

I should appreciate it very much if you will come here and if possible bring a lawyer of some criminal experience, the more experience the better, to assist my present counsel. If you like come down and talk it over first.

Shall be waiting for you.

Sincerely,
George

After military school in New Mexico, David Whittington had followed in his father's footsteps to law school, taking his own degree from the University of Arkansas and passing the bar in 1939. Like George, David Whittington was stationed in France, a major on assignment to British Field Marshal Montgomery's staff. He was in a position to help his brother and assist Joseph Greene.

To prosecute Captain Whittington, the VIII Corps wanted an officer with specific training in military justice. They brought in Lt. James Craighill from the Ninth Army. He was a pacifist minister's son from Rocky Mount, North Carolina, who had graduated from law school at the University of North Carolina at Chapel Hill and trained at the Army's Judge Advocate General's School in Ann Arbor, Michigan. *U.S. v. Whittington* was his first court-martial.

Craighill was only in Morlaix for ten days—too short a time to make friends. The town felt close to the war zone in Brest, and rumors abounded about German spies in the vicinity. Even for casual walks in the neighborhood of the VIII Corps headquarters, he was required to be armed. A few days before George Whittington went on trial, Craighill went to the mayor's home with the other VIII Corps officers and a crowd of townspeople, including many attractive young French women, for an evening of celebration after the victory at Brest. The fast-talking Joseph Greene would have been invited, and the suave Juan Sedillo, and Louis Guilloux, with his young friend from Chicago, Bill Cormier. The American officers taught the French to play "spin the bottle." The next morning, Craighill found himself without his favorite sweater. When he went back to the mayor's house to fetch it, the mayor's daughter answered the door, wearing his sweater. Many of the details of Whittington's trial have faded from James Craighill's memory, but the vision of that girl in the doorway has stayed with him, still fresh after sixty years.

Seventeen

The Case Against George Whittington

——

G EORGE WHITTINGTON'S trial began in Morlaix on the morning of September 25, 1944, a week after the surrender of Brest. On paper, at least, the Ranger captain's prospects for acquittal looked as poor or poorer than James Hendricks's had looked three weeks earlier. Hendricks had fired blindly, drunkenly. Whittington may have been drunk, but his shooting was deliberate, his target intentional. Hendricks claimed to remember nothing, while Whittington had a story, but his story was unsubstantiated. The Army had done a preliminary check, and nothing indicated that Morand was a spy.

Hendricks's fellow soldiers had found him odd and half-cracked. Whittington, too, was considered unstable and unreliable. He had a reputation for being trigger-happy, especially when he'd been drinking.

The public relations issue with French Allies in the Whittington affair was potentially even thornier than in the Hendricks case. The black quartermaster private had killed a respected local farmer, but Whittington had killed a Special Air Service paratrooper, the *crème* of the Resistance, in a sector of Brittany where the Resistance was sacred.

Beyond what they shared in the way of trouble, the difference between the two defendants was enormous. Their rank and race put them in two categories, not merely of privilege but of personhood.

James Hendricks, the twenty-one-year-old black draftee, had no military distinction, no connections, no heroic military record. A farm laborer, he was out of his element in court. He was charged with a shameful sex crime as well as a murder. Whittington, on the other hand, was a career officer and a war hero, sure to benefit from the "good soldier" defense. In his case, you would have to call it a "great soldier" defense. From his high school years at the New Mexico Military Institute to his time in the China Marines and his training as a Ranger, the military had been his world, his adopted family. He was ten years older than Hendricks and he knew how the system worked.

After his arrest and confinement, Hendricks had no one to guide him other than his chaplain, Robert Saunders, whose role was consoling rather than strategic. Religion hadn't helped him in the courtroom, except, perhaps, to inspire his defense lawyer's final request for clemency after his guilty verdict, the only slim chance of saving his life. By contrast, from the time his own commanding officer told a pre-trial investigator he was insane, George Whittington had inspired a series of clever strategies. His trial preparation was a closely plotted effort, put into place by Joseph Greene, working closely with the defendant's own brother, Maj. David Whittington. Their plan was ingenious: They hoped to convince the court that the person whose guilt should really be put to the test was not George Whittington but Francis Morand, the victim.

———

Morand was an enigma. Very few people in Lesneven had ever seen him, aside from the barmaid, the Americans in the bar, and Paul Jacopin, head of the local Resistance. The Army had neither the time nor the resources to trace his history.

Even today, that history is almost impossible to document. If we believe the stories he told to his comrades in the Resistance in the summer of 1944, Francis Morand was born in Austria and his first language was German. He had left his family, his brothers and a sister, to join the French Foreign Legion, and after several years of service, he became eligible to be naturalized as a French citizen. He may have been a Jew escaping Hitler, or a man in trouble with the law. We don't know when he changed his name to the typically French Francis Morand.

After his release from the Legion, Morand settled in the south of France and found work as a coach in a soccer club. When World War II broke out in 1939, he was drafted by the French army, and like 2 million other Frenchmen, was taken prisoner by the Germans in June 1940, when France was defeated. His comrades helped him escape the camp, and he made his way to France and then across the Pyrenees into Spain, the surest way to reach the Free French in England. There were at least a hundred refugees crossing that border every day. As soon as he crossed the border, Morand was probably arrested by General Franco's Guardia Civil and sent to Miranda de Ebro, a detention camp for aliens without visas. The camp, filthy and overcrowded, had drawn the attention of the various European consulates in Madrid, as well as the Red Cross, who lobbied for better conditions for the detainees and for their release. Franco, who saw that the Allies were winning the war, was ready to appease, and he responded to diplomatic pressure. Morand was probably released in late 1943 along with a large contingent of Frenchmen, then immediately recruited by representatives of the Free French in Spain. Able-bodied soldiers were in short supply. Many of the men leaving Miranda were too old or feeble to be of much use to the army, and even former POWs were weakened by their detention and escape. As a legionnaire with extensive combat experience, Morand would have been a highly desirable recruit.

He probably sailed to England in mid-May 1943 on the ship *Santa Rosa* with the other men who would join the 4th French Parabattalion. When he reached London, after many delays, he would have had to endure a strenuous interrogation and security clearance by the British Intelligence Service. He finally got his clearance.

When he filled out the forms for his army paybook, Morand reinvented his biography, listing his birthplace as

Casablanca and claiming his parents were French. Many of his comrades also took new names and changed their place of birth when they joined the Special Air Service. Their motivations were somewhat different than his. For them, a fictional name was a form of security, a way to prevent Nazi reprisals against family members. For Morand, long divorced from his oldest self, the French Resistance was a heroic continuation of a life on the run begun ten years earlier.

Morand was an adventurer, a sportsman, and a ladies' man. In Auchinleck, Scotland, on his time off from Special Air Service training camp, he went into town to swim and skate. He was a champion at both sports. Women were drawn to his strength, his build, and his mysterious accent, part eastern, part southern.

Pictures of him with the 4th French Parabattalion show him in full paratrooper gear, his trousers tucked into his boots. His SAS beret is perched at a jaunty angle, and at the center of the beret, directly above his high forehead, you can just make out the SAS badge, a winged dagger embroidered with the motto "Who Dares Wins." His posture is so perfect, he makes the other paratroopers look as though they're slouching.

After Auchinleck, his trajectory becomes clearer. On June 9, Morand was parachuted into an SAS base of operations called "Samwest," located in the Duault Forest, in the interior of Brittany. Separated from his unit after a Nazi attack on Samwest, he fought with the French *maquis* in the interior forests, magic places known in Arthurian legend as "Brocéliande," home to Vivian the Fairy and Merlin the Magician. In late July, Morand and several of his men joined a group of local Resistance fighters in Saint-Gilles-du-Méné. Two of the group were caught by the Nazis and tortured into revealing the location of their headquarters at the Seilla farm. In a brutal raid on the Seilla, two of Morand's fellow paratroopers died; Morand survived only because he was with a woman in town the night of the raid. On August 1, he hopped on an American truck near Dinan and crossed the Brittany peninsula with the 50th Armored Infantry Battalion of the 6th Armored Division, "The Super Sixth," who

were making their way across Brittany toward Lesneven to prepare for the battle to take Brest from General Ramcke.

Morand had told the British army he was born in
Casablanca to French parents. He told his friends in the SAS
and the *maquis* that he was originally Austrian. In Leseven, he
told Paul Jacopin that he was from the Haute-Savoie. He had
played every role a liberator could play in the summer of 1944:
he was a Free Frenchman, a paratrooper in the British army, a
fighter with the *maquis* and the FFI in the inland forests, a
liaison to the American Army who crossed the Breton countryside in a truck. His comrades had been massacred and tortured, but he had survived it all without a scratch. Perhaps by
now, lying came as naturally to him as staying alive.

No one who testified at his trial knew about his stint in the
Legion or could explain his accent by the fact that he had been
naturalized French. In death, Francis Morand became the perfect foil for George Whittington's defense.

In the opening moments of the trial, that late September
morning, Joseph Greene put his strategy on the table. Lesneven was in captured territory and enemy agents were everywhere, disguised in Allied battle dress and carrying false
identification papers. There was no reason to assume Morand
was a friend and every reason to suspect he was a spy. You
can't try someone for killing the enemy. Furthermore, Greene
had technical quibbles with the Investigator General's pre-trial
investigation. He moved to dismiss the case.

Law Member Sedillo denied the motion, while reassuring
Greene that "the accused will be accorded every privilege
which he is entitled to." Sedillo's response was a rhetorical
aside, but a significant one: the words "privilege" and "entitled" were never uttered in James Hendricks's defense.

The question of physical evidence was yet another factor that
gave Whittington's defense a distinct advantage. Victor Bignon's
body had been duly examined by the local doctor immediately

after the murder. Morand's body had been whisked away by Graves Registration to the temporary American cemetery at Saint-James immediately following the murder. No autopsy, no medical examiner's report existed on Morand. The prosecution was dependent on the testimony of the MPs who had arrived on the scene to describe the victim's wounds and the condition of his body. Whether the Ranger officer had shot Morand face to face or from the back could only be determined by testimony.

The combined testimony of four different MPs added up to a confusing set of hypotheses. Pvt. Emanuel Petrone, the first official on the scene, found Morand lying in the hotel court-yard, his carbine underneath his body and a revolver at his hip. There was a bullet in the chamber of the carbine and a full clip, but Petrone didn't check the safety on the gun. Morand was clutching his carbine—it was hard to pry it out of his hand. It looked as though he hadn't fired.

Petrone was joined in the courtyard by two other MPs. They had removed Morand's shirt and trousers, rolled him over, and looked at his wounds. There were bullet wounds to the heart, the abdomen, and one kidney. From the size of the wounds, it was impossible to tell where they had entered the body, although a small hole in Morand's back indicated that a single bullet might have entered through the back. The MPs found no stray bullets or shells in the hotel courtyard. Three of the six bullets were unaccounted for.

For two and a half hours, the members of the court asked Petrone to help them reconstruct the shooting, based on what he had learned from the position of the corpse. Did it look as though Morand had been in fighting position when he was shot? Did Petrone think Whittington had shot Morand in the front or the back? Lieutenant Craighill hoped that Petrone's answers would show the court that Whittington had intended to kill, and that he was not provoked.

Instead, what the court learned was that Emanuel Petrone knew very little about anatomy, less about forensics, and even less about proper procedure in a murder investigation.

Corp. Morris Cline had arrived after Petrone, and entered

the bar just as Whittington was demonstrating how he had dropped to the ground and killed Morand. Cline remembered that Whittington had asked him where he was from and then the two men had a friendly chat about Kentucky, where George's favorite uncle lived. It was another revealing moment: Even as he was about to be arrested, Whittington had been secure in his leadership, and young Cline remembered with pleasure that the Ranger officer had taken an interest in his civilian life. At a moment when he might have been fearful for his own future, George Whittington enjoyed an easy moment of conviviality with a lesser ranking soldier.

With no incriminating physical evidence in his way, Greene continued to defend Whittington by assailing the identity of the victim. He cross-examined an MP officer, Capt. Crien Schemering, about the existence of a small black notebook among Morand's personal effects—a notebook that Greene said contained information about U.S. Army units in the area. When Schemering referred casually to Morand as "the French soldier," Greene objected that Morand's nationality had not been established. Craighill countered patiently: "If the court please, all the evidence that has been presented in this case indicates that he was a French soldier."

Greene insisted, and his objection took on a grand, almost philosophical aura: "No sir, the statement of the Trial Judge Advocate that he is a French soldier does not make him a French soldier. I object to anything that refers to him as a French soldier. Refer to him as 'the deceased.'"

Law Member Sedillo overruled: Morand's paybook indicated French nationality. But from then on, every time someone used the phrase "French soldier," the court remembered Greene's objection.

Maneuvers were beginning to add up. An important fact that emerged during the MP testimony—that Whittington was drunk and belligerent the night of the murder—faded in the wake of Greene's dramatic suggestion that Morand carried a black book with lists of secret troop movements, the kind of notebook a spy might carry. Greene had captured the imagination of the court.

Craighill called one last witness for the prosecution, William

Runge, the Ranger captain who had gone AWOL in Lesneven with Whittington. Runge was careful and moderate in what he said, never accusatory. He denied that Whittington was drunk, contradicting what the MPs had just said. He didn't understand French, but he thought the conversation between Whittington and Morand was friendly. He really didn't remember much. Although he was a witness for the prosecution, his answers contributed to Whittington's defense.

At 3 P.M., the prosecution rested its case. Joseph Greene seized the floor to move for a direct verdict of acquittal and for a dismissal of the charge on the grounds that the prosecution failed to prove its case beyond a reasonable doubt.

He hammered against the prosecution: There was no solid evidence about the weapon of the deceased; the court didn't even learn if Morand's carbine had been fired. No shells, no empty cases had been found. No one knew if the safety on Morand's carbine was on or off. The carbine was kept for evidence, but the pistol that Morand had worn on his hip was nowhere to be found. Nor had Whittington's pistol been entered into evidence. There was no evidence presented concerning markings or powder burns on Whittington's clothing, no measurement of the distance from which the shots were fired. The court didn't learn which of the wounds were fatal. Greene summed up the situation in a rhetorical flourish, a kind of reductio ad absurdum based on the lack of evidence:

> I don't deny the fact that he [Morand] may have been dead. There is no testimony here to show the death. . . . We don't know how many bullet wounds were in the body. We don't know the measurements—what vital organs were affected. We don't know whether that bullet that went through the front came out the back. . . . It is up to the prosecution, not us, to put in such proof.

How could Greene be expected to provide George Whittington with a fair defense if the prosecution couldn't even show what had happened?

James Montgomery, the president of the court, denied the motion to acquit.

———

At 3:30 P.M., it was time for Joseph Greene to make good on his strategy. Having assailed the prosecution for its lack of hard evidence at the crime scene, he needed his witnesses to turn back the clock and refocus the court's attention on the scene at the bar, where Morand had raised the suspicions of two officers in Military Intelligence. To convince the court that Morand was a spy, he would have to introduce evidence based on conversations with the deceased.

For his first witness, Greene called Lt. Charles Zuccardy to the stand. Zuccardy was the French-language interpreter for Military Intelligence who had asked Morand for his ID papers in the bar. Zuccardy told the court the same story he had told the Inspector General. He described Morand's nervous behavior, his German accent, and his angry defensiveness when questioned about his identity.

Each time Craighill objected to hearsay conversation, Sedillo overruled. Any conversation that took place during the period leading up to the shooting counted as evidence. This included what Morand said to Zuccardy when Zuccardy asked for his papers; what Morand said to Zuccardy's sergeant, d'Etamper; what Zuccardy and d'Etamper said to each other about Morand; and what Morand's accent sounded like to each of them—his German accent in English; the way he said *"mit"* instead of "with"; his North African accent in French; what Morand's attitude was; how he said goodbye. There was protracted speculation in the court about accents, and the odd similarity of the aspirated North African "h" with the German one. True to Joe Greene's tactic, the murder trial of George Whittington was being reduced to a linguistic whodunit.

———

Louis Guilloux with his wife, Renée, and their teenage daughter, Yvonne, at their house in Saint-Brieuc in the summer of 1944. Four years of deprivations, clandestine resistance work, and the hardships of the Nazi occupation left the writer weakened and nearly emaciated, but exhilarated by the Liberation.

Louis Guilloux was officially attached to the VIII Corps headquarters as a civilian employee but was given an American uniform and the privileges of a lieutenant, with a salary of 80 francs a day—about 50 cents.

Pvt. James Hendricks in the photo he sent home to his adoptive North Carolina family from Camp Van Dorn, Mississippi. Hendricks was assigned to a sanitary company, then to a quartermaster battalion in a camp infamous for its terrible climate and the racist atmosphere in the nearby town of Centreville.

Photograph courtesy of Geraldine Bullock

The Army chose Château la Vallée, a deserted fourteenth-century manor house outside the village of Plumaudan, Brittany, for the hanging ceremony of James Hendricks.

Photograph by Alan Thomas

Jeannine Bignon in 2003, standing outside the old Bignon farm-house, its wooden door still marked by the bullets that killed her father, Victor Bignon, on August 21, 1944.

Photograph by Alan Thomas

Jeannine Bignon in her modern kitchen with a photo of Victor. The American flag on the mantel is a souvenir from a local celebration.

Photograph by Alan Thomas

Juan A. A. Sedillo, Law Member on the Morlaix Court-Martial. As a handsome young law student, he was discovered by a Fox studio executive and cast as the Cuban detective in the 1928 film *Girl from Havana*. He still cuts a dashing figure in this photo from the late 1950s, when he served as American judge of the International Court of Tangier.

American Bar Association Journal

Lt. Joseph Greene (front and center, cigarette in hand), with his Army buddies in the VIII Corps, European Theater. Greene, who loved to perform in court, was also a passionate amateur violinist.

Photograph by Don Lewis, courtesy of Eleanor Lewis McKechnie

Capt. George P. Whittington (second from left), receiving the Distinguished Service Cross with fellow Rangers on June 22, 1944, for extraordinary heroism in action on D-Day: "Captain Whittington's bravery, aggressiveness and inspired leadership are in keeping with the highest traditions of the service." Joseph Greene, Whittington's defense counsel, was convinced that the Ranger captain's decoration alone would go a long way in convincing the court-martial to acquit him.

Photograph courtesy of the National Archives and Records Administration

Francis Morand (fourth from left), the man shot by George Whittington, training with the 4th French Parabattalion, Special Air Service, in England. An Austrian naturalized after a stint with the French Foreign Legion, Morand probably took a "nom de guerre" when he joined the Free French in London. He parachuted into occupied France after D-Day and crossed Brittany with the 6th Armored Division. Morand's uncertain origins and German accent played a large part in Whittington's defense.

Photograph courtesy of Roger Schank

Lycee Kernégues, Morlaix, Brittany, an enormous H-shaped block of buildings with several courtyards, served as temporary VIII Corps headquarters. Its party room was transformed into the court-martial where James Hendricks and George Whittington were tried for murder.

Photograph by Alan Thomas

Louis Guilloux in an elegant author photo taken for his French publisher in the late 1940s. In 1949, Guilloux won one of France's top literary prizes for a novel set in Saint-Brieuc during the Nazi occupation. He only began to write about his experience with the American army in 1964.

Photograph by Roger Parry, copyright Editions Gallimard

When the cemetery for American war dead at St. James became the permanent Brittany American Cemetery and Memorial, the remains of Francis Morand and other French resistance fighters were moved to the civilian cemetery in the nearby village of St. James. Morand's tomb can be found in the company of seventeen other Free Frenchmen. A ceramic flower display at the base of his tombstone has a single word on it: "regrets."

Photograph by Jacques Adelée, courtesy of the American Battle Monuments Commission

The 96 marble squares of Plot E, the burial site for World War II dishonorable dead. The corner square in row four marks the grave of Louis Till, whose son, Emmett, was murdered in Mississippi only ten years after his father's execution. Plot E is carefully maintained by the American Battle Monuments Commission.

Photograph by Lorenzo Virgili, courtesy of the American Battle Monuments Commission

Marble square number 13: James Hendricks's grave in Plot E.

Photograph by Lorenzo Virgili, courtesy
of the American Battle Monuments Commission

The courtroom debates about language and accent would have fascinated Louis Guilloux, but the Army's novelist-interpreter wasn't in court on September 25. There were no French witnesses scheduled to testify, so no one was needed to translate. In *OK, Joe,* Guilloux wrote about how he spent his time off, sitting under the oak tree in front of the lycée gates, wandering through Morlaix. One of the officers asked him to find a bottle of perfume for his lady friend, which wasn't easy because the Germans had taken everything; the shelves in the beauty shops and boutiques were empty.

It was odd for Guilloux to walk through the town in his American uniform. "Seeing me arrive in my handsome military garb, people thought I was an American," he wrote in *OK, Joe.* "They spoke to me in jibberish or in their high school English, and when I told them that I was French they seemed to think I had played a joke on them." The courtroom was not the only place in the war zone where people wanted assurances about national identity.

By the time Guilloux got back to the Lycée Kernégues, the court-martial had recessed for the day. After nearly a month of working together, Greene and Guilloux were fast friends, and the Brooklyn lawyer recounted his first day's successes with pleasure.

Much later, when Guilloux started writing about Joe Greene, he changed the Brooklyn lawyer's name to Stone. Even without having been in the courtroom that first day, he remembered many details surrounding the Whittington case, but he wasn't sure which elements to use or how to introduce them. During the trial preparation, he had overheard David Whittington promise to give Greene a French violin if George were acquitted. Guilloux was a novelist, not an essayist, and he expressed his outrage not by accusing the Whittingtons of influence, but by transforming the promised gift into a priceless Stradivarius. To express his own disbelief, he considered turning the scene into a dream sequence:

. . . I could use a novelist's artifice and say that it was during the night, in a dream . . . that I saw Lieutenant Stone and the defendant's brother get up, shake hands, then watched the defendant's brother walk away, while Lieutenant Stone came up to me like someone bearing such good news he can't wait to tell it to the first person he sees. . . . Only it wasn't in a dream that I heard Lieutenant Stone tell me that if the defendant is acquitted, he'll be given a Stradivarius.

"I'll get a Stradivarius!"

He imparts this news with a joyous bonhomie, not at all like a cynic.

Raise your right hand and say, I swear to it!

For Guilloux, writing was always two things—a craft, and a desire to impart the truth of what he had heard and seen. The scene of the promised Stradivarius never made its way into the published version of the novel. Perhaps he decided it sounded too much like fiction.

EIGHTEEN

GEORGE WHITTINGTON'S TESTIMONY

———

"D O YOU swear to tell the truth, the whole truth, and nothing but the truth, so help you God?" Louis Guilloux was finally sworn in as interpreter in *U.S. v. Whittington* at 8:30 A.M. on September 26. In his notebook that week, he jotted down a single anguished sentence: "You're losing your boundaries, you're losing your autonomy." Now the American oath rang hollow, a refrain for his own growing discomfort. What did the truth mean if he was speaking for someone else?

Guilloux had witnessed the other trials in their entirety; this time he was entering in the middle. Like everyone else in court, he knew the day belonged to Whittington. The French civilian witnesses whose testimony he'd been called in to translate were nothing but a sideline.

Guilloux was surprised by the sight of the defendant. George Whittington looked nothing like the madman of the pre-trial documents he had read. The Ranger captain entered the makeshift courtroom with great dignity, dressed in his officer's "pinks and greens"—a dark olive green wool blouse (an overshirt) and rose-colored trousers—and carrying his overseas cap with its captain's bars. He sat quietly at the defense table, staring straight ahead. The left side of his chest was covered in ribbons, representing military achievements dating back to his years with the China Marines. To Guilloux, the swatches of color meant nothing, but to the officers of the court, every detail was significant. There was the Combat Infantryman Badge, the Distinguished Service Cross, the Bronze

Star Medal with its Oak Leaf Cluster and "V" device for valor. There were campaign ribbons for his Marine service, a pre–Pearl Harbor ribbon, and his North American Campaign ribbon with an arrowhead device to recognize his amphibious landing in Normandy. Not to mention the marksmanship badges on the left pocket of his blouse. His "Expert" badge for Rifle, Pistol, Submachine gun, and Bayonet, and his Distinguished Shot badge for pistol and rifle were all visible. On the left shoulder of his green blouse, he wore the distinctive Ranger patch, a blue diamond with a gold border and the word "Rangers" centered in the diamond; on the right, the patch of the 10th Armored Division.

A week after the surrender at Brest, the war still encroached on the court's plans. Major Sullivan, the commanding officer who had filed formal charges against Whittington and who had told the Inspector General he thought the man was insane, had asked to be excused. Unlike Donald Tucker, engaged in the supply war, Richard Sullivan was directly involved in combat, and combat had priority: The military situation for his 5th Rangers on the Brest peninsula was too complex for him to leave his command, even for a day. Craighill reserved the right to call on Sullivan later, but Whittington's CO never came to court.

The uneven responses of commanding officers to their soldiers' misconduct was a determining factor in courts-martial convictions during the 1940s. In the absence of a positive identification, Hendricks's guilt had been certified by Lieutenant Tucker, who was with him at the crime scene from the moment of his arrest. Major Sullivan's absence from Whittington's trial might well have been an automatic boon to Whittington's defense. We can only speculate about his opinion of the case. He may have believed that Whittington's shooting wasn't serious enough to merit his testimony, or, whatever his misgivings about Whittington, he may have found in his own combat duties a good excuse to help a fellow Ranger in trouble.

Two other important witnesses were unavailable: Michel d'Etamper, the MI sergeant who had clashed with Morand in the bar, and Jacques La Rus, his superior officer—the man who heard Morand and Whittington's bilingual adieux from the WC. Upon the agreement of both prosecution and defense, a statement would be read to the court from each, cobbled together from their pre-trial testimony. Sullivan's damning words about Whittington's bad behavior in his pre-trial statement, far more controversial, were not stipulated. His condemnation of Whittington was never heard by the court.

———

Louis Guilloux took his familiar position behind the witness's chair. The defense had called its first witness, Yvonne Pichon, the barmaid from the Hôtel de France. Guilloux portrayed her in *OK, Joe* in a meeting with the lieutenants a few days before the trial, a rosy-faced country girl who had dolled up for the Americans and giggled whenever she spoke. In the years after the trial, the people of Lesneven would speculate that Yvonne was at the heart of the altercation between the Frenchman and the American officer. In court, her testimony served primarily to support the American officers' opinions.

Greene began by asking her to repeat the conversation she had had with Morand at the bar. Yvonne Pichon testified that d'Etamper had asked her if she thought Morand had a strange accent and that Morand had shot her a dirty look. *"Il m'a regardée avec des yeux terribles."* It wasn't an expression Guilloux knew in English, so he translated, "He was looking at me with terrible eyes."

Joe Greene asked what she meant by "terrible eyes."

"He looked at me in a very stern way meaning, 'say nothing,'" she replied.

Next, Greene wanted to know if Morand spoke like a Frenchman. Her answer was incriminating: "He didn't look French and didn't speak . . . he searched for his words when he spoke French."

Craighill was annoyed: all this was opinion, none of it was fact, all of it was hearsay. Sedillo sided with Greene. Yvonne

Pichon's impressions counted. Yet the court had never asked about the one question she would be the expert to answer: the extent to which the two men might have been fighting about her.

———

An impatient court listened halfheartedly as the two lawyers read statements by d'Etamper and La Rus, the Military Intelligence officers. D'Etamper's text made Morand sound like a spy; La Rus's made him sound like a gentleman. Nothing was gained or lost for either side.

Finally, at 10:45 A.M., the focus was on George Whittington. Here, as in the Hendricks trial, military law required Law Member Juan Sedillo to present the defendant with his three options. He could take the stand and be sworn in like any other person, in which case he could be fully cross-examined. Or he or his counsel could make an unsworn statement on which he could not be cross-examined. It did not count as evidence and would only have as much weight as the court gave it. Third, George Whittington could remain silent. That was the right James Hendricks had exercised. It was an option chosen by defendants who believed that testifying could only damage them. Hendricks had appeared mute before the court, the man no one could identify.

Guilloux had put it well, in the philosophical language that marked his generation. Hendricks's gaze in court was empty, "as if he was no longer anything but an object." For Guilloux, Hendricks was Bigger Thomas in Richard Wright's *Native Son*, the murderer who signs a coerced confession, then refuses to speak.

Whittington was a character out of another tradition. Guilloux would make him into an ogre in a fairy tale, but to the Americans in Morlaix, he was the hero of a western. "I wish to take the stand and make a sworn statement," he announced to the court. To anyone who knew him, it came as no surprise. Captain Whittington had elected the strongest and riskiest option.

John Silbernagel, a friend of Joseph Greene's in the officers' quarters at Morlaix, remembers the lawyer agonizing about whether to allow Whittington to speak in his own defense. Whittington had a reputation for going off half-cocked—wasn't that what this case was about in the first place? And if he lost his temper in court and resorted to physical violence, he could damage his defense beyond repair.

What convinced Greene to have his client testify was something simple and visceral: Whittington's decorations. He told Silbernagel he wanted the court to have to look at the ribbons on Whittington's chest as he told his story. He didn't think these men, many of whom had landed in Normandy during the bloody week of June 6, were capable of finding anyone who had won the Distinguished Service Cross guilty.

George Whittington's performance surprised and delighted Joseph Greene. He had feared his client's temper but he had completely underestimated his intelligence. Whittington was as eloquent and calm in court as he had been flustered in the pre-trial investigation. Even his facial tics—the twitching eyes, the occasional sniffle—now made him seem discerning. Not only that, he had a story to tell that no one had heard, a revelation. It was not only his defense or decorations or even the nature of his crime that made his trial so different from James Hendricks's. It was the fact that he spoke in his own defense, and that he was fully prepared to take control of the trial, to steer its narration on the right course.

While they were having their second bottle of champagne, Whittington explained, he and Morand began to converse in Spanish. Whittington loved to play with languages and he had learned a bit of Spanish from the ranch hands in New Mexico when he was a boy. His Spanish was better than his schoolbook French, and he was pleased when Morand answered him in kind. He asked Morand how he knew the language, and Morand answered that he had learned it in Spain.

Whittington continued:

I asked him what he had done in Spain and he told me he
had served with the Fascists. He did not say "served." He
said "with the Fascists." I said to him, "with or against the
Fascists?" He told me he was with the Fascists in the Condor Legion, and as I knew that the Condor Legion was
made up of German troops in the German Army, I wondered about that but I did not pay too much attention
to it.

Like so much of the information in the trial, the story was
hearsay; Whittington was reporting what the deceased had
told him. Although Craighill let Whittington speak uninter-
rupted, there were obvious problems with his testimony. Whittington's tale wasn't merely hearsay, it was hearsay involving a
language the defendant may not have understood. But no one
in the court asked Whittington how well he really understood
Spanish, or how well Morand himself spoke the language—
not even Law Member Juan Sedillo, a native of New Mexico
whose fluency in Spanish had served him in his early law
practice.

For Guilloux, who had worked with refugees from the
Spanish Civil War since 1936 and knew the history of the conflict in its smallest details, there was an even bigger problem
with Whittington's account. The Condor Legion, whose very
name connoted flight, had consisted of aviators, not ground
troops—the phrase "German troops in the German Army"
didn't make sense.

Along with the language problem, along with the historical
inaccuracy of Whittington's account, was another issue so simple, so basic, it was astonishing that no one raised it: Would a
man who was a Nazi spy have confessed openly to an American officer that he had fought along with the Nazis?

Louis Guilloux, who had plenty of time to observe the proceedings and whose ear for language and narrative was highly
refined, must have been astonished that Whittington's story

wasn't challenged, but he had no advisory capacity in the court. He was only the interpreter.

Whittington's conclusion was as odd as the story itself. "I wondered about that [the Condor Legion] but I did not pay too much attention to it." It wasn't the response you'd expect from a man who was so quick to fight. Why didn't Whittington say anything about the Condor Legion to the Military Intelligence officers when he and Runge went up to the bar? Why didn't he have Morand arrested?

By his own account, Whittington was only gradually figuring out who Morand might be and preparing in a secret way to defend himself:

> I had heard of Germans occasionally, or people supposed not to be Germans, walking in places and shooting up troops and I didn't know whether that was his intention or not, so I walked over to the corner, took my pistol out and looked at it to see whether it was locked and on safety. I normally carry it that way. It was and I went back and we had another glass of liquor and we talked for a while.

He was giving the court an image of himself as a man who took his time, a man who was careful and skeptical.

Then he came to the courtyard scene, and the moment of the shooting itself. When he described the cordial words he and Morand exchanged in the courtyard—the conversation Jacques La Rus heard from the toilet—Whittington made Morand seem menacing, the kind of guy who would say good night and good luck in the kindest terms, then aim his gun at you. "He did not make a verbal threat," Whittington explained simply. "The only threat he made was the attempt to shoot me."

Craighill poked a few holes in his story, but they were small. If Whittington wasn't sure that Morand was going to shoot him inside the bar, what made him so sure that Morand was going to shoot him outside? Why did he go out in the courtyard in the first place? Whittington responded that he thought his friends were following him. Besides, he wasn't afraid of the paratrooper. He didn't trust him, but he wasn't afraid.

Next came the issue that had caused all the trouble in the pre-trial investigation: Was Whittington standing up or lying down when he fired at Morand? Here Whittington drew on his authority as an infantryman. He referred not just to what he did, but to his technique:

> Because I ducked down as I told you . . . I am not sure that I hit the ground or not but I ducked down and the way that is done is merely to flash the holster up with the thumb, grasp the pistol and use the same motion as you bring it forward, knocking the safety off with the thumb.

"The way that is done": One of the officers on the court took the bait. How, he asked, had Whittington learned to draw his pistol in the way he described?

D-Day wasn't even four months behind them, but the Rangers' feats at Omaha Beach, crawling under enemy fire, scaling the cliffs, were already legendary. The officer wanted to see what an expert Ranger marksman, a Distinguished Shot, looked like in action. Who could be a better model than Whittington?

Colonel Montgomery, the president of the court, ruled: "The witness is certainly under an entirely different mental situation so much so to render such a demonstration of little or no value to the evidence."

The officers on the court-martial would have to imagine George Whittington in action. Their desire to do so gives us another insight into the court's understanding of James Hendricks in comparison to George Whittington. Hendricks had fired through a door, chased and assaulted Noémie Bignon, and run from the scene. Afterwards, he couldn't even remember what happened. His actions and confession showed him to be a person without self-control, overwhelmed by events. By his own account, Whittington had done everything deliberately, with calculation and self-control. His fellow officers perceived him as an agent of his destiny.

If they couldn't watch him perform, the court wanted to learn more about Whittington's experience in the war. He explained that his battalion hadn't been in action since D-Day + 8, when they finished fighting in some towns along the Normandy-Brittany coast. From then until August, they'd been jumped a few times and dealt with snipers, but they hadn't made any attacks. They were waiting for replacements for the men they'd lost in battle, getting ready to go back into combat at Brest. The 2nd Ranger Battalion had been ambushed, shot up pretty bad, Whittington told them, the night before the shooting, and his 5th Rangers, too, were on the watch for enemy patrols operating near their bivouac area.

In this atmosphere of fear and suspicion of spies, an officer asked, why did Whittington suspect Morand in particular? Because of his speech, Whittington answered, because of what the MI officers said at the bar, and because of what Morand had told him about fighting with the Condor Legion. Again, the Condor story went unchallenged.

The last officer on the panel asked a last question that allowed the Ranger captain to summarize his own defense:

> "In other words your action was done in order to preserve your own life. Is that right?"
>
> "That's what it was, sir. I thought he was going to kill me and my only thought there was to prevent him."
>
> "What decorations do you hold?"
>
> "The Distinguished Service Cross and the Unit Citation."

———

Guilloux took the interpreter's oath a second time for the final witness in the Whittington trial. Paul Jacopin from the local FFI testified for the prosecution.

After Whittington's heroics, it was dull testimony. Jacopin merely repeated what he told the pre-trial investigators and the French police. He had known Morand for twenty-four hours. He had had supper with him, accompanied him to the bar but only stayed a few minutes; he had work to do. He remembered that Morand was in high spirits but very nervous. Jacopin thought Morand spoke with a North African accent—it sounded a little bit like the Breton way of talking, a little bit German, with an aspirated "h." He didn't really like North Africans.

Yes, Jacopin had believed Morand; he was dressed like any Free Frenchman would be (Jacopin himself wore the British uniform) and he seemed to know Captain Sicot, a Special Air Service officer who had taken over the command of Jacopin's FFI unit. There was only one thing that was odd, but Jacopin didn't learn it until after Morand was dead. Morand told him he was born in the Haute-Savoie but his paybook said he was born in Casablanca.

Jacopin's last comment damaged the prosecution's case, or what was left of it. The man best qualified to defend his fellow Frenchman, his comrade in the Resistance, was admitting that his comrade had lied.

After a day and a half of court time and thirteen witnesses, the prosecution and defense were ready to rest their cases. Juan Sedillo, the Law Member, took a moment to comment on the situation. The court was stymied by lack of information, and by a surfeit of contradictory information:

> His identity may or may not be pertinent to the fundamental issues in this case but a man has been killed. He must have been a citizen of some country and the court is still in doubt, I believe, as to who this person was.

Sedillo's perplexity was Joseph Greene's triumph. During the course of the trial, Morand's identity had disintegrated to the point where the idea that he might actually be the person his papers said he was now seemed almost preposterous. A shadowy, suspicious figure, he could be German, Savoyard, or North African. It was anybody's guess.

For George Whittington, an entirely different dynamic had taken place. While some of the officers on the court-martial had initially questioned his motives, even his sanity, by 11 A.M. on September 26 they were certain who George Whittington was. He was everything a soldier and an officer should be: deliberate, willful, brave, a risk taker, a man in control. Thanks to men like George Whittington, the Allies were winning the war in Europe.

Nineteen

The Aftermath

CRAIGHILL AND GREENE made their closing statements in under ten minutes; the court's deliberation was equally swift. At 11:30 A.M. on September 26, George Whittington was acquitted of all charges.

That evening, the 5th Rangers threw a party for Joseph Greene to celebrate his courtroom victory. As promised, the Whittington brothers presented him with a French violin that had won a prize in the 1931 Exposition Coloniale Internationale in Paris. The gift was given after the trial was over, so it wasn't technically a bribe, but it was against basic Army regulations. Court-martial personnel were never to be compensated for their work beyond their regular pay.

John Runge was fined $50, one quarter of his monthly salary, for having gone AWOL. In his letter of reprimand, Major General Middleton hoped Runge would profit from the lesson learned by this first offense. If his case had gone to trial, he might well have been dismissed from the service.

As for George Whittington, his honor was intact. But his stint with the Rangers was over; he was too much trouble to keep. Major Sullivan reassigned him to the 10th Infantry, where he served as the commander of an infantry rifle company.

Whittington and his men raced east on Patton time, through the Lorraine and the Ardennes, straight into the eye of the Battle of the Bulge. There, on an icy Luxembourg day, Whittington led Company G across the Sure River under intense fire, and in the midst of an enemy mine field, he managed to destroy four automatic weapon emplacements and capture eighteen prisoners without risking the lives of his men. During that same fierce battle, he barely escaped death. He was standing between two engineers when the Germans opened mortar fire. He came to and found his helmet split open, his skull filled with shrapnel. The men on either side of him were mangled to pieces. Whittington was recovering in a Luxembourg hospital when the transcript of his court-martial reached him on January 27, 1945. He didn't yet know he had earned a Silver Star for his valor at the Bulge.

As for the VIII Corps Judge Advocate officers, they left the Morlaix boys' lycée on August 28; Guilloux headed out with them. James Craighill, who had been with them on temporary assignment, returned to his duties with the Ninth Army. William Scully sent Craighill's commanding officer a special note of commendation. Craighill had fulfilled his task with intelligence, efficiency, and professionalism. *U.S. v. Whittington*, his first trial, was, he recalls, "one of the few cases I ever had bad luck on."

Ralph Fogarty, who had defended James Hendricks and assisted Joe Greene in his defense of Whittington, stayed longer with the VIII Corps, but was later transferred to the First Army. He rose in the Judge Advocate office to the rank of major and participated in the prosecution of the major Nazi war criminals at Nuremberg.

Scully signed off on his review of *U.S. v. Whittington* a month after the trial; by now, his VIII Corps JAG office had reached Belgium. As Staff Judge Advocate, it was Scully's prerogative to express his own opinion of the quality of the judgment rendered by the court, just as he had done after James Hendricks's trial and after the gang rape trial at Morlaix. Scully was vehement: Sedillo had been wrong to allow so much hearsay from conversations in the Hôtel de France prior to the shooting.

Yet in the end, Scully acknowledged, the court had enough evidence to justify its conclusion that Whittington had acted in self-defense. He quibbled with the way the evidence had come to the table and he took serious issue with Joseph Greene's achievement—the change in the focus of the trial from Whittington to Morand: "The erroneous construction of the hearsay rule by the Law Member permitted the defense to succeed in virtually trying the deceased as a spy, rather than trying the accused for murder."

Scully could not ask for a new trial after an acquittal. His critique was merely analytic and no further review was permitted.

In the course of a single month Guilloux had watched his boss and friend, Joseph Greene, win two stunning courtroom victories. As a prosecutor, Greene had condemned James Hendricks to hang for shooting through a door and killing a French farmer. Three weeks later, assigned as defense counsel, he had gotten George Whittington acquitted in the shooting of a Resistance fighter in a hotel courtyard. Greene was so gifted, Guilloux might well have wondered what would have happened to poor James Hendricks if the Brooklyn lawyer had been assigned as his defense counsel rather than his prosecutor. Yet the real culprit and difference between the trials was the unfairness of a system that could assign such different fates to two trigger-happy drunken soldiers.

Ultimately, attitudes much deeper than the tactics of a single trial resulted in Hendricks's hanging, Whittington's acquittal. The court saw what it knew how to see: in one case a hapless mute criminal that no one could recognize; a mere servant of the Liberation, assumed to be dispensable. And in the other an indispensable war hero, fully accountable for his actions. The world that had made Whittington a victor and Hendricks a condemned man had been invented long before 1944.

The French interpreter left no diary notes about the outcome of *U.S. v. Whittington*. In *OK, Joe*, he describes watching at a distance as the newly acquitted Ranger captain entered the officers' mess hall after his legal victory with a few of the men on the court-martial panel, the very men who had just voted to acquit him, "who acted as a kind of escort." Guilloux's metaphor is clear: The Army hadn't tried Whittington so much as it had protected him. While Hendricks waited to hang, Whittington broke bread with his judges.

TWENTY

WHITTINGTON'S PEACE

J AMES HENDRICKS was dead at age twenty-one, hanged as a convicted murderer and rapist. George Whittington went home from the war a hero. He lived to the age of eighty-three, making full use of the eloquence he had deployed so well in the courtroom at Morlaix.

Whittington attended journalism school at the University of Missouri in 1948, in a class full of veterans on the GI Bill. One of his classmates, a cartoonist named Mort Walker, put Whittington's caricature in the school humor magazine. Walker was on his way to inventing Beetle Bailey.

Whittington married a vivacious, independent-minded brunette named Agnes. After journalism school, he bought and ran a Missouri newspaper called *The Cole County Enterprise*. In an Army publication, *The Infantry Journal*, he published an essay entitled "The Miracle of Marching Fire," arguing how much infantrymen under attack had to gain, psychologically and strategically, by firing their own weapons continuously as they moved forward.

Whittington was called back to Korea for another tour of duty in 1951 and served at the rank of major as a battalion commander. In 1953, he learned that his favorite uncle, Charlie Burbank, had left him the bulk of his oil-rich estate in Kentucky. George moved his family to Henderson, where, as a respected farmer-investor, he raised four children. Later, he bought a 1,900-acre beef ranch in Costa Rica, near the Nicaraguan border, then sold it after trouble with squatters. During the Iran-contra scandal, one of his farm managers, a native of the Henderson area, was accused of running drugs at his own nearby ranch, but he denied the charges. Whittington wasn't implicated.

George and Agnes Whittington were leaders in the Henderson community, taking independent positions on every issue. In 1956, white parents in Henderson ordered a walkout of their children to protest the integration of a county school. George Whittington walked his son Charles right into his classroom to protest the racism. And in 1985, when the Unison Corporation tried to put a PCB processing plant in Henderson County, he gave a speech entitled "Welcome to Bhopal," skewering the corporation and making common cause with young environmentalists. Though he had left the newspaper business, his regular editorials in *The Henderson Gleaner* were legendary in his town.

A Republican in a solidly Democratic county, Whittington ran for commissioner of agriculture in 1959, state senate in 1961, city commission in 1963, and county judge executive in 1985, never winning an election. In 1992, he made the local news when he and his wife left the Republican Party in protest of the party's strong anti-abortion position. He told the press he could no longer recognize his fellow Republicans. "They are a radical right religion party. They've gone with the fundamentalists."

To the end of his life, George Whittington took principled and controversial stands. An atheist in the Bible Belt, he supported free speech, choice, gay rights, and abhorred government interference. "Everyone in Henderson liked George," his friend Roy Pullam recalled, "but people did a lot of praying for his soul."

By the 1990s, Whittington looked the part of a sophisticated country philosopher, with the round, ruddy face and white beard of a Papa Hemingway. From his early days as a boxer, all that remained was the neurological damage that left him with a facial tic. He lived in a grand modernist house filled with hunting trophies he had brought home from Africa—elephant tusks, elk heads, zebra rugs. The walls of his living room were hung with landscapes of New Mexico, and in a gallery were some of the bronzes he had sculpted, including a head he called *Angry Man,* for which he had won a prize. There were books everywhere: Bibles, John O'Hara novels, the *Odyssey,* an album of Leni Riefenstahl's photos of the Nubi Tribe.

———

One thing the larger-than-life Kentucky farmer-investor never bragged about was his exploits in World War II. His son Charles only learned about his father's D-Day landing from a newspaper article when he was twelve. And when a student came to interview George Whittington about his extraordinary life, Whittington refused to talk about the war. "There are two kinds of stories I won't tell," he said; "war stories and hunting stories." To Roy Pullam, he was even more adamant: "I don't talk about the things I kill—animal or man."

He knew his war literature and could recite the last paragraph of *All Quiet on the Western Front* from memory, in both German and English. On the terror of combat, he loved to quote Turenne, one of Louis XIV's greatest generals: "You tremble, carcass, but you'd tremble even more if you knew where I was taking you." Turenne was supposed to have muttered the line to himself whenever he began to shiver with fear before a battle.

In the last years of his life, Whittington finally told his wife about his court-martial in Brittany. He didn't say much about it, but he wanted her to know.

———

After George Whittington's death in 1996, Mitch McConnell, U.S. senator from the state of Kentucky, rose on the Senate floor to pay tribute to George Whittington's contributions to the life of his state and nation. He described Whittington's heroism on Omaha Beach, his contributions to the Henderson community college and the County Air Board, his Costa Rican cattle ranch, his big-game hunting and private plane, his love of reading and the arts. "A civic leader, decorated veteran, adventurer, and extraordinary Kentuckian. . . . George P. Whittington, who passed away January 27, was all of these things, and more."

— PART IV —

HISTORY
AND MEMORY

TWENTY-ONE

DEPARTURE

—

W HEN THE VIII Corps headquarters left Morlaix on September 29, 1944, at the end of the Brittany campaign, Louis Guilloux went with them. Although he had explained that his German was rudimentary, the men in the Judge Advocate office wanted their French interpreter to continue to work with them in Belgium and Germany. For three days, he experienced life in the field with the U.S. Army, traveling in boxcars, taking breaks along the side of the tracks for K- and C-rations, trading with the locals for fresh bread, eggs, and fruit, drinking captured vodka at night and sleeping in tents in the newly threshed fields of northern France. Guilloux had a chance to speak with peasants and villagers, from Rennes to Paris, who told harrowing tales of Nazi reprisals and attacks on local Resistance fighters by the Vichy militia. From eyewitnesses and survivors, he learned of the extent of the atrocities committed throughout France: "Stories of houses burned," he wrote, "young men hanged under balconies in village squares, roundups and massacres as in the darkest hours of ancient history."

Guilloux's health was declining. Severe malnourishment from the war years followed by eating too much with the Americans may have been to blame. His friend Joe Greene noticed how poorly he looked and asked an Army doctor to examine the French interpreter when the VIII Corps reached Saint-Quentin, north of Paris. The doctor speculated that another week with an Army on the move would send him straight into the hospital, and he advised the officers not to take the risk that Guilloux might collapse or even die en route. Just like that, he was officially discharged. He had served for a month, a civilian employee with a uniform and lieutenant's pay. Colonel Scully gave him a letter addressed "To Whom it May Concern," certifying his loyal and valuable service, promising him the rest of his wages, and guaranteeing him U.S. transportation and subsistence as far as Saint-Brieuc.

It wasn't easy to get home—the roads of France were jammed with refugees looking for transport. Guilloux wandered about Saint-Quentin searching for help. He felt strange in his American uniform. He was stopped by Military Police who suspected him of being AWOL and had to explain to them who he was: a French volunteer, released from his unit. They took him to a garage, where he boarded a jeep for Paris. From there he was sent to Versailles, to an organization in charge of official transports. An English truck took him as far as Laval, halfway between Paris and Saint-Brieuc. He was still a hundred miles from home.

"What I felt most of all," he wrote about the trip, "was a profound desire to sleep that was not easy to satisfy . . . now that the tension had disappeared, everything was giving way within me. There were long moments of melancholy at the idea that . . . I wouldn't be in on it." Driven by the sense of being "in on it"—being part of the liberation of his country— he had worked well beyond his physical capacity. His hair had turned gray, he noted, giving him a new authority with the other stragglers he encountered on the road.

Finally, on October 6, Guilloux reached Saint-Brieuc. He spent the next four months in convalescence, too tired to write in his diary or to work on *Le Jeu de Patience*, his novel in progress.

He heard from a few of his American friends. Joe Greene wrote to him in October, from the new VIII Corps headquarters in Belgium, with a cavalier, if chilling statement: "I am still hanging them."

Greene went on to describe the violin he had received for getting Whittington acquitted, a Mangenot from Mirecourt, near Strasbourg. It had a beautiful tone. Always ambitious, Greene told Guilloux he wanted to become a literary agent in civilian life, specializing in getting French authors like Guilloux good contracts. He had yet another story idea for Louis, based on one of his American trials.

Samuel Putnam, the American translator of *Le Sang noir,* wrote the same month: Did Guilloux have a new war novel in the works? Putnam was sure he could find him a publisher. And Bill Cormier, his faithful friend, wrote to say how sorry he was to have lost his companion.

In January 1945, before he could recover his strength, Guilloux came down with a severe case of pulmonary congestion: "It seems I was very badly off, that I almost died. If that's true, it wouldn't have been difficult, because I hardly suspected anything was wrong."

After his recovery, he went back to recording the events of the day, his progress in his writing, trips planned or taken, meals with friends. Some of his subsequent diary entries from that period consisted of a single line, as though the events were so important, no comment was required: "May 1945: Surrender of Germany"; "August: Hiroshima and Nagasaki."

———

While Guilloux recovered, the VIII Corps continued on its advance toward Germany. In his war memoirs, Bill Cormier recounted the Battle of the Bulge, the liberation of a German slave labor camp in Ohrdruf, then a move to Weimar, where the men surveyed the Buchenwald concentration camp three weeks after it was liberated. Corpses too numerous to bury were piled up everywhere. In April at Possneck, near the Czech border, Cormier received a long-awaited package from his father—a Christmas fruitcake soaked in bourbon.

After the Germans surrendered on May 8, 1945, discharge was on the minds of every American soldier. Cormier worked in a Redeployment unit, sending some men home and transferring others to duty in the Pacific according to a point system based on length of service, time overseas, battle decorations, and number of children. Major General Middleton left on May 19. In June, it was Cormier's turn to go home. A truck took him from Frankfurt past the ruined French cathedral at Reims. The stones had already been organized and numbered for restoration. "The building probably took hundreds of years to rise," Cormier wrote. "I wonder how long to restore." Then, to his great amusement, there was a bureaucratic mix-up. The men in his unit were supposed to go directly to the Pacific, but they'd been ordered to depart via Camp Twenty Grand, one of the GI transit camps named after an American cigarette—part of a constellation that included Camp Lucky Strike, Pall Mall, Old Gold, Wins, Herbert Tareyton. But the only available ships out of Twenty Grand were headed stateside. Along with the GIs, 6,000 French war brides would sail for the United States from these camps, after rigorous administrative screenings and civic instruction. Each young woman received a trousseau of lingerie; a priceless gift in a country where textiles were still carefully rationed. On the SS *Bienville* from Le Havre to Boston, his own "liberty ship," Cormier read *Anna Karenina,* the longest book he could find. His war was over.

Twenty-two

OK, Joe

—

B Y 1948, with life restored to a semblance of normalcy, Louis Guilloux accompanied his friend and editor Albert Camus on a trip to Algeria. In 1949, he finished *Le Jeu de Patience*. It won the Prix Renaudot, one of France's three top literary prizes.

Louis Guilloux lived another three decades without ever crossing the Atlantic. His month with the Army remained his only direct experience of American life.

He never forgot his stint as interpreter. For the next twenty years, as France recovered from the trauma of occupation, as the relationship of France and the United States evolved through the Cold War, as France's empire was dismantled, and as he grew older, Louis Guilloux thought back on the month he spent with the Americans in Morlaix, about the cases he witnessed and what they signified. Certain events faded; others came more clearly into focus. The writer altered, magnified, omitted what he once experienced, giving value and shape to a bygone world. His sources were his own: he had nothing but the sketchy notes he had kept in Morlaix, his few letters from the officers on the court-martial, and his prodigious memory for scenes and voices. No archives, no interviews, no fact checking.

Today, an extensive body of literature and documentary is available to anyone interested in the history of the Jim Crow Army. It makes Guilloux's achievement clear: through his art, he was able to delve deeper and come closer to the meaning of that history than any one of the actual trials could.

Guilloux started taking notes for a novel about his experience in 1964. Nineteen sixty-four was the height of the civil rights movement in the United States, the year Lyndon Johnson pushed the Civil Rights Act through the Congress. The summer of 1964 was known to civil rights workers, who flooded the South like so many liberators, as "freedom summer." In June, the bodies of three civil rights workers were found slain in Mississippi. The world's attention was riveted on the American South.

It seemed to Guilloux, as he worked, that the turbulent present offered clues for understanding the essence of the past. On the international stage, the American image had changed since World War II. No longer the young, idealistic liberator of Europe, the United States was slipping into a war it could not win in Vietnam, ten years after the French defeat at Dien Bien Phu. The Army Guilloux had known was gone, but the United States had kept a strong military presence in France, with NATO bases that brought a new generation of American soldiers and their way of life to many French towns. In 1966, de Gaulle announced France's withdrawal from the integrated military command system of NATO, but asked that the NATO governing council remain in Paris. All American bases on French soil were relocated to other parts of Europe. An angry Lyndon Johnson refused de Gaulle's request and pulled NATO's governing council out of Paris. It was a low point for French-American relations.

Guilloux followed American politics through the French press and debated world politics with many companions in the course of his travels throughout Europe. On July 16, 1966, thinking, perhaps, of his American friend Bill Cormier, he wrote in his diary: "This morning's papers are full of the riots in Chicago." The trouble had started when police turned off a fire hydrant that black children had opened, trying to cool off from the summer heat.

The young people in his own country, attuned to the struggles of Algerian and African independence movements, vocal in their opposition to the American war in Vietnam, moved to unite with workers against the French state. Guilloux, nearly seventy years old, took to the streets with them. Marching in the Latin Quarter, he was tear-gassed along with the students.

In 1968, in the thick of the French social revolution, Guilloux traveled to Orléans to participate in a debate on French and American violence. Students showed slides of the assassinations of John and Robert Kennedy and Martin Luther King, Jr., as well as scenes of French police clubbing students at the Sorbonne. In his diaries, Guilloux criticized the French press for downplaying the severity of police violence against demonstrators.

His sense of injustice, sparked by a cascade of world events, made Guilloux think hard about what could account for a society where so much turmoil was possible. He had witnessed racial segregation firsthand in the U.S. Army, and now, as he searched his memory, his own experience took on new weight; even the great fatigue and melancholy that had precipitated his departure from the Army took on meaning.

In the 1930s, Guilloux had been disillusioned with the Soviet Union. With the United States, his disappointment was more intimate. Men like Joe Greene and Bill Cormier had been his friends, his fellow soldiers in the Liberation. In his novel, he wanted to show how closely their optimism was tied to a dangerous sense of the world being theirs to shape, and to a blindness about their own shortcomings. It was a difficult challenge: What he wanted to convey, he said later, was the sense he had in 1944, at the moment of the Allied landing, that the future promised a great new happiness, and to combine that expectation of happiness with his retrospective knowledge that the dream of a better society had not come to pass.

Guilloux worked on his American story for twelve years, looking for the right form and tone. He chose fiction rather than essay, not only because fiction was his principal form of expression but because writers of his generation considered the novel a powerful—perhaps even the most powerful—genre for social commentary. He came up with a kind of *roman noir*, using what the French considered American style and technique: short sentences, quick repartee and reactions, an interior psychology that was implicit, never explicit.

The main character and narrator of his novel was the Army interpreter. At first he called him François Marmier, then Bernard Corley, finally just Louis. Guilloux kept Bill Cormier's real name, but Lieutenants Fogarty and Greene become Bradford and Greenwood, then Bradford and Stone. Juan Sedillo was Lieutenant Colonel Marquez, the bon vivant who always seemed to be studying his manicure in the courtroom. "All right!" the officers repeated to one another, then "OK!" In the very last draft, Guilloux found his title: "OK, Joe."

As he thought back on the trials and on what he had translated, he streamlined his memories. His decisions were literary, but also political. Hendricks became "the only black man in the assembly of whites"; Donald Tucker, the black commanding officer who testified for four hours in his trial, did not fit the story. And although Hendricks's crime against Victor Bignon is transposed with remarkable fidelity—even the bullet holes in the wooden door of the Bignon farmhouse are included—Guilloux left out the details of Hendricks's attempted rape on Noémie Bignon, making Hendricks a purer victim. In *OK, Joe*, the Ranger captain is a killer who guns down an entire row of prisoners of war rather than three men emerging from a gun nest, or a single German colonel who had just been taken prisoner. There is no scene from the Ranger captain's trial because the French interpreter isn't allowed to participate. Military Intelligence officers take over Louis's job. But he hears them strategizing: they're going to argue that the Free Frenchman was a Nazi spy.

In his work with the U.S. Army, Guilloux had no direct contact with the accused men. His closest contact had been with French civilian victims of crimes, the people whose testimony he translated into English. He knew little about the accused soldiers other than what he observed in court. In his novel, they appear as symbols, iconic images. He gave them epithets rather than proper names. Hendricks becomes "the idol"; "the cat who didn't even dream of taking a leap"; Whittington, "the ogre, grinning from ear to ear." It was the system that was rotten, and Guilloux's defendants were expressions of that system.

———

When *OK, Joe* was published in France in 1976, the reviewers agreed. What was remarkable about this author, one of the great political writers in a cohort that included Gide, Camus, and Malraux, was that he never preached or judged overtly. The plot of *OK, Joe,* as they described it, was simple: a series of black GIs condemned to death; a single white officer acquitted.

One reviewer compared Guilloux to a boxer who never loses his nerve, who keeps his adversary at a distance, waits patiently for an opening to place his punch.

> "But why always blacks, Bob?"
> "Ah! That's a hell of a problem!"
> "I know, Bob. Apparently you have to be an American to understand it. But why only blacks? It isn't a special tribunal for blacks?"

Guilloux had always been a deeply political writer. Yet he recoiled at the idea of a "committed literature." A writer's responsibility was above all to be lucid. In his novel, his narrator asks the simplest questions, but never answers them. Nonetheless, the sketches and dialogues in *OK, Joe* provided quiet ballast for an underlying argument—a profoundly simple one. The black GIs were guilty of their crimes, but so was the white officer, who went free.

Guilloux had a reputation in the Parisian press as a sphinx, a willfully elliptical writer who revealed nothing to anyone who tried to sound him out. But in speaking about *OK, Joe* with writer Gilles Lapouge in the summer of 1976, he was unusually forthcoming. Despite his disappointments in world politics, he told Lapouge, he retained a fervent belief in social action: "It's my misfortune not to believe in God, so I don't count on eternity. I count on people." At seventy-six, looking, as another reviewer put it, just the way an owl would look if owls smiled, Louis Guilloux explained why he had set his novel in a court of justice: "Society reinforces monstrous differences among people. And gives itself permission to punish some and not others."

TWENTY-THREE

THE QUESTION

—

BUT WHY always blacks?" That was the question in *OK, Joe,* the question never answered. It goes to the heart of racism and segregation in the U.S. Army during World War II. Black soldiers were considered unfit to fight from the time they entered the armed forces, and the assumption of their inferiority became a prophecy fulfilled by their arrest.

With sixty years' remove, we can pinpoint a series of specific reasons for the racial disparity in the sentencing of soldiers in the European Theater of Operations.

Before the trials themselves, command discretion in bringing men before courts-martial and underreported white crime played a large role. Cases that should have been brought against white perpetrators, but weren't, are difficult but not impossible to find in the archives today.

Once the cases went to trial, the inexperience of many of the men appointed as defense counsel—what Judge Advocate historian Robert Gonzales has called "the weak link in the system" of military justice—resulted in poor representation for accused soldiers. The Army was the first to admit that officers had an easier time and lighter sentences than enlisted men on trial. Nor should it come as any surprise that an Army which undervalued the contribution of black service troops to the war effort might be less than vigilant in protecting the legal rights of those same troops in a military court.

There remains a final factor, crucial yet intangible: the effect of conditions in the Jim Crow Army on black service troops and the unknowable extent to which these men sought refuge in alcohol and acts of violence.

There are no clear-cut examples in the historical record of men brought to trial for crimes they did not commit. Instead, there are countless examples of conditions that would produce extreme demoralization, even rage, in the gentlest soul.

Thomas Russell Jones, the African American lieutenant who served as executive officer for plans and training of the 369th Ordnance Company, describes watching German prisoners of war near his Louisiana training camp march cheerfully to the local movie house as they sang the traditional Nazi anthem, the *Horst Wessel Lied*: "They were going to a theater where people of color were denied access—and specifically, our black soldiers. What an incredible contradiction in the midst of the war!"

Russell Jones later saw two of his men die from dehydration brought on by drinking calvados in Normandy. He served as a legal defense counsel for black prisoners held in the garrison at Cherbourg, in Normandy. He is proud to have saved several of his men from death sentences.

Twenty-four

After the Liberation

—

T WO MONTHS after D-Day, a civil affairs officer in the 30th Infantry Division sent his commanding officer a memo entitled "Analysis of Civilian Attitude." In towns where the FFI—the interior French Resistance army—had done a good job preparing the locals, he reported, the Americans felt appreciated. In other towns, the French seemed to watch the convoy of liberators coming through as though it were any old circus parade, waiting passively for their share of cigarettes, candy, and K-rations. He added: "A conversation with a local inhabitant might be boiled down to his saying: 'Glad to see you. How soon are you leaving?'"

How soon were the liberators leaving? That was the question the French kept asking. What mattered to them in 1944 was sovereignty and recovery. While Americans worried about the Communist tendencies of undisciplined Resistance fighters, the French worried that the Americans weren't respecting their autonomy. An effort by the United States and Great Britain to impose Allied currency in France had been successfully scuttled by General de Gaulle. But complaints of interference persisted in reports from officials in northern France to their superiors in Paris: The Americans were meddling in French financial affairs; they hung their flag on French administrative buildings, treated French property as their own war booty, requisitioned hospitals needed by civilians.

Behind the local aggravations stood the larger political issue: The United States was one of the first nations to recognize the Vichy government in 1940 and had kept an ambas-

sador at Vichy until April 1942, almost two years after de
Gaulle had set up his Free French government-in-exile in London. The Allies had excluded de Gaulle from their D-Day
plans, then asked for his endorsement as the invasion began.
President Roosevelt was wary of de Gaulle's upstart movement
and mistrusted the fact that, at the Liberation, the French general had declared himself head of state without holding elec-
tions. In July 1944, de Gaulle visited Roosevelt in Washington,
but it wasn't until September 23, a month after the liberation
of Paris—at the height of de Gaulle's popular acclaim—that
Roosevelt officially recognized de Gaulle's provisional government.

An enormous task of reconstruction awaited the French,
as soon as the battles to rid their country of the Nazis were
over. Allied bombings in support of the Liberation had destroyed cities all over northern France. French casualties from
the Liberation itself were enormous—13,000 civilians died in
Normandy alone. In Brittany, the U.S. Army left behind a landscape nearly as devastated as Normandy: 45,000 houses were
in ruins, another 85,000 damaged. The Breton ports of Saint-
Malo, Brest, Lorient, and Saint-Nazaire were leveled by Allied
bombs.

In the midst of the ruins, internal French conflicts—the violent expression of a deep ideological rift that would shape the
future of France—preoccupied a nation struggling to regain its
footing. In Brittany, between June and August, Resistance
fighters executed 587 French men and women who had collaborated with the Nazis in summary executions. The liberation
governments' official courts of justice, established in October
1944, carried out thirty-one additional death sentences.

French commissioners in Brittany and Normandy reported
on evolving relations with the Americans to their administrative superiors in Paris throughout the summer and fall of
1944. Relations with the American troops were in general excellent, but there was tension between the GIs and the internal
French liberation army, the FFI. The U.S. Army seemed to
treat the German prisoners with great respect, while the

French Resistance registered the Americans' distrust or even disdain, despite the fact that FFI escorts, some twenty thousand strong, had allowed Patton's army to cross the Brittany peninsula safely and in record time. American soldiers, in turn, didn't know what to make of armed men with neither the uniforms nor the discipline of a regular army.

Behind the stories of GIs throwing candy and Nescafé from tanks to crowds of grateful citizens were other tales of French disappointment in the aid brought by the United States. In the final battle-weary months, the French Resistance, in particular, lacked food, supplies, and weapons. And the survivors of four years of food shortages did not understand why the Americans threw away quantities of perfectly good food, supposedly for reasons of hygiene.

Official French reports also registered complaints about bad GI behavior and crimes against civilians. In regions where episodes of GI drunkenness, looting, and rape were reported, some Frenchmen took refuge in the old cliché, left over from Vichy propaganda: "At least the Germans were well behaved . . ." (*Les Allemands, eux, au moins, étaient corrects*). The German soldiers billeted in French towns and villages over the past four years had, indeed, often appeared calmer, more disciplined, and more polite than the young GIs, who, crazed by the stress of combat, flew through towns in a matter of days.

But no one could ignore the reports of massacres of thousands of French civilians and Resistance fighters by the retreating German armies in the summer of 1944. In July, in Oradour-sur-Glane, the Waffen SS shot every man in the village and locked the women and children in a church, burning them alive. Nazi war crimes such as these put the misdeeds of individual GIs in perspective.

The U.S. Army in the European Theater of Operations kept careful records of the crimes and punishments of its soldiers, and worried about the reasons for those crimes. The resulting record is unusual for the World War II era, maybe even singular. Meticulous Judge Advocate reports show that the number of rapes of civilian women increased and involved a higher incidence of violence in France than in England, especially during the period from August to September 1944, after the bloody Normandy landing, as the Army was moving west into Brittany through hedgerow country: this was the period of Guilloux's employment. Once the soldiers reached Germany, the number of rapes increased still further, and although soldiers who raped were convicted and sentenced to life in prison by courts-martial, no GI was executed for raping a German woman.

Historians have speculated that the U.S. Army tolerated GI crimes against conquered enemy women better than it tolerated crimes against liberated Allied women, whose goodwill was needed in the war effort. Although the number of rapes is well documented, it remains relatively small compared to other World War II–era armies. Nine hundred and four American soldiers were tried for rape in Europe, and even if the actual numbers were much higher, they do not compare with a terrible legacy of World War II–era rapes, often officially sanctioned, including the rape of the women of Nanking by the Japanese, rapes by Nazi soldiers throughout the German sphere of occupation, the rape of Italian women by the French army during its campaign to liberate Italy, and hundreds of thousands of rapes by the Red Army across Eastern Europe and Germany. German, Soviet, and French rapes were punished unevenly by these armies—sometimes with a death sentence, or a summary execution, sometimes not at all.

The U.S. Army was both visionary and reactionary in its sensitivity to rape. A half century before the International Court at the Hague classified rape as a war crime, punishable under international law, the U.S. Army was punishing rape systematically, according to its Articles of War, with two severe sentences: life in prison or death. After the war, the Vanderbilt Commission, appointed to investigate inequities in Army courts-martial, criticized the severity of court-martial sentencing in cases of rape: its all-or-nothing character had discouraged commanders from bringing men to trial in the first place. In 1977, a Supreme Court ruling declared the death sentence for rape cruel and unjust—it was "an excessive penalty" to condemn someone to death who had not taken a life.

The Army has not executed a soldier since 1961, though the death penalty is still a possible sentence in courts-martial, as it is in civilian courts at the federal level and in thirty-eight states.

While we can argue that in terms of reported statistics, the behavior of American GIs compares favorably with that of other armies, the World War II executions remain a sad chapter in the Army's history, the culmination of acts of violence committed by the condemned men and, in a much larger sense, by the Army itself.

In a series of postwar reports, the Judge Advocate General's Department tried to understand GI crimes in the European Theater. Rape increased in France, they speculated, "because many soldiers had the notion that French women were both generally attractive and free with their love." A chapter on sex crimes in "The Military Offender in the Theater of Operations" argued that making brothels off limits to GIs had been a mistake. All other national armies recognized the need for recreational sex for their soldiers; the Germans always made sure an official brothel in each town was kept clean. The high venereal disease rate for U.S. soldiers was proof that the off-limits system was counterproductive.

The Army acknowledged that alcohol was to blame in most cases of violent crime. Raw calvados estimated by the Army as "140 proof," readily available in Brittany and Normandy, was "successfully used by the troops as fluid for cigarette lighters." The soldiers drank it like regular whiskey.

The most difficult aspect the Judge Advocate General's Department had to deal with in its analysis of GI criminality was the preponderance of African Americans who were prose-cuted and condemned. In France, 130 of the 180 men charged with rape were African Americans; in Europe as a whole, 55 of the 70 men executed for rape and murder were African Ameri-cans. The paternalistic tone taken by the U.S. Army in grap-pling with these statistics is chilling:

> Negro Troops were responsible in gross disproportion for crime and indiscipline among U.S. forces. It is not recom-mended that Negroes be barred from overseas service. That would be manifestly unfair. It is hoped that before Americans are sent overseas to fight again, if ever they must, the standard of intelligence and morality among Negro Americans will be no lower than among White Americans. But until that ideal is realized, selection of Negroes for overseas service should have other basis than the ratio to total population. There should be no other reasons but the same reasons, for discrimination among Negroes as among their White compatriots.

Nowhere in these postwar documents is there even the shadow of a suspicion that segregation itself might have played a role in creating a racial disparity in sentencing. No one, as yet, was willing to venture the obvious: it was patently absurd that 8.5 percent of the armed forces could be responsi-ble for committing 79 percent of all capital crimes.

A series of articles published in *The Crisis* in the fall of 1944 by a black chaplain named Grant Reynolds illuminates the social psychology of the Jim Crow Army. Black GIs experi-enced the Army as a plantation where black soldiers were re-duced to menial laborers and black officers to act as their foremen. White southerners set the tone in southern training camps, which established the Jim Crow standards that were perpetuated in Europe. Reynolds complained in *The Crisis* that the deeds of thousands of black soldiers who did participate in combat were unknown to the general public: there was never a picture of a black fighter in the newspaper, never a story of black heroism. The heroism of the service units, too, remained invisible. Whatever their contribution, African Americans were excluded from the story of "the Greatest Generation."

When black service units were offered a chance to participate in combat at the Battle of the Bulge, their performance was excellent. All After Action Reports and investigations showed that they had earned the esteem of their fellow soldiers, including southerners. From that emergency, the Army discovered that desegregation allowed for black heroism and for enhancing the Army's efficiency.

———

"There shall be equality of treatment and opportunity for all persons in the armed services without regard to race, color, religion, or national origin": On July 26, 1948, President Harry Truman desegregated the armed forces in a single grand gesture. Historians explain his decision by citing mounting pressures from a powerful black leadership, the terrible publicity about wartime incidents in the World War II training camps, and the influence of strong and principled personalities like Eleanor Roosevelt. The practical enforcement of desegregation was as long a process in the Army as it was in civil society, implemented with varying degrees of success during the Korean War and throughout the American civil rights movement. The ultimate motivation for integration of the Army wasn't justice; it was usable manpower.

Today, the Army is probably the most fully integrated sector of American society. You can be court-martialed for using a racial epithet. And when people think about leadership in the American military, they think first of Colin Powell, the first black chairman of the Joint Chiefs of Staff in the Gulf War and the first black secretary of state.

Today's volunteer Army is 24 percent black and includes 7,469 black officers. That integration has come with its own form of sacrifice. Beginning with the war in Vietnam, over 13,000 African American men have died on active duty in military service—18.4 percent of the total number of reported deaths.

———

Today, you can't travel far in Brittany without finding signs of the battles of the Liberation. An engraved stone in a clearing overlooking the bay of Morlaix reminds the passing hiker of the exact spot where British and French Special Air Service paratroopers landed just after D-Day. At the Seilla farm in Saint-Gilles-du-Méné, a granite marker commemorates the two SAS paratroopers and five French Resistance fighters who were murdered by Nazis on July 28, 1944. And on the long road stretching past Brittany's black mountains, a roadside plaque recalls that the 6th Armored Division of the U.S. Army, Francis Morand's temporary unit, liberated this territory with the help of the Free French.

The biggest monument of all to the war in Brittany stands at the westernmost edge of the Crozon peninsula, at the Pointe de Pen-Hir. A giant granite Croix de Lorraine, meant to resemble an ancient Breton standing stone or "dolmen," was dedicated by Charles de Gaulle in 1951 in honor of the region's extraordinary contribution to the Resistance. The monolith is as sturdy and uncompromising as the leader who imposed upon his nation a vision of an "eternal France" that had never collaborated with the Germans.

The people and places that inspired Guilloux's *OK, Joe* have made their mark on the Breton landscape. Victor Bignon is buried in the church cemetery at Plumaudan, 100 meters from the château where James Hendricks hanged on a November morning in 1944. The château, now a summer rental property advertised among the official vacation guides for the Côtes d'Armor region, has been beautifully restored. Anyone visiting this idyllic spot would be hard-pressed to conjure a history of occupation, war, liberation—of justice delivered or denied.

EPILOGUE

TWENTY-FIVE

A VISIT TO PLUMAUDAN

—

I FIRST VISITED the village of Plumaudan in the summer of 2002, after doing research on U.S. Army court-martial transcripts. I wanted some contact with the survivors of the trials Guilloux had witnessed, and Plumaudan seemed like my best possibility.

One of the youngest people portrayed in *OK, Joe* was Jeannine Bignon, the daughter of Victor Bignon, the farmer who was shot to death behind the door of his stone house by the young Quartermaster Pvt. James Hendricks. Jeannine was only eighteen in 1944; if she were alive, she would be seventy-six. And if she still lived in Plumaudan, I might be able to find her.

My hotel was fifteen minutes away, in Dinan, a tourist town famous for its medieval ramparts. Plumaudan's own claim to fame was the dry cup-shaped biscuits called *craquelins,* manufactured in a factory on the outskirts of the village since the 1930s. I drove off the main road past the factory and turned right onto a smaller road that led to the center of town. The first building on my right was the Château la Vallée.

I parked my car and walked into an elegant gravel courtyard, trying to imagine the gallows and the witnesses who had gathered there on that distant November morning. The village church and its small, walled cemetery were only a few feet away. It was easy to find Victor Bignon's tomb, part of a family plot with three names inscribed in the dark gray stone: BIGNON, BOUGIS, and PEROUX. The trial transcript had indicated that Bougis was Jeannine's mother's maiden name. Peroux might be Jeannine's married name.

After I left the cemetery, I drove up the hill behind the town hall to the hamlet of Le Percoul and walked down the narrow lane, admiring the stone farmhouses. As I was thinking about the continuity of life in those small French villages, a farmer came out from his house to ask if I was interested in buying property. I looked like a foreigner, and Breton stone houses were all the rage among the British.

I headed back down the hill to a tiny French post office, located in the center of Plumaudan next to a municipal building that advertised video conferencing. I asked the postman about Jeannine Bignon, whose married name might be Peroux, and whose father had been killed by a GI in 1944. He had only worked in Plumaudan for a decade and he didn't know the old stories, but he knew exactly who I was looking for. "Ah, you must mean Madame Peroux!" he said. He looked her up in his records: "Madame Jeannine Peroux, born Jeannine Bignon, July 14, 1926." She'd been a widow since 1995.

He told me where her house was, and he promised to arrange for an interview when he saw her on his afternoon mail delivery. He liked her, but he warned me that she was a little tense, and he said that her language might be hard for me to follow.

He called me at my hotel in Dinan, as promised: Madame Peroux expected me at five.

"You've come about the American, have you?" she asked me when I arrived at her yellow stucco house, the first in the row of farmhouses on the narrow country lane that traversed Le Percoul. "When the postman asked me, I couldn't figure out why, and then I realized it must be that. No one has come since he was hanged—they wanted to know if we wanted to go to the hanging at the Château la Vallée, but we didn't."

She looked younger than seventy-six, though the sun exposure from years of farming had thickened her skin, like women you see in Florida. She looked very strong. She smiled at me right away, a gentle smile.

She took me to the abandoned stone building across from her house—"that's where it happened." She pointed to the bullet holes in the door, never repaired. We walked inside a musty space full of cobwebs. Old farm equipment hung on the walls. I could still make out where the stove had been, where Guilloux had first seen "a handsome country girl about twenty years old" stoking the fire, when he visited the farmhouse with the American lieutenants. It was hard to imagine that four people—Jeannine, her parents, and the farmboy—had all lived in this tiny space.

Without saying much, we walked up the side stairs of the modern house across the courtyard. Jeannine and her husband had built it in the 1960s. She welcomed me into a large kitchen with a table, a TV, photos on the wall—the room where she spent most of her time. She invited me to sit down. She had a picture of her father to show me, a fine-looking gentleman with thick hair and a mustache.

When Madame Peroux began to tell her story, I had trouble understanding her: "I wanted to be a schoolteacher but I had to stay at the farm; I was the only child. So I didn't go beyond the *certificat d'études* at eleven. I wanted my son to be able to go to school; he's the financial manager at LDC, the poultry slaughterhouse in Rennes. And my eldest granddaughter is at a *grande école* in Paris, studying to be an engineer."

I took out my tape recorder and asked to record her voice, knowing I would only be able to decipher some of her sentences later. I told her how difficult it was for me to understand her; was it a regional dialect? She explained that everyone had trouble understanding her. It had been that way since her father's death—something had happened to her voice, her language.

When she talked about her father, her eyes filled with tears but she didn't cry. She had very unusual eyes—the color of light caramel—and her hair was dyed to match them perfectly. "I was blonde as a child," she said, and she showed me a photo of herself at thirteen, a pretty country girl dressed in finery.

I had brought the trial transcript and a copy of *OK, Joe* in French. She couldn't read the trial transcript because it was in English, but she looked at the French police report and said, "Yes, they got it right."

I opened Louis Guilloux's novel. Madame Peroux hadn't heard of Louis Guilloux. I told her he was one of the great writers of Brittany and that her tragedy had entered into French literature. She was surprised. Her face betrayed something positive—a sense of acknowledgment.

As I started to read to her from *OK, Joe,* her eyes again filled with tears. I read from the courtroom scene first, her mother's testimony. She disagreed with a few details in the story, and we talked about the difference between fiction and history. It was strange but gratifying to read and watch her react to what Guilloux made of her story. I stopped and asked if she could understand my foreign accent. She said she could. I read from the scene where the Americans first came to her house to get her testimony.

When I was done reading, I told her that I would send her a copy of the book. She said her granddaughter might like to read it. I warned her that Guilloux had changed a lot of details for the purposes of the novel. "He interpreted your testimony and your mother's and he was inspired by his memories," I explained. She tried to remember the interpreter at the trial, but she couldn't.

I also visited another person the postman had recommended I talk to: Louis Dalibot, who became the Bignon family doctor after the war. In the summer of 1944, Dalibot had fought with the *maquis* in the Boquen Forest—one of the places where Francis Morand was supposed to have trained Resistance fighters. But he hadn't known him.

Dalibot returned to Plumaudan in the fall of 1944. He had been one of the townspeople standing on the road the day of the hanging. He believed then, and still believes, that the Americans were doing the right thing by executing Victor Bignon's murderer. He didn't think the hanging had left an indelible mark on the memory of the town. "You have to understand," he told me, "we had seen so many deaths. An episode like that one was quickly swallowed up in the dramas of the moment."

When I returned to Plumaudan a year later, Jeannine Bignon reported that everyone in the family had read *OK, Joe*. It was important for them to learn about an event she had rarely mentioned.

On that second visit, she told me more of her story. After her father was killed, she said, "her blood turned." Peritonitis. She had head lice, toxic blood; her feet were infected. When she washed, her skin came off in the water. The family received 950 francs from the Americans. They had hoped for a pension, but as she remembers it, the American said: "Take the 950 francs or nothing." For two years, she and her mother seldom left the house. She married a distant cousin at age twenty. She had worked as a farmer for forty-seven years, then retired. Today, her farm was leased: she still owned 25 hectares.

One of the last things we discussed was the problem of reparations. The family had done well after the war, but the death of her father had meant a struggle. If the family had had a lawyer or a priest to help them, they might have applied for reparations—a pension for Jeannine and her mother. They had come through it all and their farm had thrived, but Jeannine shook her head as she recalled, once again, the Americans' invitation to attend the hanging—a symbol, for her, of how much they had misunderstood. What she and her mother had needed in 1944 was not to watch James Hendricks hang. They needed help in running the farm.

Suddenly, my eye was caught by something surprising. There was an American flag sticking out of a family photo on the mantel behind her. Jeannine explained that a friend had given it to her in Dinan at an American celebration. They were handing them out. I wondered if the celebration had been the anniversary of D-Day? She didn't know.

"You don't mind having an American flag, after what happened to you?"

"Oh, why not!" Madame Peroux said. She laughed, but her laughter wasn't bitter.

TWENTY-SIX

SOLDIER TROUBLE

———

JAMES HENDRICKS's Deceased Personnel File listed two next of kin: Geneva Henderson Irby in Washington, D.C., and Annie Henderson in Macon, North Carolina. Hendricks and Henderson are both common North Carolina names, but on the 1930 Census rolls for Macon there appeared a six-year-old boy named James Hendricks, the adopted son of Annie and Ed Henderson. He was a member of a large household that included their six children and two grandchildren.

With this news, my French search suddenly became local. Macon, a farm town in Warren County, not far from the Virginia border, was only a ninety-minute drive from my home in Durham.

I went to the two black-owned funeral homes in Warrenton, the county seat, then to the wills and deeds department at the county courthouse, to fill in the family tree and find names and addresses for the Hendersons still living in Macon. The Hendersons were one of the leading families in the county, a courthouse clerk said, known for their hard work and independence.

Thurston and Thurletta Brown at the Brown Funeral Home in Warrenton introduced me to James's classmate Robert Daniels. Daniels told me the rumor that had gone around Macon after the war: James Hendricks had been shot by a firing squad for striking a white officer. Another funeral home director, Richard Greene, who had buried Henderson family members, suggested that Evelyn Henderson Echols, the daughter of James's stepbrother Alex, was the person to contact. She had moved back home from Maryland, and she worked for the Social Security Administration in the nearby town of Henderson.

In September 2003, I sent a letter to Mrs. Echols, asking if I could meet with her to discuss James Hendricks. It was hard to get the letter right, and I suspected she might not want to answer. I was surprised a month later to find her message on the answering machine at my office. She had hesitated, she later told me, but finally decided to respond because of one phrase in my letter: "Jim Crow Army."

When we first spoke on the phone to arrange my visit, she asked how James had died. I told her he had hanged after a court-martial. She asked about the charges and other aspects of the case. She took in my words and encouraged me to say more. Her own parents had never discussed James openly—"Older people didn't talk around kids." She guessed that if they were still alive, they would not have cared to speak to me. At the end of our conversation, she asked if James was guilty. I told her I hadn't fully answered the question, even for myself, and promised to bring her the full trial transcript.

On a rainy day in November 2003, I traveled up Interstate 85, then along winding country roads where new ranch houses alternated with a few 1920s-era farmhouses, to a town that consisted of a single street of storefronts. We had arranged to meet at the Macon post office, which was almost as small as the one in Plumaudan. Mrs. Echols got out of her car to shake hands, coming toward me with a deliberate gait and a twinkle in her dark, velvety eyes. She was an attractive, youthful woman in her early sixties, wearing a soft blue and white pants suit. Another woman was there too, Evelyn Echols's first cousin Geraldine Bullock, one of the grandchildren who had grown up with James on the Henderson farm in the 1930s and 1940s. Mrs. Bullock, a woman in her seventies, was wearing a trench coat and a silk neck scarf with a leopard pattern; I had the feeling she had always been glamorous.

Mrs. Echols offered to drive. She and Geraldine Bullock

sat in the front seat and I sat in back. We passed fields where the soy and tobacco had recently been harvested and talked about James Hendricks. His best friend from childhood had just passed away, and there weren't many people left who had known him well. We stopped at the new home Mrs. Echols and her husband had recently built; it was luxurious, with a large welcoming living room and plenty of room for guests. We were joined by two of Mrs. Echols's siblings, one of whom challenged me from the start: "Why do you even care about this?" she asked. I started to raise some of the larger issues of war and justice, then Evelyn moved the conversation back to James Hendricks. She pushed me, in her gently persistent way, to tell them everything I knew.

When Geraldine Bullock spoke about growing up with James, her melodious voice filled with tenderness. As a child, she had thought of him as her own big brother; he was a tease and a smart aleck, who "liked to joke and carry on all the time." By coincidence, James was later stationed with Geraldine's husband, Junius Bullock, at Camp Van Dorn. In her house in nearby Manson, North Carolina, she keeps a memento from Junius's military service—a handkerchief embossed with the name of his laundry detachment.

In 1944, James had written to her from France saying he'd had some trouble and wasn't coming home. He asked her to tell Neva, her aunt, to go to the NAACP. "I never throw anything away," she told me. After our first talk, she looked everywhere for the letter, but it had disappeared in her last move, after her husband's death. She had a few precious pictures to share: the snapshot James had sent her from Mississippi wearing his quartermaster uniform, and a picture of his girlfriend, Jeannette Wright, who died young of typhoid fever.

Mrs. Bullock remembered the family's attempts to get information about James. Geneva Irby and her husband wrote to the NAACP after the war, but they didn't get any answers. When Geraldine moved to Washington to live with her aunt Neva, she looked for James's file in the War Department, where she had a job after school. There was no file under his name—it looked to her as though the file had been removed or transferred to another department.

"We were under the impression he went before a firing squad," Mrs. Bullock told me. "This story touched me and I have always wondered what happened to him."

Through my ongoing conversations with Evelyn Echols and Geraldine Bullock, I tried to reconstruct what the Army might have told the older generation about James's death, and how the rumor started around Macon that James had been executed for striking a white officer. His Deceased Personnel File contained no letters to the family. There was one document left to consult: his 201 Personnel File, a much more detailed Army record. Millions of such files had been destroyed in a 1973 fire, but the Personnel Records Center in St. Louis, Missouri, was able to salvage the remains of James's papers. In July, the file arrived in the mail. In it, we finally found some answers to our questions.

James was hanged at Plumaudan on November 24, 1944. Twelve days later, on December 6, the War Department sent the following telegram to Geneva Henderson Irby, Evelyn and Geraldine's aunt:

OFFICIAL REPORT RECEIVED STATES YOUR NEPHEW PRIVATE JAMES E. HENDRICKS DIED TWENTY FOUR NOVEMBER IN THE EUROPEAN THEATER OF OPERATIONS LETTER FOLLOWS

The letter that followed, sent the same day, didn't say much more

Dear Mrs. Irby:
This letter is to confirm the report previously sent you that your nephew died on 24 November 1944 in the European Theater of Operations. Death was due to your nephews [sic] wilful [sic] misconduct.
                                        Sincerely yours

There was another family communication in the file. Joseph

Hendricks, separated from his brother in infancy, wrote to the Army in 1947 from his home in New Jersey to find out what happened to James. The Army responded. Again, the only explanation for his death was "willful misconduct."

For all the family might have known, James could have walked in front of a tank or killed himself by misfiring his own gun. If there had been any mention of a court-martial transcript in the letter, they could have requested a copy, but they had no idea such a document existed. The transcript sat in the Army archive in Maryland.

The rumors about James's death now began to add up. For an African American family in Macon, North Carolina, in a state that has seen over a hundred lynchings since the 1880s, "willful misconduct" isn't vague—it's a code. To anyone who knew the irreverent, fun-loving James, it made sense that he had sassed off to a white officer and was executed for insubordination. The family imagined he was shot by a firing squad, because in books and movies, that's how military men were executed.

———

In September 2004, Evelyn Echols, Geraldine Bullock, and I met again to go over the contents of the 201 Personnel File and figure out what questions remained. I had been unable to find any record in the NAACP archives of the Irbys' request for information or the organization's response. I only knew the NAACP was swamped by similar requests, which survive in voluminous files, some headed simply: "Soldier Trouble." I had located James's defense counsel, Ralph Fogarty. He was ninety-one, living in Illinois. He declined my repeated requests for an interview. We had learned from the 201 Personnel File that James had spent nearly a month in the Foster General Hospital in Jackson, Mississippi, before he was shipped overseas, and we wondered how he had been taken ill. Geraldine had visited the site of Camp Van Dorn after the war with Junius, and we knew that James's experience there was an important part of his story. But the Army hospital records were gone.

In the course of my research, I had made contact with a former Graves Registration sergeant named Emmett Bailey, who agreed to talk to me. Coincidentally, he, too, was from North Carolina. He sent me records showing he had buried James Hendricks. Bailey, who is white, said he never got over the sight of the public hangings. He had witnessed sixteen of them. "It was old KKK procedure," he said. "It was a legal lynch." Emmett Bailey lived in Henderson, North Carolina, where Evelyn Echols worked. He asked me to give Evelyn his name, so she could contact him if she wanted to.

TWENTY-SEVEN

A RESTING PLACE FOR JAMES HENDRICKS

———

T HE HENDERSON family wanted to know the location of James's grave. In 1949, James Hendricks's body had been moved from the temporary American cemetery at Marigny where Emmett Bailey had overseen his burial to "land adjacent to World War I Cemetery, Fère en Tardenois, France." The Battle Monuments Commission provided the information that Hendricks was buried in Plot E of the Oise-Aisne American Cemetery and Memorial.

Very few people know of the existence of Plot E, a small gravesite outside the walls of a cemetery reserved for the dead of World War I. Ninety-six soldiers are buried in Plot E—all of them men who were executed in Europe, North Africa, and the Mediterranean Theater of Operations during World War II. Graves Registration archives refer to these men as the "dishonorable dead." Over two hundred miles separate them from the honorable dead of World War II in the American cemeteries in Normandy and Brittany.

Plot E is described on a website called "Lesser Known Facts of WWII" as a secret place, closed to the public. It got some publicity in 1987 when the body of Eddie Slovik, the only American executed during the war for desertion, was removed from Plot E and sent home at his family's request. The plot is administered by the American Battle Monuments Commission, along with World War I and World War II monuments throughout the world, but it is not mentioned in public ABMC documents.

To get to Plot E, you travel east of Paris to a part of the

countryside where the fiercest battles of World War I were fought—a gentle landscape of rivers, woods, and farmland, interrupted by an occasional modest village. When I arrived at the cemetery on a Sunday afternoon in January 2004, I was greeted by the superintendent, a dignified American man nearing retirement after an Army career overseas. We turned our backs to the massive World War I cemetery, with its iron gates and stone entry columns, and walked out a back door in the caretaker's building to a small clearing in the woods.

A circle of laurel bushes and a few large pine trees framed the space, but there were no walls. All I could see as I approached was an expanse of manicured grass dotted with small white squares. In front of the squares was a single plain white cross. The white dots turned out to be a series of identical marble squares set in the grass. Each marble square was engraved with a gray number. There was no plaque anywhere, nothing to mark the site or explain what it was. The numbers went from 1 to 96 in four rows set about five feet apart, on land that sloped downwards.

The superintendent stood by quietly while I explored the space. I was struck by how carefully Plot E had been designed. Today, it is as impeccably maintained as the rows and rows of crosses at Omaha Beach, as though visitors were expected imminently. But aside from cemetery workers and an occasional Battle Monuments official, there has never been a visitor here.

I walked down the slope of land to the corner grave in row four, to square number 73. That number belongs to Louis Till, the person in Plot E whose story has such tragic historical resonance. Till was executed in Italy in 1945 on a charge of rape and murder. Ten years later, his son, Emmett Till, was fourteen years old when he was beaten, shot, and thrown in a river in Mississippi for whistling at a white woman. I looked at the square and thought about the young son's open casket at his funeral in Chicago. His mother had wanted the world to see the evidence of that terrible, unpunished murder.

I stopped next at marker 19, which belonged to William Davis, the GI from Virginia whom Louis Guilloux saw sentenced to hang on September 24, 1944. Two witnesses to his hanging had told me that the town crier in Guiclan stood on the cemetery wall and announced the impending event to the townspeople after Sunday mass, the day before Davis's execution. The field where he was hanged is known in Guiclan, in the Breton language still spoken by the older generation, as *"Park an hini du"*—"black man's field." In Davis's personnel file there is a form letter to his widow dated four months after his death, with no reference to his trial or execution. The letter says only what a good soldier he was.

An Army that had been so eager for French civilians to witness its punishment of criminal GIs seemed just as eager to hide those punishments from the families of the executed men. If anyone had challenged them, Army officials would have been hard-pressed to justify their policy of public hangings in Europe, ten years after every state in the Union had abolished public executions at home.

I was struck by what was missing in Plot E, everything you expect to find in a military cemetery: each soldier's name, his rank and unit, the date of his death, the state where he entered the Army, his upright marble cross or star. Plot E is a perfectly designed anti-memorial. "A house of shame," one worker at the cemetery called it.

Of the ninety-six men buried in Plot E, eighty were enlisted men who had been assigned to "colored only" units: Quartermaster Service companies, Ordnance companies, Port battalions, and a few "colored only" combat units. Thirteen men in Plot E were white, two were Hispanic, one was a Navajo Indian.

The names of the dead resonated in my mind as I walked in the hidden space: Otis B. Crews, Tommie Davison, Willie Johnson, Amos Agee, General L. Grant—named for the hero of another war. In death, their privacy is protected but their history has been erased.

I walked up the sloping lawn to the marble square that had brought me there: number 13. Buried under the neatly mowed grass, a few steps from the single marble cross that was supposed to stand for all the men, were the last remains of General Prisoner James E. Hendricks.

Evelyn Echols still hopes she might someday bring James's body home to Macon, or at the very least, bring the family together for the memorial service he never had.

———

Louis Guilloux was buried on October 18, 1980, in the Saint-Michel Cemetery at Saint-Brieuc in the company of a political, religious, and literary elite. At his funeral, the mayor of Saint-Brieuc evoked the writer's battle against social injustice, his refusal of "that oppression which affects not only the material conditions of existence, but even more the dignity of humankind." This, he said, was the meaning of Louis Guilloux's life.

"Why write?" Guilloux asked himself in a diary entry from 1951. "To transmit. . . . To jostle our ignorance, to bring the evidence home." The interpreter at the American courts-martial in Morlaix was not a religious man, but he had believed all his life in the power of testimony. "Everything I had seen came back to me," he wrote in the final pages of *OK, Joe*. "I had been a witness, and I told myself that one day, I in turn might again raise my right hand and say, 'I swear!'"

Notes

―

PART I: LIBERATION

CHAPTER 1: PLUMAUDAN

3: *No photographs could be taken:* National Archives, College Park, Standing Operating Procedure No. 54, Execution of Death Sentences Imposed by Courts-Martial, December 14, 1944, Headquarters European Theater of Operations (cited hereafter as Execution of Death Sentences). Adjutant General Operations Reports; file 250: Discipline.

4: *He arranged them in the courtyard:* National Archives, College Park, Memorandum: Orders "To Officers and Enlisted Men concerned," November 21, 1944, in Record of Trial, *U.S. v. Hendricks* (for full reference, see note below); communication from Col. Poole Rogers (formerly Captain), 610 Quartermaster Graves Registration Company, July 21, 2004.

4: *GIs who committed crimes:* National Archives, College Park, Record Group 338, VIII Corps, Adjutant General 250 series: Discipline. Memorandum dated December 1944 from Headquarters, European Theater of Operations, entitled "Procedure for Execution of Death Sentences on the Continent": "Executions of sentences of death imposed upon personnel of this command for crimes of violence against indigenous inhabitants on the Continent will take place at, or in the vicinity of, the community where the crime occurred."

4: *General Prisoner James Hendricks:* Report of Proceedings at the Execution of General Prisoner James E. Hendricks, 3345189, November 24, 1944, by Capt. Albert M. Summerfield, Recorder (cited hereafter as Execution Report), pp. 2–3.

4: *He wore his uniform:* Execution of Death Sentences, Item 6b, Preparation for Execution: "The prisoner, if a member of the military service of the United States, will be dressed in regulation uniform, from which all ornaments, insignia and evidence of membership of any branch of the military forces have been removed."

5: *The poor conditions at Camp Van Dorn:* National Archives, College Park, Record Group 247, Robert J. Saunders, Chaplain 201, Box 1596. The file gives a poignant picture of Saunders's struggle to serve as chaplain in the segregated Army. He was born in Oklahoma in 1903 and educated at Western University, Shaffer Seminary, and the Harvard Chaplain School, and became an ordained minister of the National Baptist Convention of America. On October 13, 1943, Saunders wrote the Chief of Chaplains that he was "temperamentally unfit" for service at Camp Van Dorn and requested a transfer. By November 1, he was ready to give up: "It is impossible to do effective work under these conditions since cooperation is necessary in a chaplain's work. I request that I be allowed to resign my commission at once." His request to transfer, then to resign his commission, was ignored—the Chief of Chaplains office explained that it did not have jurisdiction to accept a resignation. He would have to go through the Adjutant General's office. Saunders didn't pursue the matter. In 1944, he shipped overseas with the 366th Engineering General Service Regiment Battalion and served as their chaplain in England, France, and Belgium. His correspondence shows that he was gratified to be with the troops in Europe. He distributed testaments, conducted prayer services, met with individual soldiers, gave sex morality lectures to hundreds of men, presided over funerals. During the month of November 1944, records show that he conducted four guardhouse visits to sixty soldiers. On conflicts faced by black chaplains in the segregated Army, see Ulysses Lee, *The Employment of Negro Troops, U.S. Army in World War II: Special Studies* (Washington, D.C.: Department of the Army, 1966), pp. 225–29, 394–97.

5: *that there were to be black witnesses present:* Execution of Death Sentences, p. 2.

6: *"Do you have a last statement"* . . . *Tell all the boys:* Execution Report, p. 3.

7: *"The guilty were always":* Fonds Louis Guilloux, Bibliothèque municipale de Saint-Brieuc, LGO OK Joe 01.01.03c, 1966 manuscript (draft for the novel in progress), p. 255.

7: *"Fifty-five of them were African Americans:* National Archives, College Park, Record Group 331, Twelfth Army Group (final After Action Report), vol. 10: First United States Army, Report of Operations, Annex no. 15, Provost Marshal Section; Judge Advocate General, Box 267.

7: *He concentrated on the trial:* Record of Trial of Private First Class James E. Hendricks by General Court-Martial, Tried at Morlaix, Finistère, France, 6–7 September 1944 (courtesy J. Robert Lilly and U.S. Army Clerk of Court; cited hereafter as *U.S. v. Hendricks*); Record of Trial of Captain George P. Whittington by General Court-Martial, Tried at Morlaix, Finistère, France, 25–26 September 1944 (courtesy U.S. Army Clerk of Court: cited hereafter as *U.S. v. Whittington*). Judge Advocate reviews of these cases were published in the Judge Advocate General's Department Board of Review, Holdings and Opinions, branch office of the Judge Advocate General, European Theater of Operations (Washington, D.C.: Office of the Judge Advocate General, 1942–46). A VIII Corps Judge Advocate diary, including a list of general courts-martial, made it possible to identify each of Guilloux's cases: National Archives, College Park, Record Group 407, Entry 427, World War II Operations Reports 1940–1948, VIII Corps, Judge Advocate Journal, 1 July 1944–31 October 1945. For a comparative study of courts-martial for rape and murder in England, France, and Germany at the liberation, see J. Robert Lilly, *La Face cachée des GI's: Les viols commis par des soldats américains en France, en Angleterre et en Allemagne pendant la Seconde Guerre mondiale,* trans. Benjamin and Julien Guérif (Paris: Payot, 2003).

7: *He called it* OK, Joe: Originally published in 1976 as *OK, Joe!* in a book of two novellas, *Salido, suivi de OK, Joe!* (Paris: Gallimard/Folio, 1976), trans. with an introduction by Alice Kaplan as *OK, Joe* (Chicago: University of Chicago Press, 2003). Subsequent references are to the Chicago translation.

CHAPTER 2: OCCUPATION AND RESISTANCE

9: *"You won't be a cobbler":* Louis Guilloux, *L'Herbe d'oubli* (Paris: Gallimard, 1984), p. 53 (my translation).

9: *He had lived in several worlds:* For a biography of Guilloux, see Yves Loisel, *Louis Guilloux: Biographie* (Brest: Cooper Breizh, 1998). Among literary studies, see Mary Jean Green's pioneering *Louis Guilloux: An Artisan of Language* (Birmingham, Ala.:

Summa Publications, 1980), as well as Walter Redford, *Louis Guilloux: Ear Witness* (Amsterdam and Atlanta: Editions Rodopi, 1998), and, in French, Henri Godard's *Louis Guilloux: Romancier de la condition humaine* (Paris: Gallimard, 1999). Guilloux's diaries, published in two volumes as *Carnets 1921–1944* (Paris: Gallimard, 1978) and *Carnets 1944–1974*, eds. Roger Grenier and Françoise Lambert (Paris: Gallimard, 1982), are cited hereafter as *Carnets I* and *Carnets II*.

9: *a Dostoievskian epic:* Louis Guilloux, *Le Sang noir* (Paris: Gallimard, 1935), was translated into English by Samuel Putnam in 1936 as *Bitter Victory* (New York: R. M. McBride). Sadly, the translation is long out of print. Unless the translation can be reissued, or the novel retranslated, Guilloux's greatest literary achievement will remain lost to English-speaking readers.

9: *The book had nearly as strong:* In 1935, an enormous public meeting was held at the Salle Poissonnière in Paris to discuss the political consequences of *Le Sang noir*. Speakers included Gide, Malraux, and Aragon (Loisel, op. cit., p. 125). Guilloux also served in 1935 as secretary for a World Congress of anti-Fascist writers that brought representatives from over thirty countries to Paris. See the account by Loisel, pp. 137–42.

9: *returned from the trip:* After André Gide took a public stance against the Soviet Union in his *Retour de l'U.R.S.S.* and *Retouches à mon Retour de l'U.R.S.S.* (Paris: Gallimard, 1936 and 1937), Louis Aragon and Jean-Richard Bloch, the leading Communist intellectuals who edited *Le Soir*, pressured Guilloux to discredit Gide by writing in the newspaper about Gide's homosexual activities. Guilloux's refusal to do so cost him his job at *Le Soir*, where he was about to become editor of the literary pages. Nor did he ever second Gide by publishing his own public attack on the USSR. He felt, in the end, that the trip had been too superficial for him to draw definitive conclusions. See *Carnets I*, pp. 140–41, 152.

10: *Guilloux's native Brittany:* Luc Capdevila, *Les Bretons au lendemain de l'Occupation: Imaginaire et comportement d'une sortie de guerre, 1944–1945* (Rennes: Presses Universitaires de Rennes, 1999), gives a valuable account of the Nazi presence in Brittany as background to a social and political history of the Liberation throughout the region.

10: *Although he complained:* The novel was published after the war as *Le Jeu de Patience* (*The Patience Game*).

11: *". . . I saw some long, fat"*: *Carnets I*, p. 346.

11: *"I'm at Baratoux School"*: *Ibid.*, p. 347.

11: *the spa town of Vichy:* For a political and diplomatic history of Vichy, see Robert O. Paxton's classic *Vichy France: Old Guard and New Order 1940–1944* (New York: Knopf, 1972); for a study of intellectual and political choices in occupied France, see Philippe Burrin, *France Under the Germans: Collaboration and Compromise* (New York: New Press, 1997).

12: *Vichy suspended the French constitution:* The number of Jewish deportees was established by Serge Klarsfeld in his *Mémorial de la Déportation des Juifs de France 1940–1944* (Paris: Editions Klarsfeld, 1993). Jean-Pierre Azéma, *De Munich à la Libération 1938–1944: Nouvelle histoire de la France contemporaine* (Paris: Le Seuil, 1979), p. 189, estimates the number of people deported specifically for acts of resistance at approximately 41,000. The most recent study indicates a larger figure: In June 2004, the Fondation pour la mémoire de la Déportation (Foundation for the Memory of Deportation) published a list of 86,048 people deported from France for reasons other than their race. This number includes Resistance fighters, Frenchmen taken hostage by the Nazis in reprisal for acts of resistance, and as well those arrested for ordinary crimes. See *Le Livre-mémorial des déportés de France arrêtés par mesure de répression et dans certains cas par mesure de persécution* (Paris: Editions Tirésias, 2004).

12: *Five thousand Bretons were deported:* Jacqueline Sainclivier, *La Bretagne de 1934 jusqu'à nos jours* (Rennes: Editions Ouest-France, 1989). See also her *La Bretagne dans la guerre: 1939–1945* (Rennes: Editions Ouest-France/Mémorial de Caen, 1994) for a breakdown of these statistics.

12: *a crime punishable by death:* Claude Chabrol's 1988 film, *Une Affaire de femmes* (*A Story of Women*), dramatized the trial and execution of an abortionist under Vichy. Miranda Pollard, *Reign of Virtue: Mobilizing Gender in Vichy France* (Chicago: University of Chicago Press, 1998), provides a pioneering analysis of the centrality of gender for understanding Vichy policy.

12: *Saint-Brieuc was an important center:* This *département* of Brittany is known today as the Côtes d'Armor.

13: *"If only I could say"*: *Carnets I*, p. 277.

13: *He was forging a coalition:* Christian Bougeard, "Louis Guilloux et son temps," in Yannick Pelletier, *Louis Guilloux:*

Dossier d'articles, d'études et de témoignages (Bassac-Châteauneuf-sur-Charente: Plein Chant, 1982), pp. 131–48.

13: *linked to the Communists:* The "Front National" Resistance movement had, of course, no connection whatsoever to Le Pen's far right National Front of the 1990s.

13: *Guilloux went into hiding: Carnets I*, pp. 356–61.

14: *The first step in the process:* For a history of the invasion, see the first volume in Rick Atkinson's liberation trilogy, *The Army at Dawn: The War in North Africa 1942–1943* (New York: Henry Holt & Co., 2002).

15: *As a schoolboy:* Interview with Yvonne Guilloux, June 26, 2002, Paris.

15: *he had made ends meet:* Guilloux, *L'Herbe d'oubli,* includes moving accounts of the writer's education and first experiences with the English language. In 1921, Guilloux was hired as a translator of English-language dispatches for the Parisian newspaper *L'Intransigeant*; on his literary translation, see the note in chapter 4, below.

CHAPTER 3: THE LIBERATION

16: *Louis Guilloux's mother: Carnets I*, p. 364.

17: *Throughout northern France:* Archives de l'Ille-et-Vilaine, Rennes, 43W56, weekly reports by the Service Régional des Renseignements généraux [police intelligence]. Week of February 14–20: "There remains a psychosis around the landing and military operations outside France are followed with approval. Feelings of hostility toward the Occupation troops continue to increase." Week of February 21–27: "Public opinion: the likelihood of a landing remains one of the main subjects of conversation; it can be said that the population, tired of war, is ready to give itself body and soul to whoever will make the war stop" (my translations).

17: *"We are constantly waiting":* Archives de l'Ille-et-Vilaine, Rennes, 43W8, Prefect's report for the week of March 6–12.

17: *French intelligence reports describe:* See Hilary Footitt, *War and Liberation in France: Living with the Liberators* (London: Macmillan, 2004), on French civilian reactions to the Allied bombings in Normandy. For Brittany, see Archives du Finistère, Quimper, 31W2521, on reactions to the American bombing of Telgruc in September 1944.

17: *there were nearly 10,000 casualties:* The statistics vary. The figure of 130,000, given by the U.S. Center for Military History, refers specifically to the amphibious landings on the five Normandy beaches. U.S. forces landed only on Omaha and Utah Beaches; British and Canadian soldiers, as well as a small French contingent, landed on Juno, Gold, and Sword Beaches. The United States suffered 2,000 casualties at Omaha Beach alone.

17: *"It is a terrible and monstrous thing"*: Cornelius Ryan, *The Longest Day* (New York: Simon & Schuster, 1959), p. 197.

18: *They were known for their violent behavior:* There are also stories of Russian units who deserted the German army and joined the *maquis* in the Breton forests. Communication from Paol Keineg, November 30, 2004.

18: *"virtually reduced to dust":* Footitt, op. cit., p. 43. Footitt's book, based on a study of the French, British, and American armies, examines the varying effects of liberating armies on local populations in several different regions of France.

19: *He was not alone:* British Ministry of Economic Warfare, *French Basic Handbook, Economic Survey Since June 1940,* compiled July 1944, Imperial War Museum, London. Statistics compiled by the Ministry of Economic Warfare in July 1944 estimate 1,500 calories a day for the city dweller—half of the prewar intake.

19: *"the least effort is costly":* Carnets I, p. 390, July 10, 1944.

19: *found themselves face to face:* Papers of Don Lewis, who served with the Adjutant General unit of the U.S. Army VIII Corps in Brittany (courtesy Eleanore Lewis McKetchnie).

20:*"The typical Breton . . . naturally erotic":* Zone Handbook 8: Rennes (London: Ministry of Economic Warfare, 1943–45). Civil Affairs handbooks for each zone of France are available at the Imperial War Museum, London (call no. 28768-14) and at the Bibliothèque de Documentation Internationale, Université de Nanterre. There is a basic handbook for all of France, as well as nineteen separate Zone Handbooks; Belgium, Denmark, Italy, the Netherlands, and Norway have handbooks as well. According to Charles-Louis Foulon, *Le Pouvoir en province à la libération* (Paris: Colin, 1975), the handbooks were created by American and British officers in Civil Affairs headquarters in Pittsburgh and Wimbledon. How the books were distributed or used for the education of officers in the field has not been documented.

21: *they were likely to find:* U.S. Army Information Bulletin no.

17, May 5, 1944, Archives Nationales F1A3815, quoted in Foulon, op. cit., p. 35.

CHAPTER 4: THE INTERPRETER

22: *But the Nazis were gone: Carnets I,* pp. 401–05.

22: *"Je suis un buveur de rues":* Interview with Mona Ozouf, January 14, 2004, Paris. Ozouf, a student of Renée Guilloux in Saint-Brieuc who knew Louis Guilloux well, has written movingly about his work. See "Pour Louis Guilloux," *Le Nouvel Observateur,* 2016, June 26, 2003.

23: *all crowding around her:* Yvonne Guilloux's sketchbook, dated August 7, 1944, Fonds Louis Guilloux, Bibliothèque municipale de Saint-Brieuc.

23: *"The slight little fellow":* Bill Cormier later transcribed his war diary and entitled it "Through the Eyes of a Soldier: Memoirs of the Second World War," typescript (n.d.; courtesy Olivia Cormier; cited hereafter as Bill Cormier, War Diary), p. 66.

24: *"affected both investigations":* National Archives, College Park, Record Group 319, "Military Justice Administration in Theater of Operations," USFET monograph, file 250/1 (1946–48), Study no. 83 (1945), p. 52.

24: *already had three book-length translations:* Margaret Kennedy, *La nymphe au coeur fidèle,* trad. Louis Guilloux (Paris: Plon, 1927); G. K. Chesterton, *La vie de Robert Browning,* trad. Louis Guilloux (Paris: Gallimard, 1930); and Claude McKay, *Quartier noir,* traduit du nègre américain par Louis Guilloux (Paris: Rieder, 1933). With his wife, Renée, Guilloux translated a second Kennedy novel, *The Fool of the Family,* as *L'Idiot de la famille* (Paris: Plon, 1929), and a scholarly article about the post–World War I American novel by Gorham Munson, "Le roman d'après-guerre aux Etats-Unis," in *Europe,* 116 (August 1932), pp. 617–23.

24: *Guilloux's notebooks from the 1930s:* See e.g. *Carnets I,* pp. 80, 83.

24: *unloading shipments:* Jonathan Gawne, *Americans in Brittany: The Battle for Brest* (Paris: Histoire et Collections, 2002), pp. 3–4.

25: *"He sailed for Brest":* Claude McKay, *Home to Harlem* (New York: Harper Brothers, 1928), re-edited with a foreword by Wayne Cooper (Boston: Northeastern University Press, 1978), p. 4.

25: *"Mr. Louis Guilloux"*: National Archives, College Park, Record Group 407, Entry 427, World War II Operations Reports, 1940–1948, VIII Corps, Judge Advocate Journal, 1 July 1944–31 October 1944.

25: *Guilloux's diary says: Carnets I*, p. 414.

25: *"Only time for 'headliner'"*: Entry dated September 9, 1944. Unpublished diary fragments ("Carnet de guerre"), August–September 1944 (courtesy Leo Scheer and the Fonds Louis Guilloux, Bibliothèque municipale de Saint-Brieuc; cited hereafter as Carnet de guerre).

26: *"but who wasn't a good egg"*: Fonds Louis Guilloux, Bibliothèque municipale de Saint-Brieuc, LGO OK Joe 01.01.03, manuscript in lined notebook (*"cahier d'écolier"*), dossier b (1967?), p. 171.

26: *"See you later"*: Ibid., p. 199.

26: *He was full of ideas:* Carnet de guerre, September 5, 1944.

27: *violinist's hands: OK, Joe*, p. 2.

27: *awkward at the ordinary tasks:* Interview with Eleanore Lewis McKetchnie, May 17, 2003, Winter Park, Florida, evoking her husband Don Lewis's memories of Greene. Lewis was a colonel with the VIII Corps in Morlaix.

27: *"I am really enjoying my new situation"*: Carnet de guerre, September 1, 1944.

CHAPTER 5: JAMES HENDRICKS

28: *What part of the bad things:* Thomas Nagel, "Moral Luck," in *Mortal Questions* (Cambridge: Cambridge University Press, 1979), pp. 24–38.

28: *By the time James Hendricks was a teenager:* Interview with Evelyn Echols and Geraldine Bullock, November 15, 2003, Macon, North Carolina.

29: *for new beginning:* Interview with Thurston Brown, Thurletta Brown-Gavins, and Robert Daniels (pseudonym), September 14, 2004, Warrenton, North Carolina.

29: *farmed a large plot of land:* Warren County records don't indicate when Ed Henderson first acquired his land or how much land he owned; they do show that in 1940, Ed Henderson's son, Alex, purchased an additional 100 acres adjacent to his father's farm.

29: *Reading, writing, arithmetic:* Interview with Robert Daniels, September 14, 2004, Warrenton, North Carolina. On the Rosenwald

School project, see Tom Hatchett, "The Rosenwald Schools and Black Education in North Carolina," *North Carolina Historical Review,* vol. 65, no. 4 (October 1998), pp. 387–444.

29: *prone to violent temper tantrums:* Interview with Robert Daniels, September 14, 2003, Warrenton, North Carolina.

30: *Hendricks was finally drafted:* Interviews with Geraldine Bullock, November 15, 2003, and September 25, 2004, Macon, North Carolina.

30: *He was inducted at Fort Meyer:* James Hendricks, 201 Personnel File (courtesy Army Personnel Records Center, St. Louis, Missouri).

30: *"harvest of disorder":* Lee, op. cit., chapter 12, "Harvest of Disorder," pp. 348–79.

31: *the men were expected to learn:* National Archives, College Park, 791 Sanitary Company Unit History, Record Group 94, Adjutant General's Office, World War II Operations Reports 1940–1948: Medical, MDCO-775–0.3 to MDCO-820–0.2.

31: *The riot was barely contained:* See the account by Lee, op. cit., pp. 368–70.

31: *The fires of the legend:* Carroll Case, *The Slaughter: An American Atrocity* (Asheville, N.C.: First Biltmore Corporation, 1998).

31: *the Army issued its report:* National Archives, College Park, "A Historical Analysis of the 364th Infantry in World War II," Department of the Army, report published December 1999.

32: *What the record shows:* See Lee, op. cit., chapter 12.

32: *What followed was:* Ibid., p. 372.

32: *"They cherish a deep resentment":* April 3, 1942, quoted in ibid., p. 365. On the active role role taken by the black press in publicizing conditions in the Jim Crow Army, see Lee Finkle, *Forum for Protest: The Black Press During World War II* (Rutherford, N.J.: Fairleigh Dickinson University Press, 1975).

33: *He spent a month:* James E. Hendricks, 201 Personnel File (courtesy Army Personnel Records Center, St. Louis, Missouri).

PART II: UNITED STATES
VERSUS PRIVATE JAMES E. HENDRICKS
CHAPTER 6: THE INCIDENT

37: *"I am gravely concerned":* National Archives, College Park, Record Group 338, VIII Corps, 250 series: Discipline; 250.1:

Morals and conduct, January 1943–June 1945. Memorandum dated August 20, 1944, from Gen. George Patton to all officers under his command entitled "Crimes against Civilians."

38: *The commanders themselves were under:* Ibid.: "Some offenders have already been tried by general court-martial, and severe sentences[,] including the penalty of death, have been imposed. All offenders will be promptly tried and will be punished in a manner commensurate with their crimes. Each unit commander at a special formation held as soon as possible after the receipt of this communication will personally impress upon all members of his command the views herein expressed. Particularly, he will announce at such formation that the death penalty already has been imposed in cases of rape which took place in France." Patton's comments, as well as those of Major General Middleton and Colonel Scully, in chapter 13, are prime examples of the "unlawful command influence" that was often cited as a flaw in the World War II military justice system. Postwar reforms made it a crime for a commander to influence a court-martial.

39: *Purple Hearts:* National Archives, College Park, 3326th Quartermaster Truck Company Unit History dated January 20, 1944, Record Group 407, Adjutant General's Office, World War II Operations Reports 1940–1948.

39: *known as the "pet":* Interview with Geraldine Bullock, November 15, 2003, Macon, North Carolina, evoking her late husband Junius Bullock's memories of Hendricks at Camp Van Dorn.

39: *Some days he would talk:* U.S. v. Hendricks, testimony of Corp. Robert Manns, p. 81. The details that follow are taken from the transcript of Hendricks's court-martial and supporting documents. Subsequent notes indicate the testimony or document on which details in the text are based.

39: *supposed to keep the safety on:* U.S. v. Hendricks, testimony of Lt. Charles F. Michaels, p. 46; testimony of Lt. Donald Tucker, p. 48.

40: *Hendricks declined the cider:* U.S. v. Hendricks, testimony of René Bouton, pp. 38–39, and Charles Bouton, p. 85.

40: *He pounded on the door:* U.S. v. Hendricks, testimony of Noémie Bignon, pp. 7ff., and Jeannine Bignon, pp. 25ff.

41: *Charles ran as fast as he could:* U.S. v. Hendricks, testimony of Charles Bouton, p. 86.

41: *By the time Hendricks got inside:* U.S. v. Hendricks, testimony of Noémie Bignon, p. 16, and René Bouton, p. 41.

41: *Lieutenant Tucker had heard:* U.S. v. Hendricks, testimony of Lt. Donald Tucker, p. 74.

41: *He hadn't been on:* U.S. v. Hendricks, James Hendricks signed statement, n.d.

42: *Tucker sent for the MPs:* U.S. v. Hendricks, testimony of Lt. Donald Tucker, p. 59.

42: *Tucker told him:* Ibid.

43: *The gendarmerie informed:* Côtes d'Armor (formerly Côtes-du-Nord) regional archives, Saint-Brieuc; 2W97, Procès verbal de gendarmerie, Brigade de Caulnes, 22 September 1944, "Information on the assassination of Victor Bignon, fifty-year-old farmer in Plumaudan, by a black American soldier, James E. Hendricks," statement by Noémie Bignon (my translation).

43: *found one of the two eggs:* Question by the prosecution: "What was the condition of the egg after it was taken out?" Lt. Tucker: "Well, it was still together then, but when it came back again it had been shattered." U.S. v. Hendricks, p. 57.

43: *advised Hendricks of his rights:* The *Manual for Courts-Martial* guaranteed to each soldier the right not to incriminate him- or herself before an officer conducting an investigation.

43: *until Lieutenant Tucker came after him:* U.S. v. Hendricks, testimony of Lt. Donald Tucker, p. 60.

43: *"I'm sure it was my rifle":* U.S. v. Hendricks, signed statement of James E. Hendricks, n.d.

CHAPTER 7: THE COURT-MARTIAL

45: *"Lieutenant Stone walked up":* OK, Joe, p. 3.

46: *Guilloux translated the document:* U.S. v. Hendricks, Prosecution's exhibit no. 2, translation of physician's August 22 statement certifying the death of Victor Bignon.

46: *"This morning, in the courtyard":* Carnet de guerre, September 2, 1944. Mistakes in cross-racial identification have become a central issue in many contemporary death penalty cases. See, among the abundant literature, Sheri Lynn Johnson, "Cross-Racial Identification Errors in Criminal Cases," *Cornell Law Review*, vol. 69 (1984), pp. 934–87.

47: *There hadn't been a proper party:* Communication from Martha Le Clech, educator and historian of the Morlaix lycées and author of a history of the girls' lycée, *Du Collège de jeunes filles au collège du Château* (Plourin: Bretagne d'hier, 1999), October 5, 2003.

48: *Guilloux drew on his memory: OK, Joe,* pp. 49–50.

48: *the shortcomings of military justice:* Georges Clemenceau (1841–1929), French prime minister and minister of war, is credited with the famous quip.

48: *"Courts-martial are part":* Elizabeth Hillman, "The 'Good Soldier' Defense: Character Evidence and Military Rank at Courts-Martial," *Yale Law Journal,* vol. 108, no. 4 (January 1999), pp. 879–911.

49: *a unanimous vote was required:* World War II courts-martial proceedings were governed by *A Manual for Courts-Martial U.S. Army 1928* (Washington, D.C.: U.S Government Printing Office, 1928, cited hereafter as *Manual for Courts-Martial*). A two-thirds majority was required for conviction for most offenses; a three-fourths majority for life imprisonment or prison sentences longer than ten years; for the death penalty, a unanimous vote was required (see Article of War 43, p. 212).

49: *remembering the scene: OK, Joe,* p. 51.

49: *his only Hollywood role:* See the account of his discovery and Hollywood adventure, "Georgetown University Played a Part in Odd Career," *The Washington Post,* December 2, 1928.

49: *anthologized countless times:* "Gentleman of Río in medio," originally published in the *New Mexico Quarterly,* vol. IX, no. 3 (August 1939); reprints include Philip D. Ortega, *We Are Chicanos: An Anthology of Mexican-American Literature* (New York: Pocket Books, 1975), pp. 287–90.

49: *as a book reviewer had claimed:* Letter to the editor, *New York Times,* June 1, 1930, p. 12.

50: *a Danish countess:* 1930 U.S. Census, Santa Fe, New Mexico.

50: *squired admirals' daughters: Washington Post* society columns, December 5, 1941, p. 23; January 1, 1942, p. 12; March 13, 1942, p. 18.

50: *to great legal responsibilities:* Sedillo was named legal chief of the Stuttgart military government in August 1946; he served as a justice of the highest appeals court in occupied Germany in September 1948; he was appointed American Judge of the International Court of Justice in Tangier in 1953. On his work in Tangier, see Juan A. A. Sedillo, "The International Court of Tangier: A Unique Instrument of International Justice," *American Bar Association Journal,* vol. 43 (1957), pp. 718–20.

50: *a neighborhood of German immigrants:* 1930 U.S. Census, Wausau, Wisconsin.

50: *would rise to the rank:* U.S. Army Personnel Records for Ralph Fogarty (courtesy Army Personnel Records Center, St. Louis, Missouri).

50: *"As soon as you saw him":* OK, Joe, p. 12.

50: *By 1944 he wasn't yet:* John Marshall Law School yearbooks for 1938, 1939, and 1940, and alumni directories. On legal education at John Marshall, see William Wleklinski, *A Centennial History of John Marshall Law School* (Chicago: JMLS, 1998). Fogarty was admitted to the Chicago Bar in 1948 (information courtesy of the Illinois Bar Association).

51: *In choosing Fogarty:* The Vanderbilt Commission, which met after the war to consider problems in World War II courtsmartial and suggest reforms, decried the use of inexperienced officers as defense counsel. See Robert F. Gonzales, "Officers First: Judge Advocates During World War II," unpublished manuscript, Office of The Judge Advocate General, United States Army, referred to subsequently as Robert F. Gonzales, "Officers First: Judge Advocates During World War II."

51: *He attended law school at Fordham:* Attorney Admission papers, July 8, 1931, State of New York (courtesy Appellate Division, Supreme Court of the State of New York, Second Judicial Department).

51: *There were too many Greenbergs:* Petition: Application of Joseph D. Greenberg; Leave to Change his Name to Joseph D. Greene, City Court of the City of New York, County of Kings, Brooklyn, New York, October 8, 1941.

52: *He was drafted:* Joseph D. Greene, Army Personnel File (courtesy Army Personnel Records Center, St. Louis, Missouri).

52: *But in the absence of enough trained judge advocates:* See Gonzales, op. cit. There were 38,000 lawyers serving in the military in World War II—it was up to individual commanders, working with the Staff Judge Advocates, to identify these men and have them assigned to court-martial duty.

52: *Everyone who watched him:* Interview with Eleanor Lewis McKechnie, May 17, 2003, Winter Park, Florida, evoking her late husband Don Lewis's memories of watching Greene in the VIII Corps court-martial.

52: *"At the end of his speech":* OK, Joe, p. 51.

CHAPTER 8: THE CASE AGAINST JAMES HENDRICKS

53: *"to get some"*: *U.S. v. Hendricks*, testimony of Corp. Robert Manns, p. 82.

53: *The Bouton brothers said*: *U.S. v. Hendricks*, testimony of Charles Bouton, pp. 84–88, and René Bouton, pp. 37–41.

53: *The Bignon women . . . "no Mademoiselles"*: *U.S. v. Hendricks*, testimony of Noémie Bignon, pp. 8 and 11, and Jeannine Bignon, p. 27. Victor Bignon's cry of "We're good French people" was reported to the French gendarmes who investigated the case, but not to the Americans. See Côtes d'Armor regional archives, 2W97, Procès verbal de gendarmerie, Brigade de Caulnes, 22 September 1944, "Information on the assassination of Victor Bignon, fifty-year-old farmer in Plumaudan, by a black American soldier, James E. Hendricks," statement by Noémie Bignon.

53: *Both Noémie and her daughter*: *U.S. v. Hendricks*, testimony of Noémie and Jeannine Bignon, pp. 7–31.

53: *gave the details of his enlisted man's*: *U.S. v. Hendricks*, testimony of Lt. Donald Tucker, pp. 47–78.

54: *the man who had first knocked*: *U.S. v. Hendricks*, testimony of Jeannine Bignon, p. 26.

54: *In the courtroom*: *U.S. v. Hendricks*, testimony of Noémie Bignon, p. 23.

54: *"How was I supposed"*: Interview with Jeannine Bignon, July 22, 2002, Plumaudan, France.

54: *"the witnesses are not familiar"*: Branch Office of the Judge Advocate General, Board of Review no. 1, *U.S. v. Hendricks*, November 9, 1944, p. 9.

55: *referred to the accused*: *U.S. v. Hendricks*; on references to race in questioning, see, e.g., pp. 17, 18, 31, 39, 40.

55: *the same type of bullet*: *U.S. v. Hendricks*, p. 30.

55: *two types of manslaughter*: *Manual for Courts-Martial*, pp. 165–66.

56: *The arraignment sheet*: *U.S. v. Hendricks*, Arraignment sheet, p. 4.

56: *conviction for a felony murder meant*: There exists a large body of legal literature critical of felony murder. See, e.g., Nelson E. Roth and Scott E. Sundby, "The Felony-Murder Rule: A Doctrine at Constitutional Crossroads," *Cornell Law Review*, vol. 70, no. 446 (March 1985), pp. 446–59; and Rudolph J. Gerber, "The

Felony Murder Rule: Conundrum Without Principle," *Arizona State Law Journal*, vol. 31, no. 763 (1999), pp. 763–85.

CHAPTER 9: NOÉMIE BIGNON'S TESTIMONY

57: *"As was to be expected":* See Office of the Judge Advocate, History of the Judge Advocate General's Office in the European Theater, 18 July 1942–1 November 1945 (unpublished manuscript, on file with the Office of the Chief of Military History, Historical Manuscript file 8-3.5 AA v. 1; courtesy Madeline Morris), "Sex Offenses: Legal problems and solutions" in "Military and Civil Offenses," chapter 22, p. 244. For a comparative legal study of rape in military and civilian courts, see Madeline Morris, "By Force of Arms: Rape, War and Military Culture," in *Duke Law Journal*, vol. 45, no. 651 (February 1996), pp. 651–781.

58: *"a simple-minded peasant":* U.S. v. Hendricks, testimony of Noémie Bignon, p. 13.

58: *She sat in the makeshift court:* Interview with Jeannine Bignon, July 22, 2002, Plumaudan, France.

59: *French and Gallo:* The Celtic Breton language is spoken by the people of western Brittany; Gallo, a Latin-derived dialect, was spoken in the east of Brittany. Saint-Brieuc, Guilloux's town, is on the western edge of the region of "Gallo" speakers, so Guilloux would have understood Noémie Bignon's way of speaking. In an early version of *OK, Joe*, he described her language: "She expressed herself in her own language, just as Lieutenant Greenwood wished; which means she spoke the patois used by peasants in our region" (my translation). Fonds Louis Guilloux, Bibliothèque municipale de Saint-Brieuc, LGO OK, Joe, 01.01.03c.

59: *"I may have to use":* U.S. v. Hendricks, p. 14.

59: *"I told you about ten times":* U.S. v. Hendricks, testimony of Noémie Bignon, p. 14.

59: *to instruct the witness: U.S. v. Hendricks*, pp. 14–15.

60: *Public figures:* See Eluard's poem "Comprenne Qui Voudra" (1944), and Brassens's song "La Tondue," which became a hit song in France in the early 1960s. For an empirical and cultural analysis of the practice of the *tonte* (shaving) of women during the Occupation and the Liberation, see Fabrice Virgili's groundbreaking study, *Shorn Women: Gender and Punishment in Liberation France*, trans. John A. Flower (Oxford and New York: Berg Publishers, 2002).

60: *"shaking as violently"*: OK, Joe, p. 23.

60: *"I never should have let"*: Fonds Louis Guilloux, Bibliothèque municipale de Saint-Brieuc, LGO OK Joe 01.01.03c. First manuscript draft on school notepaper, fol. 96–329, hand-dated by Guilloux "January 2, 1966," p. 238.

60: *"I was plunged"*: Fonds Louis Guilloux, Bibliothèque municipale de Saint-Brieuc, LGO OK Joe 01.01.03a, p. 135.

61: *"Did he, at any time"*: U.S. v. Hendricks, p. 15.

61: *"He let his arms"*: OK, Joe, p. 72.

61: *"I took his private part"* . . . *hadn't entered her*. U.S. v. Hendricks, testimony of Noémie Bignon, p. 16.

62: *small translation mistakes*: U.S. v. Hendricks, pp. 9, 29.

62: *Hendricks's raincoat*: U.S. v. Hendricks, cross-examination of Noémie Bignon by the defense, p. 19.

62: *"I am going to offer"*: U.S. v. Hendricks, p. 58.

62: *"Gentlemen, let's cut"*: U.S. v. Hendricks, pp. 58–59.

CHAPTER 10: THE DEFENSE

64: *Organized opponents:* For legal critiques and opposition to the felony murder rule, see the last note on page 191, above.

66: *Psychiatric evaluations in many general courts-martial:* Col. Theodore B. Borek, Judge Advocate, "Legal Services during War: An Individual Study Project," U.S. Army War College, Carlisle Barracks, Pennsylvania, March 23, 1987. These exams applied specifically to the First U.S. Army and the Twelfth Army Group (Third, Ninth, and Fifteenth Armies). Only the Fifteenth U.S. Army required psychiatric exams for every individual tried by general courts-martial.

67: *"I have no reasonable ground"*: Maj. Jack B. Harrison, 80th QM Battalion Mobile, pre-trial investigation report, court-martial file, *U.S. v. Hendricks*.

67: *"As I stated in my opening"*: U.S. v. Hendricks, pp. 23–24.

67: *"If the court please"* . . . *"a circumstantial case"*: U.S. v. Hendricks, p. 24. After the war was over and the Judge Advocate Department analyzed its judicial decisions, the Hendricks case would be described in a summary of death sentences as evidence that a murder charge can be fairly proven by circumstantial evidence alone, without any positive identification of the criminal. See JAG Board of Review, European Theater of Operations, *Supplemental Digest of Opinions*, vols. 1–2, 1945–1946, p. 410, Article of War 92: "Murder; Rape" and "Murder in General."

CHAPTER 11: HENDRICKS'S COMMANDING OFFICER

68: *It was common knowledge:* National Archives, College Park, Record Group 407, General Correspondence, Jean Byers, "A Study of the Negro in Military Service: Report to the NAACP," June 1947, National Archives, College Park, Record Group 407, General Correspondence, esp. p. 52: "One of the principal prerequisites for the assignment of a white officer to a colored unit seemed to be that he was born and reared in the south. . . . The majority of southern white officers refused to think of the Negro as a soldier; they could think of him only as a laborer, a buffoon, a servant, a helpless child."

69: *31,000 officers in all:* See "Officers for Negro Troops," in Erna Risch and Chester L. Kieffer, *The Quartermaster Corps: Organization, Supply, and Services,* Vol. II (Washington, D.C.: Department of the Army, Office of the Chief of Military History, 1955), pp. 202–07.

69: *actually a marked improvement:* Gail Buckley, *American Patriots: The Story of Blacks in the Military from the Revolution to Desert Storm* (New York: Random House, p. 265).

69: *Black soldiers made up nearly half:* African American soldiers within the Quartermaster Corps were assigned, according to a 1940 policy, to truck and service units, a policy the Army attributed to the dearth of black soldiers with a high enough level of education or training for more specialized work. The Army's idea was to assign white officers to command these truck and service units until black officers could be trained to replace them.

69: *bandage its problems:* See "Officers for Negro Troops," in Risch and Kieffer, op. cit., pp. 202–07.

70: *in close proximity to a black officer:* Ulysses Lee, op. cit., pp. 179ff.

70: *They treated him with more respect:* Thomas Russell Jones, "J'étais un officier noir dans l'armée américaine pendant la Deuxième Guerre mondiale," interview with Claude Collin, *Guerres mondiales et conflits contemporains: Revue d'histoire,* 204 (December 2001), pp. 141–48.

70: *came from Kansas City, Missouri:* Army Personnel Records Center, St. Louis, Missouri, and 1930 U.S. Census, Kansas City.

70: *beginning ten months:* Army Personnel Records for Lt. Donald F. Tucker and 3266th Quartermaster Truck Company Unit History, January 20, 1944, op. cit.

71: :"*A confession made*": *Manual for Courts-Martial*, pp. 116–17.

71–72: *"When you had that conversation" . . . "before you got an answer"*: U.S. v. Hendricks, testimony of Lt. Donald Tucker, pp. 66–67.

72: *The men argued*: U.S. v. Hendricks, p. 67.

72: *"I am objecting to counsel"*: U.S. v. Hendricks, p. 68.

72: *"The court is very anxious"*: U.S. v. Hendricks, p. 67.

72: *"on the grounds that no proper warnings"*: U.S. v. Hendricks, p. 73.

72: *"Did you threaten"*: U.S. v. Hendricks, p. 75.

73: *"I was very pleased"*: U.S. v. Hendricks, p. 78.

74: *the "good soldier" defense*: See Hillman, "The 'Good Soldier' Defense," op. cit., pp. 879–911.

75: *Hendricks had three options*: See *Manual for Courts-Martial*, pp. 125ff.

75: *an unsworn statement*: Ibid., p. 61.

75: *frightened or intimidated*: Interview with James Craighill, February 19, 2004, Charlotte, North Carolina.

75: *The third option*: U.S. v. Hendricks, p. 17.

76: *the "cat who didn't even"*: OK, Joe, p. 49.

76: *Negro officers were very difficult to find*: National Archives, College Park, Record Group 338, VIII Corps, 250 series: Discipline; 250.1: Morals and conduct, January 1943–June 1945, Memorandum dated March 6, 1944, from Maj. Gen. John C. H. Lee, Deputy Theater Commander, reproduced December 12, 1944: "Although in this theater the ratio of Negro officers to white officers is not large, it is especially desired that wherever practicable, one or more Negro officers be detailed as members of all courts-martial before which are to be tried Negro personnel for the more serious crimes, including crimes of violence or disorder and those involving inter-racial sensibilities. . . . These instructions have been furnished in writing to all commanders exercising General Court-Martial jurisdiction, and will not be reproduced or distributed by them. Such publication as is necessary to carry this directive into effect will be done orally."

76: *New Articles of War ratified in 1948*: U.S. House of Representatives, Committee on Military Affairs, Judicial System, U.S. Army, Report no. 2722, 79th Congress, 2nd sess., 1946. See also Gonzales, op. cit., chapter 17 and Conclusion. Fogarty was indeed a qualified lawyer, though he was not a member of the bar.

77: *"As awful as it was"*: OK, Joe, p. 54.

CHAPTER 12: THE HANGING

78: *At 3:45 P.M. on September 7:* U.S. v. Hendricks, p. 99.

78: *his first offense:* U.S. v. Hendricks, p. 99.

78: *They gave no explanation:* U.S. v. Hendricks, Memo to Commanding General, VIII Corps, from Lt. Col. Juan A. A. Sedillo, Law Member, and Capt. Frederick L. Orr, entitled: "Recommendation for Clemency."

78: *"No errors injuriously affecting":* James Craighill, Staff Judge Advocate; endorsed by William Scully, VIII Corps, September 18, 1944; reviewed by David Hartman, Staff Judge Advocate at the Army level, on October 23, 1944; reviewed by the Branch Office of the Judge Advocate General, November 11, 1944.

78: *Eisenhower's order:* U.S. v. Hendricks, Headquarters, European Theater of Operations, order signed October 27, 1944, by Dwight D. Eisenhower, General, United States Army Commanding.

79: *"Insomuch as First Lieutenant":* Review of Staff Judge Advocate, September 18, 1944, p. 5.

79: *five weeks after the trial:* 3266th Quartermaster Truck Company Unit History, op. cit. Promotions came fast in wartime, and Tucker's own promotion to captain probably had little connection to his role in *U.S. v. Hendricks.*

79: *It mentions no deaths:* Ibid.

79: *In his role as interpreter:* In several drafts of *OK, Joe,* Guilloux used the words "the oath of an official interpreter—and that of an accomplice" (see, e.g., Fonds Louis Guilloux, Bibliothèque municipale de Saint-Brieuc, LGO OK Joe 01.0201b, early manuscript, p. 98). In the final draft of the novel, what remained was "The oath of an official interpreter" (p. 79). On his sense of being a spectator, see 1966 draft, LGO OK Joe 01.01.03b, p. 135.

79: *"He remained as immobile":* Fonds Louis Guilloux, Bibliothèque municipale de Saint-Brieuc, LGO OK Joe 01.01.03c (1967), p. 214, "Cahier d'écolier," fol. 96–329. The echo in this passage of the character Meursault in Camus's *The Stranger,* indifferent to his own fate in court, is striking for any French reader. Camus was Guilloux's editor at Gallimard after the war; the two men, who shared strong political and personal affinities, remained close until Camus's death in 1960.

80: *"Incidentally, where were they":* OK, Joe, pp. 78–79.

80: *"The trap mechanism":* All subsequent details are taken from the Execution Report.

80: *was sitting in his truck:* Telephone interview with Emmett Bailey, October 22, 2003, Henderson, North Carolina.

81: *men in Graves Registration:* Bailey recalled that German POWs and black GIs, thrown to the bottom of the military hierarchy, were assigned to grave digging (ibid.). Col. Poole Rogers, the commanding officer of the Graves Registration who signed off on Hendricks's burial, remembers that only white men in his unit did this work. Communication from Col. Poole Rogers (Ret.), July 21, 2004.

CHAPTER 13: VERDICTS

82: *"Friday. Yesterday and":* Carnet de guerre, September 8, 1944.

82: *"I should have lots":* Carnet de guerre, September 9, 1944.

82: *"Am tired":* Ibid.

82: *condemned to terms of life:* Record of Trial, *United States v. T/5 Freeman Davis, Pvt. Caeser Nathan, T/5 Charlie Roland, Pvt. Cornelius Harris, Pvt. Eli Chambers, Pfc. Spruil Carrol, T/5 S. T. Fellows, T/5 William Mitchell, Pvt. William Davis,* Trial convened at Morlaix, Finistère, September 20–21, 1944 (courtesy U.S. Army Clerk of Court).

82: *received the same sentence:* S. T. Fellows was sentenced to life at hard labor in a federal penitentiary. His mother was the cook for the family that owned the local newspaper. Both his parents and the white elite of his town in North Carolina petitioned the government for his release. He received a series of reduced sentences and was finally released in the mid-1950s. September 29, 2003, interview, Laurinburg, North Carolina, with Robert Dickson and his father, Paul Dickson, former owner of the *Hoke County News Journal,* whose letter of support accompanied the 1946 petition: "I have seen and studied the record and my doubt of his guilt has greatly increased, somewhat, admittedly, by my knowledge of his excellent character prior to his induction into the army. I strongly recommend a pardon for this boy and I am morally certain that he would return to his father's farm and make this county a good citizen as he was before the army got him." (*U.S. v. Davis, Nathan, et al.*).

82: *The VIII Corps court-martial:* Pvts. Searcy Howell and Clarence L. Franklin of Battery A, 696th Field Artillery Battalion, were condemned to death by the court; their sentence was confirmed by the Commanding General, ETO, who then commuted each to hard labor for life "owing to special circumstances."

83: *"The perpetrators":* U.S. v. Davis, Nathan, Roland, et al., Staff Judge Advocate Review, October 13, 1944, p. 6.

83: *"The court utterly failed":* Ibid.

83: *"Colère du Colonel S":* Carnet de guerre, September 19, 1944.

83: *still remembers the day:* Telephone interview with John Silbernagel, March 6, 2004, Middleton, Wisconsin.

83: *"I am completely at a loss":* National Archives, College Park, Record Group 338, World War II Operations Reports 1940–1948, VIII Corps, 250.4, Judge Advocate: Discipline, Memorandum from Troy H. Middleton, Major General, U.S. Army Commanding, to Claud T. Gunn, Colonel, FD, President of General Court-Martial, October 16, 1944. Middleton continues: "Unfortunately, the provisions of Article[s] of War 19 and 31 prevent me from ascertaining which of the members of the court were responsible for the adoption of life sentences rather than death sentences. However, those members who were guilty of such gross failure to vote for adequate punishments will themselves recognize the application of the foregoing reprimand."

84: *"the very polite Colonel":* OK, Joe, p. 74.

84: *France had just discontinued:* The precipitating event in this abolition was the 1938 execution of a serial killer named Edgar Weidmann, guillotined outside the prison at Versailles in full view of a passing tramway. The unexpected number of witnesses and an ensuing riot had created a scandal, and the state passed a law restricting executions to the interior of the prison. French military justice meted out its own death penalties; these were private. The forest outside the gigantic military fort at Vincennes, to the east of Paris, was the site of the firing squad that executed World War I spy Mata Hari in 1917. Five hundred and fifty men were executed by firing squad during World War I after trial by courts-martial for crimes ranging from desertion to treason. By the time James Hendricks went to the gallows, several notorious Nazi collaborators had already received the death sentences from specially designed liberation courts of Justice—what the French call "exceptional jurisdictions," neither military nor civil. These men, like the condemned traitors of the First World War, faced firing squads behind prison walls.

84: *for administering abortions:* See Miranda Pollard on the case of Marie Louise Giraud in Pollard, *Reign of Virtue,* op. cit.

84: *French criminal code:* Until 1978, rape was considered a misdemeanor (a *délit*) rather than a crime, and was adjudicated by a panel of judges in a lower court, the *chambre correctionnelle.* Since it has been reclassified as a crime, it has been adjudicated in the *Cour d'Assises,* a criminal court with a jury of citizens. See Georges Vigarello, *A History of Rape: Sexual Violence in France from the 16th to the 20th Century,* trans. Jean Birrell (Oxford: Blackwell/Polity Press, 2001).

85: *according to the Eighth Amendment:* See *Coker v. Georgia,* 433 U.S. 584 (1977), argued March 28, 1977. The state of Louisiana still adjudges death for the rape of children under twelve.

85: *a fine line:* Stuart Banner, *The Death Penalty* (Cambridge, Mass.: Harvard University Press, 2002), p. 229: "the line between a lynching and an official execution could be thin."

85: *sixteen men were executed:* Statistics from State of North Carolina, Department of Corrections, including the name, race, and date of each prisoner executed since 1910, are available on a website: http://www.doc.state.nc.us/DOP/deathpenalty.

85: *"the death penalty was a form":* Banner, op. cit., p. 320.

85: *was sentenced to hang:* Record of Trial, *United States v. Pvts. William E. Davis and J. C. Potts,* Trial convened at Morlaix, Finistère, September 23–24, 1944 (courtesy U.S. Army Clerk of Court).

85: *"You're doing a good":* Fonds Louis Guilloux, Bibliothèque municipale de Saint-Brieuc, LGO OK Joe 01.01.03c, p. 222.

86: *After the trial: U.S. v. Hendricks,* witness pay vouchers.

86: *had established claims commissions:* Gonzales, op. cit., see chapter 5, "The Special Foreign Claims Detachment," and chapter 12, "Judge Advocates as Claims Officers." Gonzales interviewed Lt. Lawrence Lougee, a claims officer stationed with the VIII Corps in Morlaix, France. Lougee wrote a comic short story based on his experience, about a brothel owner who wanted to be reimbursed for additions to her *maison close* after the Americans had declared it off limits (unpublished manuscripts, courtesy Robert Gonzales). See also December 27, 1944, letter from the Morlaix Claims Office to the regional prefecture, outlining the types of claims: "Claims by French civilians in the case of death will be taken into consideration by the Claims Office on the condition that the deaths do not result from combat activity by the American Army. These claims will be considered according to the rules of the U.S. Army and French law applicable in these cases." Archives départementales des Côtes d'Armor, series 5W, "Réclamations" (my translation).

86: *The Army paid:* Interview with Jacqueline Nicole, December 27, 2002, Saint-Thégonnec, France.

86: *"The peasants needed me":* Fonds Louis Guilloux, Bibliothèque municipale de Saint-Brieuc, LGO OK Joe 01.01.03c, 1966 draft, p. 238.

87: *"On August 16, 1944, around":* Archives de l'Ille-et-Vilaine, Rennes 43W218 Police et gendarmerie: Rapports quotidiens, report for August 18, 1944 (Fougères); Service Historique de la Gendarmerie Nationale, rapport du maréchal des logis-chef Brien, brigade de Louvigné-du-Désert, August 18, 1944, "Report of the murder of Monsieur Velé, farmer, committed by two American soldiers in the village of L'Epine in La Bazouges-du-Désert."

88: *That was the last that the Velé family heard:* Communication from Auguste Velé, the grandson of the Frenchman killed in Bazouges, March 29, 2004.

88: *In either scenario:* The Velé family never received a letter telling them that the soldiers were tried for the killing—the kind of formal letter of apology that Noémie and Jeannine Bignon received after James Hendricks was tried, convicted, and hanged in Plumaudan. The letter from Colonel Warden, VIII Corps Adjutant General, written on behalf of the Commanding General, notifies Madam Bignon of Hendricks's conviction and hanging, and concludes: "The Corps Commander desires to express his deepest regret that such heinous crimes should be committed by a member of his command against law abiding citizens of France. Further he wishes to express his great sympathy for you in respect of the untimely death of your husband" (December 12, 1944).

PART III: UNITED STATES VERSUS CAPTAIN GEORGE P. WHITTINGTON
CHAPTER 14: LESNEVEN

91: *the Hôtel de France:* Louis Le Guennec, *Le Finistère monumental—Brest et sa région* (Quimper: Les Amis de Louis Le Guennec, 1981), p. 378.

91: *Lesneven was declared:* U.S. v. Whittington, Inspector General's investigation, and Record of Trial, pp. 49, 57.

92: *The 5th Rangers, for whom:* See Jonathan Gawne, *Americans in Brittany*, p. 62, on the role of the 5th Rangers in the Battle of Brest. Henry S. Glassman, *"Lead the Way, Rangers": A History of the Fifth Ranger Battalion* (first printed in Germany, 1945; repr. Washington, D.C.: Ranger Associates, 1980), gives the number of 5th Ranger Battalion casualties on D-Day itself as 60, with an additional 70 deaths over the following five days.

92: *known as a goody-goody:* Interview with John Raaen, May 18, 2004, Winter Park, Florida.

92: *The liquor was in the cellar:* A photograph of the bar, with its empty shelves, is part of the Record of Trial, *U.S. v. Whittington.*

93: *In the skies overhead:* Jean-Yves Le Goff, ed., *Lesneven, destinées d'une capitale* (Lesneven: Musée du Léon-Lesneven, 1992), p. 287.

93: *a thick, sweet after-dinner drink:* Subsequent details have been gleaned from testimony by Sergeant d'Etamper (pp. 73–74, stipulated testimony), Lieutenant Zuccardy (pp. 48–60), Captain Runge (pp. 40–46), Yvonne Pichon (pp. 66–73), and Captain Whittington (pp. 76–85), *U.S. v. Whittington.*

94: *"I studied it":* U.S. v. Whittington, testimony of Lt. Charles Zuccardy, p. 51.

95: *It was as impressive a credential:* On the Special Air Service at the liberation, see Paul Golder's informative website: http://www.lerot.net.

95: *Capt. Jacques La Rus also from Military Intelligence:* testimony of Capt. Jacques La Rus (stipulated from pre-trial statement), *U.S. v. Whittington,* pp. 75–76.

CHAPTER 15: GEORGE WHITTINGTON

97: *It was a boy's dream:* Interview with Agnes Whittington, April 12, 2004, Henderson, Kentucky, and telephone interview with Susan Batterton, April 27, 2004, Hot Springs, Arkansas. Pictures of George and David Whittington as children on the New Mexico ranch are included in Susan Batterton's genealogical website:http://wolves.dsc.k12.ar.us/cyberace/sbgone/gen/fam1/whittington/whit.htm.

97: *He could have gone:* Interview with Agnes Whittington, April 12, 2004, Henderson, Kentucky.

97 *cut his high school education:* This according to Bill Sulli-

van, George Whittington's friend and attorney, in a speech at Whittington's memorial service in Henderson, Kentucky, June 23, 1996 (videocassette courtesy of Charles Whittington). Nonetheless, the school claimed him proudly. See "Military Heroes of New Mexico Military Institute," Lt. Col. Joseph D. Posz, U.S. Army (Ret.), NMMI class of 1955 (Roswell, N. Mex.: New Mexico Military Institute Alumni Association, 1994): "George Whittington came to NMMI in the fall of 1928 and graduated six years later on June 5, 1934. At NMMI he not only excelled as a writer for cadet publications but also showed great proficiency in boxing. . . . "

98: *In China he acquired:* Communication from Charles Whittington, May 29, 2004.

98: *They were fast:* Whittington's hands were so quick, his son remembers, he could still catch flies out of the air when he was in his seventies. Communication from Charles Whittington, May 12, 2004.

98: *They set up base:* Henry S. Glassman, *"Lead the Way, Rangers,"* op. cit.

98: *Schneider invited Whittington:* Interview with John Raaen, May 18, 2003, Winter Park, Florida; and Carl Weast, oral history transcript, n.d. (1988?), Peter Kalikow World War II Collection, National D-Day Museum Foundation, p. 3. John Raaen, who was a captain and battalion staff officer for the 5th and who trained with Whittington, remembered the incident. His feeling at the time was that Whittington had done the right thing, but he had done it the wrong way. Or at least, not the Army's way.

99: *"Whitt, that's what":* Communication from John Raaen, February 7, 2003.

99: *the beginning of northern France's liberation:* See Jonathan Gawne, *Spearheading D-Day* (Paris: Histoire et Collections, 1998).

100: *"a duck shoot":* Weast, Oral history transcript, p. 8. For an account of the near disaster at Omaha Beach, see Jean-Pierre Azéma, Robert O. Paxton, and Philippe Burrin, "La Bataille des plages," *6 Juin 1944* (Paris: Perrin/Le Mémorial de Caen, 2004), pp. 108–17.

100: *"George Whittington was a hell":* Weast, oral history transcript, p. 19.

100: *Whittington reminded him:* Whittington quoted by Weast, oral history transcript, pp. 18–19.

101: *"What does 'bitte' mean?":* Whittington told his son he didn't remember if the incident occurred, but that, in any case, neither side was taking prisoners that day. Correspondence from Charles Whittington, June 6, 2004.

101: *Some Rangers were bringing a German:* Interview with John Raaen, May 18, 2003, Winter Park, Florida. Thinking back on the incident, with his own experience as a general in Vietnam, Raaen tried to imagine Whittington's point of view: "You commanded the soldiers who tried to kill me, therefore I can kill you."

101: *"His peers thought":* Communication from John Raaen, December 4, 2004.

101: *killed twenty Canadian prisoners of war:* The Canadians have placed a monument on the site of the murders. Killing of prisoners on both sides is discussed by Paul Fussell in *The Boys' Crusade* (New York: Modern Library, 2003).

101: *The Army commemorated:* Gawne, *Spearheading D-Day,* pp. 212–13.

CHAPTER 16: THE INVESTIGATION

102: *After the events of August 22: U.S. v. Whittington,* 127th General Hospital, report filed September 1, 1944.

102: *"When the officer in question":* Thomas G. Petrich, undated pre-trial statement, *U.S. v. Whittington.*

103 *"I believe the man":* Pre-trial statement by Major Sullivan, Commanding Officer, 5th Rangers, *U.S. v. Whittington,* August 23, 1944.

103: *it was standard procedure:* On psychiatric evaluation for defendants in courts-martial, see chapter 10.

103: *The hospital commander: U.S. v. Whittington,* 127th General Hospital report filed September 1, 1944.

103: *the Frenchman's temporary duty:* Inspector General, Report of Investigation of Killing of Francis Morand, 4th French Parachutist Battalion, by Capt. George P. Whittington, 5th Ranger Battalion, August 27, 1944.

104: *and "retreat as far as": Manual for Courts-Martial,* p. 163. The Inspector General's report understood the Whittington situation as a brawl or sudden affray, which the manual defined as "a fight in a public place to the terror of the people, in which acts of violence occur or dangerous weapons are exhibited or threatened to be used." The report explained: "Captain Whittington's expressed excuse of self-defense does not fall within the limiting conditions imposed under discussion of Article of War 92, p. 163,

M.C.M., heading 'Without legal excuse,' in that he, if he believed himself to be in danger, did not 'retreat as far as he safely can.' On the other hand, he appears to 'have been the aggressor and intentionally provoked the difficulty,' in that he deliberately followed his victim, who had withdrawn to the outside of the building. This would indicate the presence of 'malice aforethought' within the provisions of the paragraph entitled 'malice aforethought,' p. 163, M.C.M."

104: *The Americans scaled:* Jonathan Gawne, *The Americans in Brittany,* pp. 138ff. After the evacuation of Brest, 3,000 citizens chose to remain; many perished in the bombings of the week of September 9. See *Le Finistère en guerre: 1940–1950* (Rennes: Editions Ouest France, 2004), p. 40.

104: *"The deepest silence":* OK, Joe, p. 95.

105: *Since the siege of Brest:* Gawne, *The Americans in Brittany,* p. 156.

105: *"I was with some officers":* Carnet de guerre, September 19, 1944.

105: Sebastopol Sketches: Leo Tolstoy, *Sebastopol Sketches* (1855–56) (New York: Penguin, 1986).

105: *was entirely pulverized:* Gawne, *The Americans in Brittany,* p. 156.

105: *to get ready for another trial:* Journey to Lesneven noted in Guilloux's Carnet de guerre, September 22, 1944.

106: *James Montgomery acted:* U.S. v. Whittington, p. 3.

106: *Whittington had the right:* Hendricks had also had this right; he chose Lt. Norman Porr, whose presence at the trial left no traces.

106: *"Dear David":* National Archives, College Park, Record Group 339, World War II Operations Reports 1940–1948, VIII Corps, file 250.4, Judge Advocate: Discipline: Courts-Martial, January 1944–November 1944. Memorandum from George P. Whittington to Maj. David B. Whittington, Subject: Request for Individual Counsel in General Court-Martial Trial.

107: *David Whittington:* Telephone interview with Susan Batterton, April 27, 2004, Hot Springs, Arkansas.

107: *his first court-martial:* Interview with James Craighill, February 19, 2004, Charlotte, North Carolina. On September 18, Craighill had drafted the first Staff Judge Advocate Review of *U.S. v. Hendricks.*

CHAPTER 17: THE CASE AGAINST GEORGE WHITTINGTON

108: *nothing indicated that Morand: U.S. v. Whittington,* Inspector General's pre-trial investigation, op. cit.

108: *a reputation for being trigger-happy:* Ibid., and interview with John Raaen, May 18, 2003, Winter Park, Florida.

110: *when he changed his name:* Morand told the story of his Austrian origins and career in the French Legion to Roger Schank (letter to the author, February 28, 2003) and Jean Poilvert (interview, Saint-Gilles-du-Méné, July 27, 2003). Schank was in the SAS training camp at Auchinleck, Scotland, with Morand; Poilvert knew him in the *maquis* in the summer of 1944.

110: *There were at least a hundred:* British National Archives, Foreign Office, London, 371 34737.

110: *Miranda de Ebro:* July 9, 2004, Communication from David Portier, author of a forthcoming book on the SAS, *Les Parachutistes SAS de la France Libre 1940–1945* (Grasse, France: David Portier, Edition d'auteur, 2004).

110: *join the 4th French Parabattalion:* Communication from David Portier, July 9, 2004.

110: *he would have had to endure:* On the process of interrogation of French refugees arriving in England from Spain, see British National Archives, Foreign Office, 371 34737. The British Intelligence Service set great stock in its strenuous interrogation of Free Frenchmen; the goal was to prevent spies from entering the Resistance. In 1943, the service faced a rush of volunteers who would have to endure excruciating waiting periods. Some of the Frenchmen were interrogated at the Royal Patriotic School. Morand may have gone through the Camberwell Centre, a former work camp that the War Office had transformed into a clearinghouse. A few of the men were so demoralized by the long wait that they resorted to hunger strikes in protest. British National Archives, Foreign Office 371 36093.

111: *the French Resistance was a heroic continuation:* Morand may have chosen his name only upon entering the SAS. The name "Francis Morand" appears neither in the archives of the French Legion, nor in the lists of French soldiers drafted in 1939, nor in the list of French prisoners of war, nor in the archives of the French resistance. Neither the British army nor the Royal Air Force can find his name in their records, despite the fact that the paybook found on Morand's body gave a matriculation number in the British army. Communication from Bernadette P. Hand,

British Army and Historical Disclosures, Army Personnel Centre, August 24, 2004; letter from Teresa Barnes, Royal Air Force Personnel Management Agency, October 12, 2004; and communication from Paule René-Bazin, Directeur, Ministère de la Défense et des anciennes combattants (France), September 14, 2004. On the influx of European Jews into the Legion during the 1930s, see Douglas Porch, *The French Foreign Legion* (New York: Harper-Collins, 1991), pp. 436, 443ff.

111: *Women were drawn:* Letter from Roger Schank to the author, February 28, 2003.

111: *magic places known in Arthurian legend:* "All of France resembled Brocéliande," wrote the great Resistance poet Louis Aragon in 1942. After his friend Georges Politzer was assassinated by the Gestapo, Aragon composed a poem in which he imagined his entire nation under the evil spell of "the witches of Vichy and the dragons of Germany." See Louis Aragon, "De l'exactitude historique en poésie," *Poésie 45* (Paris: Seghers, 1945). The forests that served as bases for the French Resistance in Brittany had long been considered magic places by the Breton people. Still today, the lush quality of the underbrush, the fog, and the light make them seem so. In this beautifully eerie landscape, the SAS, with its sophisticated training at the hands of the British army, helped transform the scrappy French *maquis* into the *Forces Françaises de l'Intérieur* (FFI), who would participate in the liberation of Brittany throughout the month of August. After the raid on the Samwest base in Duault Forest, Morand and his paratrooper comrades trained their fellow Frenchmen in the Boquen and Hardouinais Forests; their work included armed combat with Nazi collaborators. On Morand's unit, see "Operations of the 4th French Parabattalion," Papers of Sir Roderick William McLeod, Liddell Hart Centre for Military Archives, Kings College London. The legendary "Brocéliande" is based on a real place, the Paimpont Forest, due south of Dinan.

111: *two of Morand's fellow paratroopers died:* On July 27, two of the men in Morand's group went out on a mission. Their car broke down on the road to Dinan and they were stopped by a German patrol. The Germans noticed that one of the Frenchmen had on Nazi boots. They figured, correctly, that he was a *maquisard*, wearing the boots of a Nazi he had executed. So they took both men to Gestapo headquarters in Dinan for interrogation. One of them broke down under torture and revealed the whereabouts of the rest of their group, who were hiding on a farm in Seilla, near Saint-Gilles-du-Méné.

At dawn on July 28, the Germans launched a surprise attack on Seilla. After twenty minutes of combat, they killed all the *maquis* and paratroopers in the house, including Serville and Coquette from Morand's SAS stick, then set the house on fire. The event lives on in the memory of Saint-Gilles, where on the final Sunday of every July, an outdoor mass is held in homage to those Resistance fighters. "Le drame du 28 juillet," a detailed account of the Seilla massacre, including testimony by Jean Poilvert, was published by the mayor's office of Saint-Gilles-du-Méné in the *Saint-Gilleois* (2003), pp. 13–18. Jean Poilvert, interviewed on July 27, 2003, at the Seilla commemoration, recalled with a smile that Morand was with a woman in town when the farm was attacked. Seduction had saved his life that night.

112: *the battle to take Brest:* Morand's papers note that he was assigned as a French liaison to the 50th Armored Infantry Battalion of the Sixth Armored Division. *U.S. v. Whittington,* information on Francis Morand.

112: *He moved to dismiss: U.S. v. Whittington,* pp. 5–7.

112: *while reassuring Greene: U.S. v. Whittington,* p. 7.

113: *Morand's body had been whisked:* After St. James became a permanent American cemetery for World War II dead, Morand's body was moved to the civil cemetery of the town of Saint-James, along with the remains of seventeen Free French fighters killed during the summer of 1944. All the tombs are marked with white metal crosses of Lorraine, symbols of the Resistance, and marble plaques provided by the 2ème Division Blindée of the French army. At the foot of Morand's cross of Lorraine, someone has placed a ceramic flower assortment with a single word on it: "regrets."

113: *It looked as though he hadn't fired:* The details that follow are culled from *U.S. v. Whittington,* testimony of Private Petrone (pp. 8–27), Corporal Cline (pp. 27–31), Captain Schemering (pp. 31–39), and Lieutenant Lutz (pp. 39–40).

114: *He cross-examined an MP officer:* After several exchanges of bickering between prosecution and defense about the relevancy of the black book, Sedillo ruled that Schemering could testify to its contents only if he could identify it. He couldn't.

114: *"If the court please": U.S. v. Whittington,* p. 34.

114: *Craighill called: U.S. v. Whittington,* testimony of Captain Runge, pp. 40–46.

115: *"I don't deny": U.S. v. Whittington,* p. 47.

116: *Morand's nervous behavior: U.S. v. Whittington,* testimony of Lt. Charles Zuccardy, pp. 48–60.

116: *Any conversation that took place:* Sedillo invoked the legal doctrine known as *res gestae,* by which evidence can be introduced when it contributes to the knowledge of events leading up to a crime. Hearsay evidence is often excluded because its validity can't be measured by the jurors; *res gestae* allows evidence to be admitted if it appears reliable for some additional reasons.

116: *True to Joe Greene's tactic:* James Craighill, interviewed on February 19, 2004, in Charlotte, North Carolina, had vivid memories of the linguistic mysteries presented in the Whittington trial.

117: *a bottle of perfume:* In the published novel, Lieutenant Stone has requested the perfume, *OK, Joe* (p. 85); in earlier drafts, Lieutenant Colonel Marquez, Sedillo's fictional counterpart, makes the request. Fonds Louis Guilloux, Bibliothèque municipale de Saint-Brieuc, LGO 01.02.01c, p. 101.

117: *"Seeing me arrive": OK, Joe,* p. 85.

118: *"I could use":* Fonds Louis Guilloux, Bibliothèque municipale de Saint-Brieuc, LGO OK Joe 02.02.01, section entitled "Américains."

CHAPTER 18: GEORGE WHITTINGTON'S TESTIMONY

119: *"You're losing your boundaries":* Carnet de guerre, last undated entry, five pages after the last dated entry of September 22, 1944: "tu perds ton autonomie, tu perds tes frontières." The word *frontières* in French refers to national borders even more than to personal boundaries; Guilloux is feeling the loss of his national identity.

120: *On the left shoulder:* Communication from John Raaen, June 8, 2004.

120: *The military situation for his 5th Rangers: U.S. v. Whittington,* p. 65.

120: *uneven responses of commanding officers:* In chapter 19 (Gonzales, op. cit.), Gonzales names "unlawful command influence" and "harsh and inconsistent court-martial sentences" as the major problems stemming from the Articles of War system of military justice in place during World War II: "In the aftermath of the war, stories of misuse of command authority, unfairness in punishments, and inadequate protection of a soldier's basic rights before a court-martial, fueled a movement by veterans and civic organizations alike to eliminate these deficiencies." The resulting reform was new Articles of War in 1948, followed by a Uniform Code of Military Justice in 1950.

120: *Two other important witnesses:* It wasn't unusual for the court to ask for "stipulated" testimony based on pre-trial statements, when witnesses were no longer in the area or unavailable due to other duties, such as combat. Both defense counsel and trial judge advocate (prosecutor) had to agree on any given stipulation.

121: *a rosy-faced country:* OK, Joe, p. 89.

121: *Yvonne was at the heart of the altercation:* Interview with Claude Le Menn, adjunct to the mayor of Lesneven, December 8, 2003.

121: "Il m'a regardée": *U.S. v. Whittington,* testimony of Yvonne Pichon, pp. 66–73.

121: *Her answer was incriminating:* Yvonne Pichon's critical remark was odd, given how many inhabitants of Lesneven in the 1940s, native Breton speakers who learned French only in school, would also have searched for words in French. Communication from Paol Keineg, November 30, 2004.

122: *Nothing was gained or lost:* U.S. v. Whittington, stipulated testimony of Sergeant d'Etamper and Captain La Rus, pp. 73–76.

122: *Finally, at 10:45 A.M.:* The details and dialogue that follow are from *U.S. v. Whittington,* testimony of Capt. George Whittington, pp. 76–85.

122: *Hendricks's gaze:* Quoted on text page 79.

123: *remembers the lawyer agonizing:* John Silbernagel, telephone interview, March 6, 2004, Middleton, Wisconsin.

123: *Whittington loved to play with languages:* This information on Whittington's knowledge of Spanish comes from interviews with his widow, not from the court-martial transcript.

124: "I asked him what": *U.S. v. Whittington,* p. 77.

124: *But no one in the court:* Sedillo's 1939 short story, "Gentleman of Río en medio," inspired by his law practice in Santa Fe, is narrated by a lawyer who must negotiate a land deal in Spanish.

124: *The Condor Legion:* See Georges Roux, *La Guerre d'Espagne* (Paris: Fayard, 1963). The Condor Legion consisted of a dozen air squadrons; Hitler sent fewer than five or six thousand men on the ground, and no organized ground divisions.

125: "I had heard of Germans": *U.S. v. Whittington,* p. 78.

125: *"He did not make":* U.S. v. Whittington, p. 80.

126: *"Because I ducked":* U.S. v. Whittington, p. 82.

126: *"The witness is certainly":* U.S. v. Whittington, p. 85.

127: *"In other words":* U.S. v. Whittington, p. 85.

127: *Paul Jacopin from the local:* U.S. v. Whittington, testimony of Paul Jacopin, pp. 85–89.

128: *"His identity may":* U.S. v. Whittington, p. 88.

CHAPTER 19: THE AFTERMATH

130: *At 11:30 A.M. on September 26:* U.S. v. Whittington, p. 89.

130: *threw a party:* Interview with Eleanor Lewis McKechnie, May 17, 2003, Winter Park, Florida, evoking Don Lewis's memories of the Whittington trial and its aftermath.

130: *The gift was given:* Joseph Greene to Louis Guilloux, October 28, 1944, Fonds Louis Guilloux, Bibliothèque municipale de Saint-Brieuc, LGC 5.1.8, Letters in English; see text pages 140–41.

130: *William Runge was fined:* Conmunication from John Raaen, July 13, 2004: "A captain made $220 a month, so a $50 penalty was nearly 25 percent of Runge's monthly pay. Rather severe in the final analysis."

130: *In his letter of reprimand:* National Archives, College Park, Record Group 338, World War II Operations Reports 1940–1948, VIII Corps, 250 series: Discipline. Memorandum from Maj. Gen. Troy Middleton to Lt. William Runge (no date): "I hereby severely reprimand you for your offense. Your behavior shows that you lack the conscious appreciation of the responsibilities of your rank and raises grave doubts as to your qualifications as an officer and your usefulness to the Army. Absence of an officer from his unit without authority and also involving violation of standing orders all occurring in the combat zone, would amply justify a court-martial sentence of dismissal from the service were such offenses referred for trial. Were it not for the fact that this is your first offense and that you have heretofore a good record, I would be inclined to deal more severely with you. Leniency is shown because it is hoped that you will profit by this experience and so conduct yourself in the future as to merit the confidence that has been placed in you."

131: *Whittington was recovering:* U.S. v. Whittington, Receipt for record of trial, delivered at Hoscheiderhof, Luxembourg, January 27, 1945.

131: *for his valor at the Bulge:* Interview with Agnes Whittington, April 12, 2004, Henderson, Kentucky. See also: National Archives, College Park, Record Group 407, WWII Operations Reports, Headquarters, U.S. Forces, European Theater, General Order No. 217, July 26, 1946; Silver Star Medal Citation, Captain George P. Whittington, Company G, 10th Infantry Regiment, for gallantry in action on January 17, 1945.

131: *Craighill had fulfilled:* William S. Scully to Stanley W. Jones, JAGD, September 27, 1944 (courtesy James Craighill). "He reflects excellent training and a well grounded professional background. I was particularly impressed by his reviews of two complicated cases which were excellently done. Further he performed his duties as trial judge advocate in the Whittington case in an equally efficient and intelligent manner."

131: *his first trial:* Interview with James Craighill, February 19, 2004, Charlotte, North Carolina.

131: *He rose in the Judge Advocate office:* John Marshall Law School alumni directories; and communication from Jane Fogarty Nesbit, October 6, 2004.

132: *"The erroneous construction":* U.S. v. Whittington, Review of Staff Judge Advocate, October 31, 1944, p. 3.

132: *"who acted as a kind of escort":* OK, Joe, p. 101.

CHAPTER 20: WHITTINGTON'S PEACE

133: *Beetle Bailey:* Interview with Agnes Whittington, April 12, 2004, Henderson, Kentucky.

133: *published an essay:* George Whittington, "The Miracle of Marching Fire," *The Infantry Journal* 65 (September 1949), pp. 6–7.

133: *the bulk of his oil-rich estate:* Henderson welcomed Whittington with a newspaper profile, "Meet Charlie Burbank's Nephew and Heir: A Tale of Presses, Philosophies, Ribbons, Rifles," *The Henderson Gleaner,* February 1, 1953.

134: *Whittington wasn't implicated:* Whittington was interviewed about the situation on the Costa Rica–Nicaraguan border in *The Henderson Gleaner,* December 23, 1984 ("They've shot paradise all to hell").

134: *white parents in Henderson:* On the walkout, see *The Washington Post,* September 25, 1956.

134: *walked his son Charles:* Interview with Agnes Whittington, April 12, 2004, Henderson, Kentucky, and telephone interview with Charles Whittington, April 15, 2004.

134: *he gave a speech:* Interview with Roy Pullam, April 10, 2004, Henderson, Kentucky. See also *The Henderson Gleaner,* October 25, 1985.

134: *"They are a radical right religion":* Frank Boyett, "Long-time Local GOP Couple Change Their Party Affiliation," *The Henderson Gleaner,* September 1, 1992.

134: *"Everyone in Henderson":* Interview with Roy Pullam, April 10, 2004, Henderson, Kentucky.

134: *a Papa Hemingway:* Video interview, Bonnet Productions, Henderson High School, cassette (courtesy Roy Pullam, n.d.).

134: *He lived in a grand:* Details are taken from a tour of the house on April 12, 2004 (courtesy Agnes Whittington).

135: *"There are two kinds of stories":* Video interview, Bonnet Productions.

135: *"I don't talk":* Interview with Roy Pullam, April 10, 2004, Henderson, Kentucky.

135: *He knew his war literature:* Communication from Charles Whittington, June 6, 2004.

135: *"You tremble":* Agnes Whittington remembers the line as one of his favorites (interview, April 12, 2004, Henderson, Kentucky). In George Whittington's generation, Turenne's phrase was familiar to every French schoolchild: "Quelquefois, pendant une bataille, il [Turenne] ne pouvait s'empêcher de trembler . . . alors il parlait à son corps comme on parle à un serviteur. Il lui disait: 'Tu trembles, carcasse, mais si tu savais où je vais te mener tout à l'heure, tu tremblerais bien d'avantage.'" Lavisse, *Histoire de France, Cours moyen* (Paris: A. Colin, 1912), p. 107.

136: *"A civic leader":* *Congressional Record,* proceedings and debates of the 104th Congress, 2nd sess., vol. 142, Washington, D.C., Friday, March 15, 1996, no. 36, Senate Tribute to George Whittington.

PART IV: HISTORY AND MEMORY
CHAPTER 21: DEPARTURE

139: *For three days:* Details of the VIII Corps departure from Bill Cormier, War Diary, pp. 74–75.

139: *"Stories of houses":* OK, Joe, p. 116.

140: *Colonel Scully gave him:* Guilloux experimented with the story of his interview with the Army doctor in an unpublished version of the last chapter of *OK, Joe,* Fonds Louis Guilloux, Bibliothèque municipale de Saint-Brieuc, LGO OK, Joe, 02.01.01, "OK, Joe, dernier chapitre, première manière," p. 16. Scully's letter to Guilloux has been preserved in the writer's archives, LGPP 01.01.017, Dossier papiers personnels: certificats de l'armée américaine, Scully, William:

> This is to certify that Louis-François-Marie Guilloux has recently been a civilian employee of Headquarters VIII Corps APO 308 U.S. Army as interpreter-translator. His home is in Saint-Brieuc, Côtes-du-Nord, France, and he started to accompany such headquarters from Morlaix, Finistère, France, on a change of station. At Saint-Quentin he became ill and it is both his opinion and that of the undersigned that he cannot withstand the rigors of field service. Therefore, he has left the employ of the U.S. voluntarily and is en route to his home at Saint-Brieuc. He is entitled to pay from 16 September to 30 September 1944, at 2400 francs per month (i.e., 80 francs per day)—Mr. Guilloux is entitled to transportation from St. Quentin to his home at St. Brieuc at U.S. expense and to necessary subsistence at Government expense for such journey.
>
> —I request all U.S. military authorities to assist Mr. Guilloux to obtain necessary transportation and subsistence—including quarters if necessary. He has left Government employ in good standing and has rendered both loyal and highly valuable service in all respects.
>
> —William S. Scully, Colonel, JAGD, Hq VIII Corps APO 308, U.S. Army

140: *He was still a hundred miles: Carnets II*, pp. 9–12.

140: *"What I felt":* Ibid., p. 11.

140: *"I am still hanging them":* Fonds Louis Guilloux, Bibliothèque municipale de Saint-Brieuc, LGC 5.1.8. Letters in English, typed letter from Lt. Greene, October 28, 1944.

141: *It had a beautiful tone:* Jonathan Bagg of the Ciompi Quartet calls Paul Mangenot (1862–1942) an excellent craftsman, who produced a large number of instruments and sold them for less money than the top-level violin makers. It was standard practice to put a "Stradivarius" label on violins, with the name of the actual craftsman underneath. Today, Mangenot violins, described in advertisements as copies of the Stradivarius, sell for between 1,500 and 1,800 euros.

141: *And Bill Cormier:* Fonds Louis Guilloux, Bibliothèque municipale de Saint-Brieuc, LGC 5.1.8., Letters in English, typed letter from Samuel Putnam, November 4, 1944.

141: *"It seems I was very badly off":* Carnets II, p. 13.

141: *"May 1945":* Carnets II, pp. 13–14.

141: *Cormier received:* Bill Cormier, War Diary, p. 105.

142: *an American cigarette:* For a history of these camps, see
Jean-Claude Marquis, Valérie Herson, and Jean-Louis Jourdainne,
*Les Camps cigarette: Les Américains en Haute Normandie à la
Libération* (Rouen: Editions Médianes, 1994). By 1945, 100,000
men had passed through the cigarette camps. The book includes
photos of the graffiti carved by the GIs in the trees near the camp,
as well as an analysis by Jean-Claude Marquis of the changing
image of the American soldiers in Normandy.

142: *Each young woman received:* Elizabeth Coquart, *La France
des GIs: histoire d'un amour déçu.* (Paris: Albin Michel, 2003),
p. 176. Hilary Kaiser, *Des amour de GI's: les petites fiancées du dé-
barquement* (Paris: Tallendier, 2004), estimates 6,000 as a total
for the number of war brides.

142: *On the SS* Bienville: Bill Cormier, War Diary, p. 119.

CHAPTER 22: *OK, JOE*

143: *Today, an extensive body of literature:* The best starting place is
still Ulysses Lee, *The Employment of Negro Troops*; and Jean Byers, "A
Study of the Negro in Military Service: Report to the NAACP," op. cit.

144: *"This morning's papers":* Carnets II, p. 401.

145: *In his diaries:* Ibid., p. 468. On police violence in May '68,
see Kristin Ross, *May '68 and Its Afterlives* (Chicago: University of
Chicago Press, 2002), pp. 27ff.

145: *What he wanted to convey:* "Louis Guilloux s'explique," *Lire
Magazine* (nos. 11 and 12, double issue, summer 1976), interview
by Gilles Lapouge, pp. 10–26.

146: *In the very last draft:* Fonds Louis Guilloux, Bibliothèque
municipale de Saint-Brieuc. In a manuscript dated 1968 (LGO
01.01.03d), he's still using the phrase "All right" instead of "OK."
In LGO 01.01.06 (incomplete manuscript on school notepaper),
he writes on the cover a new idea for a title: "O.K. Joe! Why not?"

146: *three men emerging:* See text pages 100–101.

146: *"the idol":* OK, Joe, pp. 199, 49, and 101.

147: *One reviewer compared:* Paul Morelle in *Le Monde,* July 30,
1976, p. 10.

147: *"But why always blacks"*: OK, Joe, p. 75.

147: *unusually forthcoming:* Lapouge interview, p. 17 and *L'Express*, June 21, 1976, p. 26.

CHAPTER 23: THE QUESTION

149: *Before the trials themselves:* On the issue of command discretion in a postwar context, see the analysis of Elizabeth Hillman in her forthcoming *Defending America: Military Culture and the Cold War Court-Martial* (Princeton, N.J.: Princeton University Press, 2005), chapter 5, "Commanding Discretion: Race, Sex, and Military Crime."

149: *Cases that should have been:* Interviews with French civilians, French police reports, and U.S. military police reports of arrests, never taken to the next level, would be the place to start. See, e.g., the case of the shooting of Auguste Velé by white officers, pp. 88–87. Cases of white officers acquitted in courts-martial are also difficult to locate, since trial transcripts can only be requested from the U.S. Army Clerk of Court by the name of the defendant.

149: *"the weak link"*: Gonzales, op cit., chapter 19.

149: *The Army was the first to admit:* See the discussion of leniency of courts-martial toward officers in the study prepared by the Judge Advocate Section, General Board of the United States Forces, European Theater: "Military Justice Administration in Theater of Operations," National Archives, College Park, Record Group 319, USFET monograph, file 250/1 (1946–48), Study no. 83 (1945), pp. 37–38. For a study of officer privilege in the postwar era courts-martial, see Hillman's forthcoming *Defending America: Military Culture and the Cold War Court-Martial,* chapter 6, "'Gentlemen Under all Conditions': Officers on Trial."

150: *"They were going to a theater"*: Thomas Russell Jones, "J'étais un officier noir dans l'armée américaine pendant la Deuxième Guerre mondiale," interview with Claude Collin, *Guerres mondiales et conflits contemporains: Revue d'histoire,* 204 (December 2001), pp. 141–48. For a portrait of Thomas Russell Jones, see Claude Collin's memoir, *Mon Amérique à moi* (Paris: L'Harmattan, 2002), pp. 128–37. Jones, op. cit., and letter to the author, September 9, 2002.

CHAPTER 24: AFTER THE LIBERATION

151: *a memo entitled:* National Archives, College Park, Record

Group 94 World War II Operations Reports 1940–1948, file 330-1.2. 8/1/44–9/30/44, box 8733. Memorandum from Lt. Col. M. Campbell, Civil Affairs, 30th Infantry Division, entitled "Analysis of Civilian Attitude."

151: *An effort by the United States and Great Britain:* On Allied plans to establish a military government in France, see, from the French perspective, Charles-Louis Foulon, *Le Pouvoir en province à la libération,* and François Bédarida, "Les Alliés et le pouvoir," in *Les Pouvoirs en France à la libération,* eds. P. Buton and J. M. Guillon (Paris: Belin, 1994), pp. 60–76. From the American perspective, see Harry L. Coles, *Civil Affairs: Soldiers Become Governors* (Washington, D.C.: Office of the Chief of Military History, Department of the Army, 1964), and Merritt Y. Hughes, "Civil Affairs in France," in Carl J. Friedrich et al., *American Experiences in Military Government in World War II* (New York: Rinehart & Co., 1948), chapter VII, pp. 148–68. See also the diary of a Civil Affairs Division officer in Normandy: Maj. Gen. John J. Maginnis, *Military Government Journal: Normandy to Berlin,* ed. Robert A. Hart (Amherst, MA: University of Massachusetts Press, 1971).

151: *The Americans were meddling:* Archives Nationales, Paris, Relations avec les Autorités Alliées: Rapports des Commissaires Régionaux; F1a 3304–F1a 3308: Diverse reports and memos for the period October 1944–September 1945.

152: *French casualties from the Liberation itself:* See Azéma, Paxton, and Burrin, op. cit., p. 134.

152: *45,000 houses were in ruins: Histoire de la Bretagne,* ed. Jean Delumeau (Toulouse: Privat, 1969), pp. 503–06.

152: *carried out thirty-one additional:* The figures are from Christian Bougeard, "L'Épuration: 587 exécutions en Bretagne," *La Bretagne Libérée* (Rennes: Le Télégramme, 2004), p. 106. On the purge of collaborators in Brittany, see Capdevila, op. cit., pp. 197–218.

153: *FFI escorts, some twenty thousand strong:* Azéma, Paxton, and Burrin, op. cit., p. 165.

153: *why the Americans threw away:* See Harold Callender's November 5, 1944, article for the *New York Times.* "Transition for France Is a Painful Process: Her People Believe That Allies Do Not Appreciate Extent of Her Suffering" offers a summary of French attitudes and is quoted approvingly in a French government report on relations with the Allies (Archives Nationales, F1a 3304,

November 14, 1944, Ministère de l'Intérieur, service des relations interalliées, report on the American press). On American food habits from the point of view of an undernourished Frenchman, see Guilloux's descriptions in *OK, Joe,* esp. pp. 58–59: "As I left I passed the kitchens and saw heaps of food, especially pastries, which the flies and yellow jackets were assailing, and I thought it was leftovers about to be thrown away. I asked a passerby if all that was really going into the trash? He burst out laughing. Of course it was all going to be thrown away. Leftovers? No. Surplus. It was the same every day. I was reluctant to tell him that it was very regrettable, there was enough there to feed at least twenty poor families. I told him anyway, and he started to laugh again. 'That may be,' he answered. But what I was asking for was against regulations. And what about sanitary precautions?"

153: *"At least the Germans were well behaved":* See, e.g., Archives Nationales, F1a 3304, letter from the Regional Commissioner of the Republic in Rouen to the Minister of War, undated, quoting an article in the *Journal de Cherbourg*: "In the regions occupied by the Americans, the women no longer dare milk their cows without being accompanied by a man. . . . Many times, I've been surprised to hear people say, 'At least the Germans were well behaved.' The American authorities have declared houses of prostitution off limits. If the Americans cannot import American women to satisfy the needs of their men, may they at least respect French women" (my translation).

153: *the Waffen SS shot:* On the massacre at Oradour and the place of the Oradour tragedy in French national consciousness, see Sarah Farmer, *Martyred Village: Commemorating the 1944 Massacre at Oradour-sur-Glane* (Berkeley: University of California Press, 1999). On the hanging of ninety-seven Resistance fighters on the streets of Tulle, see Adam Nossiter, *The Algeria Hotel: France, Memory and the Second World War* (New York: Houghton Mifflin, 2001).

154: *Once the soldiers reached Germany:* See J. Robert Lilly, *La Face cachée des GI's,* op. cit.

154: *Although the number of rapes:* The History Branch office of the Judge Advocate General with the United States Forces European Theater (July 18, 1942 through November 1, 1945) reports 904 soldiers charged with rape and 461 condemned on rape charges. Reported cases do not correspond to actual cases. In his study of sexual criminality in World War II, Lilly, op. cit., p. 40, estimates that there may have been as many as 17,000 GI rapes in the European Theater; he bases his figure on the theory that only 5 percent of rapes were reported. It's extremely difficult to extrapolate from reported rapes or rape convictions to actual incidents; Lilly's figure of 5 percent is often cited, while other analysts estimate that approximately 50 percent of actual rapes are reported. Morris, op. cit., emphasizes a crucial difference between rape cases that come to trial in courts-martial and in civilian courts. In the case of a rape committed by a soldier in Europe during World War II, it was the commanding officer, not the victim, who brought charges—a situation that would make unreported rapes more likely.

154: *German, Soviet, and French rapes:* Fabrice Virgili's preface to Lilly, op. cit., pp. 9–49, gives a theoretical overview and review of the literature on war and rape in the World War II era. On the punishment of ordinary crimes committed by Wehrmacht soldiers, see Birgit Beck, "Rape: The Military Trials of Sexual Crimes Committed by Soldiers in the Wehrmacht, 1938–1944," in Karen Hagemann and Stefanie Schüler Springorum, eds., *Home/Front: The Military, War and Gender in Twentieth-Century Germany* (New York and Oxford: Berg Publishers, 2002), pp. 255–73. Manfred Messerschmidt and Fritz Wöllner, *Die Wehrmachtjustiz in Dienste des Nationalsozialismus: Zerstörung einer Legende* (Baden-Baden: Nomos Verlagsgesellschaft, 1987), estimate that some 21,000 Wehrmacht soldiers were executed for desertion, most of them in the final months of the war, but figures on punishments for rapes and murders committed by Nazi soldiers are not available. On crimes committed by Soviet troops, see Norman Naimark, *The Russians in Germany: A History of the Soviet Zone of Occupation, 1945–1949* (Cambridge, MA: Harvard University Press, 1995), pp. 74ff. On the French side, in an infamous episode of liberation history, Moroccan and Algerian infantrymen in the French army committed hundreds of rapes in Tuscany in 1943–44. The Italian government later awarded pensions to the victims of these crimes (Lilly, op. cit., p. 14); rapes of German women by French soldiers in Stuttgart are reported by Christophe Notin in his history of the French zone of occupation in Germany: *Les Vaincus seront les vainqueurs* (Paris: Perrin, 2004), pp. 267ff, 369ff. What is missing from the existing literature is any clear sense of how the various national armies punished such crimes.

154: *After the war, the Vanderbilt Commission:* See Office of the

Judge Advocate General, "History of the Judge Advocate General's Office in the European Theater," 18 July 1942–1 November 1945, p. 248, and "The Military Offender in the Theater of Operations," Study no. 84, p. 21: "The reluctance of a court-martial to convict an American soldier for the rape of a foreign woman which was unaccompanied by brutality and violence is said to be the direct result of the inability to impose moderate punishment." For a summary of the Vanderbilt Commission's recommendations and subsequent reforms, see Gonzales, op. cit., chapter 17, "The Revision of the Articles of War."

155: *The Army has not executed:* Private John A. Bennett was hanged for rape and attempted murder of an eleven-year-old Austrian girl in 1961. As of 2004, seven service members sat on military death row (five of them African American men). On the military death penalty, see Dwight H. Sullivan, "The Last Line of Defense: Federal Habeas Review of Military Death Penalty Cases," *Military Law Review,* vol. 144 (Spring 1994), pp. 1–76 and "A Matter of Life and Death: Examining the Military Death Penalty's Fairness," *The Federal Lawyer,* vol. 45, no. 5, pp. 38–44.

155: *"because many soldiers":* Office of the Judge Advocate General, "History of the Judge Advocate General's Office in the European Theater," p. 241, quoted in Morris, op. cit., p. 667.

155: *the need for recreational sex:* "The Military Offender in the Theater of Operations," Chief Military History, file 250/2, study no. 84, June 17, 1945, p. 13.

155: *"successfully used by the troops":* Ibid., p. 8.

156: *"Negro Troops were responsible":* Ibid., p. 26.

156: *A series of articles:* Grant Reynolds, "What the Negro Soldier Thinks About This War," *The Crisis,* vol. 51, no. 9 (Sept. 1944), pp. 289–91; no. 10 (Oct. 1944), pp. 316–18; no. 11 (Nov. 1944), pp. 352–357.

157: *The heroism of the service units:* Jean Byers, "A Study of the Negro in Military Service, Report to the NAACP," op. cit. See chapter V, "Non-Combattant Troops": "The European battle of supply was largely won by Negro skills and Negro strength." Byers's report singled out the record of truck drivers in what was known as the Red Ball Express, "unequalled in military trucking history" (p. 106).

157: *From that emergency:* On black combat units in World War II, see Lee, op. cit, pp. 644–87, and Gail Buckley, *American Patri-*

ots (New York: Random House, 2001). Kareem Abdul-Jabbar and Anthony Walton's *Brothers in Arms: The Epic Story of the 761st Tank Battalion, World War II's Forgotten Heroes* (New York: Broadway Books, 2004) gives a vivid narrative history of the first black armored tank battalion called to fight in the Battle of the Bulge.

157: *the influence of strong:* See Richard Dalfiume, *Desegregation of the U.S. Armed Forces: Fighting on Two Fronts* (Columbia, Mo.: University of Missouri Press, 1969); and Bernard C. Nalty, *Strength for the Fight: A History of Black Americans in the Military* (New York: Free Press, 1986).

157: *Today's volunteer Army:* For the overall percentage of blacks in the military, see Sidney Freedberg, Jr., and Peter H. Stone, "The Price," *National Journal*, vol. 36, no. 22, May 29, 2004, pp. 1,688–93. The black officers figure of 7,469 was given for the Army in August 2004; it includes active duty officers, warrant officers, Army Guard and Army Reserve officers, out of a total officer strength of 80,835—in other words, 9.2 percent (courtesy Samantha Walker, Department of Defense Manpower Department). Progress has been slow: in 1962, black officers represented only 1.6 percent of the total armed forces; by 1971, that percentage had risen only to 2.3 percent. See Hillman, "Commanding Discretion: Race, Sex, and Military Crime," in *Defending America; Military Culture and the Cold War Court-Martial,* op. cit.

157: *Beginning with the war in Vietnam:* Secretary of Defense website, "Active Military Deaths/race-ethnicity summary" (as of March 15, 2003). The exact figure, including Vietnam, is 13,777. African American casualty statistics for World War II are not available. The total number of active duty military deaths of all races/ethnicities, male and female, including Vietnam, was 92,980 in March 2003.

EPILOGUE
CHAPTER 25: A VISIT TO PLUMAUDAN
163: *"a handsome country girl":* OK, Joe, p. 4.

165: *When I returned:* Interview with Jeannine Bignon, June 30, 2003, Plumaudan, France.

CHAPTER 26: SOLDIER TROUBLE
166: *I went to the two:* I'm grateful to Professor Maurice Wallace, who advised me that if I wanted to learn about the African American

community in any southern town, I needed to talk to funeral home directors. More than preachers, they have a long-standing relationship with the community and know the family stories.

169: *The letter that followed:* Only the in-house documents specified that Hendricks had been a General Prisoner and that death occurred by "judicial asphyxia (execution by hanging)" at Plumaudan. James Hendricks, 201 Personnel File (courtesy Army Personnel Records Center, St. Louis, Missouri).

170: *The Army responded:* Letter from Joseph Hendricks, Orange, New Jersey, to Adjutant General's Office, Washington, D.C. (n.d.), received March 13, 1947 (James Hendricks, 201 Personnel file, op. cit.).

170: *the NAACP was swamped:* NAACP microfilm, part 9, "Discrimination in the U.S. Armed Forces 1918–1955," series B, Armed Forces Legal Affairs.

171: *"It was old KKK procedure":* Emmett Bailey, telephone interview, October 22, 2003, Henderson, North Carolina. Bailey served as a topographical draftsman in two different Graves Registration companies.

CHAPTER 27: A RESTING PLACE FOR JAMES HENDRICKS

172: *James Hendricks's body had been moved:* Disinterment Directive, James E. Hendricks, Individual Deceased Personnel File, Department of the Army.

172: *Ninety-six soldiers are buried:* Two of the graves are empty: Miranda and Slovik were repatriated by request of their families.

172: *website called:* See http://members.iinet.net.au/rgduncan/Facts-2.html. In November 2004, the entry on Plot E in George Duncan's site on "Historical Facts of the Second World War" was no longer available on the Web.

172: *It got some publicity in 1987:* Larry D. Hatfield, "Executed Deserter Now Home," *San Francisco Examiner,* July 11, 1987.

173: *I was struck by how carefully:* National Archives, College Park, Record Group 92, Office of the Quartermaster General, General Correspondence, Miscellaneous File 1946–48, Graves Registration, box 278, esp. the November 9, 1948, letter from Brig. Gen. Kester L. Hastings, QMC, Chief, Memories Division, to Brig. Gen. Howard Peckham, discussing the decision to segregate the dishonorable dead with inconspicuous markers. Many of the men in Plot E had previously been buried in the temporary

American cemetery at Marigny; others were transferred from the Mediterranean and North African theaters.

173: *Till was executed in Italy: United States v. Privates Fred A. McMurray and Louis Till,* both of 177th Port Company, 379th Port Battalion, Transportation Corps, convened at Leghorn, Italy, February 17, 1945. One of the rare references to Till's execution can be found in Ezra Pound's *Pisan Cantos,* 74, ll. 171–72, 178–79), written in 1945. Pound was confined to the same U.S. military detention center as Till, awaiting his own trial and possible death sentence for his Fascist radio broadcasts in wartime Italy. See Richard Sieburth's introduction and edition of the *Pisan Cantos* (New York: New Directions, 2004).

173: *his son, Emmett Till:* On the murder of Emmett Till, see Stephen J. Whitfield, *A Death in the Delta: The Story of Emmett Till* (New York: The Free Press, 1988), and most recently, the television documentary directed by Stanley Nelson, *The Murder of Emmett Till* (PBS/WGBH Educational Foundation: American Experience, 2003).

173: *His mother had wanted:* On Till's funeral, see the *Chicago Defender,* September 1, 1955. Till's mutilated body could only be identified by his father's signet ring, with the initials L.T.

174: *Two witnesses to his hanging:* Interviews with Louis Keruzec, July 26, 2002, December 27, 2002, and July 1, 2003, Locmenven, France; interview with François Prigent, October 15, 2002, Tours, France.

174: *The field where he was hanged:* Ibid.

174: *The letter says only:* William Davis, Individual Deceased Personnel File, Department of the Army, letter to Mrs. Madeline Davis, April 6, 1945: "Prior to his death your husband was performing duties, the nature of which cannot now be disclosed, which contributed immeasurably to the winning of this War. He always performed his tasks eagerly, cheerfully and efficiently. . . . "

174: *ten years after every state:* In the United States, where capital punishment was under the jurisdiction of individual states, the public hangings of the nineteenth century had given way to jail-yard gallows, and finally, to new technologies of death: electrocution and the gas chamber. By 1930, only a few states continued to hang condemned men, and public executions had been outlawed in all states but Kentucky. The 1936 hanging of Rainey Bethea in a carnival atmosphere in Owensboro, Kentucky, before a crowd of

10,000–20,000 bystanders so revolted public opinion that the Kentucky state legislature abolished the practice. In both countries, the old function of catharsis and expiation through public execution no longer seemed viable. See Banner, op. cit., pp. 154–68.

174: *"A house of shame":* Since my first visit to Oise-Aisne Cemetery, the Battle Monuments Commission has responded promptly to every request I have made for information. Using the list they sent me, I was able to compile information about each of the ninety-six men in Plot E—their division, their crime, and their date of execution.

175: *At his funeral:* See the account of the service in Loisel, op. cit., pp. 278–79.

175: *"To transmit . . .":* *Carnets II,* p. 126.

175: *"Everything I had seen":* *OK, Joe,* p. 119.

ACKNOWLEDGMENTS

—

Roger Grenier first told me about the French writer who had worked for the U.S. Army in their courts-martial during the summer of 1944. Without his support and guidance, his deep knowledge of French literature and culture, this book would not have seen the light.

The National Endowment for the Humanities awarded me the research fellowship that enabled me to finish *The Interpreter.* I am grateful to my deans at Duke, Karla F. C. Holloway and William H. Chafe, for their support.

My appreciation goes to Robert O. Paxton, whose work on France has been a model for me of probing and judicious history.

Learning about military justice and the Army was akin to learning a new language, and I am indebted to the generosity of experts in these fields. Richard Boylan, senior military archivist at the National Archives in College Park, Maryland, guided me to the VIII Corps Judge Advocate's journal and to a treasure trove of documents. Col. Robert F. Gonzales (U.S.A., Ret.), Judge Advocate and historian of the Judge Advocate Department in WWII, corresponded with me over the course of several years about everything from military justice reforms to claims commissions and Army structures. Maj. Gen. John C. Raaen, Jr. (U.S.A., Ret.), former 5th Ranger and a veteran of the D-Day landings at Omaha Beach, was unstinting in his generosity. His own eloquent and vivid recollections of WWII deserve their own book. George Chalou, retired archivist and consultant to the United States Court of Military Appeals, guided me in the National Archives and consulted with me on many details of my research. Criminologist J. Robert Lilly shared his own documents and his perspective. Linda Erickson at the office of the Clerk of Court, U.S. Army, answered countless queries and provided me with the transcripts that formed the basis for my study.

I am grateful to the following individuals and institutions for scholarly advice, assistance with documentation, and research support: Steve Anders at the Quartermaster Museum; Carolyn Lacky; Jennifer Barrett, Stick Research Agency, London; Ben Kimmel; Michael Radulescu at the Marly Rusoff Agency; Shelley Green and Mary Lou McCarten, genealogists in Wausau, Wisconsin; Christopher Hunt at the Imperial War Museum, London; Betsy Lauren Plumb at the National D-Day Museum, New Orleans; Jacques Adelée, St. James Military Cemetery; John Aust, Oise-Aisne American Military Cemetery; Bernadette Hand and Beverly Hutchinson, Historical Disclosures, British Army; Daniel C. Lavering at the Judge Advocate General's Legal Center and School; Kurt Maier at the Library of Congress; Sara Merkle at Northern Kentucky University; Deirdre McConathy; Kadzi Mutizwa at the Free Press; David Portier and Paul A. Golder, historians of the Special Air Service; Winston James, historian and biographer of Claude McKay; French sociologist Caroline Douki; James Pelzer, Clerk of the Court, Appellate Division, Supreme Court of the State of New York; Marthe LeClech, Morlaix, Brittany; Arthur Phillips; Olivier Ranger; Chris Robinson; Ben Kimmel; Tyler Stovall, historian at U.C. Berkeley; Hans Wollstein, film critic, Copenhagen; Kevin Hull and William Wleklinski at the John Marshall Law School; Jane Fogarty Nesbit; Ellen Davis, Maurice Bradford, and Mary Looney of the National Personnel Records Center; Thomas Sole, Martha Sell, and Margaret Flott of the American Battle Monuments Commission.

Eleanor Lewis McKechnie generously shared the papers of her first husband, Don Lewis, including his photographs of Lesneven and his notes for a detective novel based on *U.S. v. Whittington.* Col. Poole Rogers (U.S.A., Ret.) and former Sgt. Emmett Bailey of the Graves Registration Company, shared their memories. Col. John Silbernagel (U.S.A., Ret.), who served on the Court Martial at Morlaix, and James B. Craighill, trial judge advocate in *U.S. v. Whittington,* shared their vivid recollections of events over sixty years past.

The encouragement and challenges provided by several legal scholars greatly enriched my thinking about Guilloux's cases: Madeline Morris, Professor of Law at Duke University, shared her files from a research project on war and rape. Robinson Everett, Professor Emeritus at the Duke University Law School and former chief judge, United States Court of Military Appeals, consulted with me on the Board of Review documents for both the Hendricks and Whittington trials. Elizabeth Hillman, historian and professor at the Rutgers School of Law–Camden, shared her work and perspective on military justice, race, and gender, and entered into dialogue with me about my specific cases, opening up new worlds of reflection.

Thomas Russell Jones, former judge on the New York State Supreme Court, corresponded with me about his experience in the Army. Claude Collin of Grenoble, whose published interview with Thomas Russell Jones provides a unique testimony to the experience of African American officers in World War II, facilitated our contact.

I am grateful to Agnes Whittington of Henderson, Kentucky, for the chance to learn more from her about the postwar life of her extraordinary husband. My thanks go as well to Roy Pullam, Henderson County North Junior High School, to Frank Boyett, staff writer at *The Gleaner*, to William Sullivan, and to Charles Whittington and Susan Whittington Batterton.

In France, I benefited from the kind assistance of Bruno Isbled in the Archives Départementales de l'Ille-et-Vilaine at Rennes; Geneviève Danion and Claude Fagnen in the Archives Départementales du Finistère at Quimper; Paule René-Bazin at the Archives of the French Ministry of Defense; and the staff at the Archives Départementales des Côtes d'Armor in Saint-Brieuc. The Archives Nationales in Paris granted me special permission to consult holdings pertaining to inter-allied relations in 1944–46.

At the Institut Histoire du Temps Présent, an unparalleled resource for research on World War II–era France, I am grateful to Director Henry Rousso and to Fabrice Virgili and Luc Capdevila for their generous counsel, as well as to IHTP librarian Jean Astruc, who has yet to be stumped by a researcher's question. At the Bibliothèque Municipale de Saint-Brieuc, I am indebted to Marie-Noelle LeBour and Pierre-Yves Kerloch for guidance in the Guilloux archives, as well as to Dominique Grellard, director of the Saint-Brieuc libraries. My thanks go to Roland Fichet and Annie Lucas of the Théâtre de Folle Pensée in Saint-Brieuc, and to my colleague Paol Keineg, who first introduced me to the riches of Brittany.

To understand the summer of 1944 and Louis Guilloux's experience as interpreter in four different trials, I am indebted to many people in France, both those who helped facilitate interviews and those who shared their own memories, beginning with Yvonne Guilloux, Louis Guilloux's daughter. In Plumaudan, Jean-Pierre Davenet introduced me to Jeannine Bignon Peroux; I am also grateful to Madame Peroux's son, Pierrick Peroux, for his help. In Dinan, Dr. Louis Dalibot spoke to me about his experiences in the *maquis* and shared his deep knowledge of the community of Plumaudan. In the Finistère region of Brittany, in Guiclan and Locmenven, Jean Kergoat, adjunct mayor, arranged for a number of interviews; his father, Alain Kergoat, and their neighbor, Louis Keruzec, evoked their vivid memories of the murder of Germaine Pouliquen. Germaine Pouliquen's daughter, Jacqueline Nicole, was kind enough to speak to me with the assistance of her daughter, Michèle. In Tours, Gen. François Prigent (French Army, Ret.), who, as an adolescent, witnessed the execution of William Davis, spoke to me at length about his memories. In Lesneven, I was fortunate to work with Claude LeMenn, deputy mayor, who welcomed me to Lesneven over a period of several years of research and assisted me in my interviews with Yvonne Pichon and Fernand Jacopin, to whom I am also grateful. Claude LeMenn and Mayor Jean-Yves Le Goff kindly invited me to participate in the commemoration of the liberation of Lesneven in August 2004 and to speak to the community about my research. In Paris, historian Mona Ozouf shared her memories of Louis and Renée Guilloux, her former teacher. In Paris, Roger Schank spoke to me and wrote to me at the end of his life about his memories of Francis Morand, providing rare photos of Morand at their SAS training camp at Camberley. In Saint-Gilles-du-Méné, journalist Pierre-Yves Joyaux facilitated my interview with Jean Poilvert, former member of the *maquis,* who fought with Morand in the summer of 1944. I am grateful to Auguste Velé, who interviewed his family members about the tragic death of his grandfather, also named Auguste Velé, in August 1944, in Bazouges-du-Désert, France.

My colleague Maurice Wallace helped me plan my interviews with the families of black GIs; he and his assistant, Lottie Sneed, made important initial contacts for me in Macon and Raeford, North Carolina. In Laurinburg, Paul Dickson spoke to me with the assistance of his son Robert "Bubba" Dickson, about his memories of Jim Crow–era Raeford and his efforts to obtain a pardon for S. T. Fellows. In Warrenton, Vaughan, and Macon, North Carolina, I am grateful to the people who helped me reconstruct James Hendricks's childhood story and the history of Macon in the 1930s and 1940s: Thurletta Brown-Gavins, who arranged an interview with her father, Thurston Brown, director of Brown's Funeral Service, and Robert Daniels (pseudonym), James Hendricks's classmate at the Embro School. Richard Greene, director of the R. H. Greene Funeral Home, helped me contact James Hendricks's adoptive siblings. I am grateful for the generosity and openness of the members of James Hendricks's adoptive family: Evelyn Henderson Echols and her husband, Otis Echols, Regina Ryan, Benjamin Henderson, and Geraldine Edwards Bullock. Olivia Cormier, whose husband, Bill, was Louis Guilloux's closest American friend in the summer of 1944, generously provided copies of her husband's World War II memoirs.

My research assistants in Duke's Program in Literature during the past four years, Jennifer Rhee, Shilyh Warren, Sara Appel, and Corina Stan, did background research on topics ranging from military law to Breton history and American wills and probate records. Their own perspectives on my cases always taught me something new.

For their careful reading of the manuscript, I owe an enormous debt of gratitude to Col. Robert F. Gonzales (USA, Ret.), Elizabeth Hillman, Paol Keineg, Robert O. Paxton, Donald Reid, Kristin Ross, Virginia Vander Jagt, and Maurice Wallace.

My agent, Marly Rusoff, enabled me to find the right home for my book and encouraged me throughout my research and writing with her keen eye and her steady sense of values. She understood both the potential of my subject and its challenges. I feel very lucky to have her support. Bruce Nichols, my editor at The Free Press, gave me the greatest gift—an overall structure that enabled me to find my way amidst a mass of primary sources. He is proof that the hands-on editor, who cares deeply both about language and ideas, is alive and well in New York City.

I was fortunate to have the support of two talented photographers: Alan Thomas (also the editor of *OK, Joe* at the University of Chicago Press), who, with his wife, Julia, traveled with me throughout Brittany to capture images connected with my research; and Lorenzo Virgili, who photographed Plot E.

Laurel Goldman's Tuesday writing workshop and its members, Alex Charns, Kathleen O'Keeffe, Martha Pentecost, David Levine, and Mia Bray, gave me the opportunity to read aloud from my work in progress. Their ear for language, their sense of argument and intention, always challenged me, and their responses invariably led me from a new awareness of individual words and sentences to the very largest issues at stake.

Dee Gunn followed the progress of this book from Chapel Hill to the Pointe de Pen-Hir. His affection and support nurtured my work. I am thankful, too, for the friendship and intellectual guidance of Michèle Longino, Helen Solterer, Anne Garréta, Kristin Ross, Monique Middleton, and David Auerbach, and for the wise counsel of Terry Vance, Vivian Foushee, and our Wednesday group.

Finally, my thanks go to Cathy Davidson, who has been my writing partner for over fifteen years. There's no way I can begin to thank her adequately in a few sentences. She has seen nearly every version and draft of my manuscript. Her genius for structure, her sense of justice and her clarity, all challenge and inspire me, and I never stop learning and delighting in our work together.

INDEX

—

About the Author

ALICE KAPLAN is the Gilbert, Louis and Edward Lehrman Professor of Romance Studies and Professor of Literature and History at Duke University. She is the author of *The Collaborator: The Trial and Execution of Robert Brasillach,* winner of a Los Angeles Times Book Prize and a finalist for the National Book Award and the National Book Critics Circle Award. Her previous book, *French Lessons: A Memoir,* was a finalist for the National Book Critics Circle Award. The recipient of a fellowship from the National Endowment for the Humanities for *The Interpreter,* she traveled throughout Brittany, France, and the southern United States for her research. A native of Minneapolis, Kaplan divides her time between Durham, North Carolina, and Paris, France.